Action Research in Software Engineering

Miroslaw Staron

Action Research in Software Engineering

Theory and Applications

 Springer

Miroslaw Staron
Department of Computer Science
and Engineering
University of Gothenburg
Gothenburg, Sweden

ISBN 978-3-030-32612-8   ISBN 978-3-030-32610-4   (eBook)
https://doi.org/10.1007/978-3-030-32610-4

This Springer imprint is published by the registered company Springer Nature Switzerland AG.
The registered company address is: Gewerbestrasse 11, 6330 Cham, Switzerland

To my family

Foreword

Action! It is what engineered projects demand. As stated by the Cambridge Dictionary,[1] the action is *"the process of doing something, especially when dealing with a problem or difficulty."* Usually, the engineering of any product involves a plan of actions. Such a plan must consider the different dimensions of the problem and the context variables (physical, environmental, technical, and social) that someway influence product construction. However, only effective actions can guarantee the success of projects and the reduction of engineering risks. That is what engineers learned along the centuries.[2] At least four stages of (r)evolution (pre-scientific, first industrial, second industrial, information) can be observed regarding the understanding of the instruments, technology limits, and properties of different products. The interaction between theory (research) and practice (action) has been vital to acquire evidence to support this learning process. There are indeed plenty of challenges to face in contemporary products and many lessons to learn. In whatever way, the evolution of engineering knowledge allows engineers to offer and build more and more complex solutions to the benefit of society.

The Cambridge Dictionary states that research is *"a detailed study of a subject, especially in order to discover (new) information or reach a (new) understanding."* The learning process in the engineering field has been supported by research, in its different formats and configurations. In this case, a researcher expects *"to study a subject in detail, especially in order to discover new information or reach a new understanding."* It is possible to notice the contribution of experimentation strategies in the evolution of engineering by observing the growth of some domains. For instance, some well-established engineering fields, such as automobile, civil,

---

[1] https://dictionary.cambridge.org/dictionary/english/.

[2] http://www.creatingtechnology.org/history.htm.

chemistry, or electrical engineering, have identified the primary challenges and context variables that can influence the plan of actions to build their conventional products and that could contribute to risky contemporary ones. The commonality of properties offered by their products (discovered by research) indeed makes the plan of actions less challenging.

Software engineering and its related products are young when compared with other engineering fields. The expected commonality and somehow stable properties presented by conventional engineered products become less tangible when talking about software products. There are many context variables involved in the engineering of a particular software product or software technology. The planning of actions is risky since software products differ from each other in at least one of their planning dimensions (peopleware, processes, and product). Perhaps, part of the challenge comes from the difficulties software engineers face in defining and showing the product they use to build. Besides, there are unknown context variables that can influence the plan of actions (software processes, in this case) and affect the result of the project. Therefore, observation, experimentation, and learning are vital to support the evolution of our capacity of engineering software products and technologies for the benefit of society.

Each software project or software technology development represents an unmissable opportunity to research, learn, and evolve! Software engineers and practitioners indeed learned a lot since the 1950s when software products started to be delivered. However, all of this learning is (and maybe it will never be) not enough to support the building of new products. Software is everywhere. Its costs are concerned with its engineering, on which manufacturing is not possible. It needs to evolve to keep itself valuable and useful, but it deteriorates at the same time. New problems and solutions demand custom-built components, inserting quality risks. Besides, all software systems can fail, introducing damage risks depending on the problem domain. All of these issues can challenge building and maintenance actions. However, they vary according to the features of the different software projects and their context variables. Therefore, they need to be observed, characterized, and mitigated.

As previously demonstrated in other engineering fields, research represents an essential instrument to support the understanding of the software-related phenomena and the mitigation of issues in the software processes. Empirical Software Engineering is an area of software engineering that has intensively worked to understand the application and evolution of software processes and technologies by applying the scientific method (experimentation) and other observation strategies. Nowadays, experimentation is the realm of software engineering when discussing the combination of theory (researchers) and practice (software practitioners) in favor of learning and evolution of the field.

Along the years, the application of software engineering and experimentation principles and strategies in the software projects have been a reality in my professional life. I indeed started doing much more software engineering than experimentation, next begun to do much more experimentation than engineering software products, and so realized that the merging of actions with research could be great to support development, learning (in general), and the decision-making (in particular) in software projects (mainly those really challenging and unexpected in terms of requirements, technology, innovation, and organization). These experiences were reported in some publications, which intended to make clear (even that not completely) the collaboration involved in those experiences and to share with the software engineering community what we learned and applied in the projects. It was in 2009. The impact of using action and research in our projects was so intense that we decided to call for this strength in the title of one of our publications. Since then, action research became a strategy of engineering in all of the software projects of the Experimental Software Engineering Group at COPPE/UFRJ with the industry that this combination of approaches (action and research) is feasible and makes sense.

It was June 16, 2019, when I received an initial message from Prof. Dr. Miroslaw Staron, from the University of Gothenburg, Sweden, talking about the experiences that Paulo Sérgio Medeiros dos Santos and I reported in one of our previous publications in 2011 and the similarities with his current experiences on using action research in the industry. The sequence of messages was full of kindness and included a link to the draft of this book, which I read with great interest and pleasure. It was possible to understand why he sent that initial (and other) messages to me. I felt honored and pleased by receiving the messages, an invitation to prepare this foreword, besides being able to be one of the first readers of his book.

Action Research in Software Engineering: Theory and Applications, by Prof. Miroslaw Staron, is a must-read book for those researchers and practitioners interested and concerned with strengthening the collaboration between academia and industry, building a plan of actions based on evidence, or making decisions supported by science in their software projects. It offers 12 chapters full of information and relevant discussions regarding the use and limits of action research in software engineering. The chapters present concrete examples, which make the understanding of concepts easy for those not wholly involved with the empirical software engineering context.

The book covers the cycles of action research. It organizes the chapters in the way an action research strategy is usually introduced into the software projects. The instruments used throughout the cycles of action research can be easily realized or captured from the discussions and examples. This material is of great value for those that need to speed up the introduction of action research and guarantee the effectiveness of actions in their software projects.

This book is also a contribution to the empirical software engineering community. It registers and tailors the processes and principles involved in action research to the software engineering field, describing the methodology and making explicit the limits of action research when applied in the area. Besides, this book also represents an adequate material to support graduate courses regarding action research in software engineering.

Thanks, Miroslaw, for sharing with the software engineers your experiences and knowledge regarding action and research!

I hope the reader enjoys reading this book as much as I did.

Professor of Software Engineering   Guilherme Horta Travassos
CNPq Researcher, ISERN Member
Experimental Software Engineering Group
PESC/COPPE/Federal University of Rio de Janeiro
Rio de Janeiro, Brazil
August 2019

Preface

Every scientist has his and her own favorite research topics, types of studies, and research methodology. It's natural, and it's something that is very important for all kinds of researchers. I see it as a part of academic freedom. For me, the favorite research methodology is action research.

I started with action research without knowing that it is a valid research methodology. A company was looking for a researcher who could help them with research on software metrics. I was interested and met with the company, and so we started. The company asked me to spend all my research project time at their premises, not in my office (which is ca. 300 m away in another building). Colleagues from my department called this a consultancy and not research (at that time), but they supported me.

I'm very grateful for their support, because this kind of working with research turned out to be "my thing," and I've been working according to action research since then. I've learned that the first problem formulation is often symptomatic, the real problem is hidden, and we need to run some diagnostics to find it. At the beginning, this diagnostics took me a lot of time, several interviews, and data collection. In the course of time, it became easier as I learned where to look for. I've also learned how to work with practitioners. Many of my students are now working for the companies that I collaborate with, so we have a common language thanks to the knowledge I got from their older colleagues. I'm very grateful for that.

Today, it's obvious that action research is the methodology that my research team uses. Our industrial partners expect us to work with them, solve their industrial problems, and contribute to theories in software engineering. I wrote this book to help young and experienced researchers, scientists, and software engineers. I would like to inspire them to action and to encourage them to try action research, because it requires courage. As an action researcher, you need to listen to your industrial colleagues; sometimes you need to admit to making a mistake or not knowing how things work in industry.

In this book, I start with the description of action research, its history, and purpose in Chaps. 1 and 2. I provide examples of how a research proposal looks like and why we need to write it in this particular way. In Chap. 3 I go into detail of how to diagnose the "real" problem that needs to be solved. Chapter 4 is all about the planning of the action, and Chap. 5 is about action taking. Chapter 6 helps with the evaluation and discusses methods for analyzing qualitative and quantitative data. Chapter 7 elaborates on the methods for identifying knowledge which is important for dissemination at the company and in the academic community. Chapter 8 provides an alternative research methodology to action research as a methodology— design science research—and discusses their differences and similarities. Chapter 9 helps to ensure that the knowledge developed in action research lasts longer than one specific project. Chapter 10 is about evaluating the validity of an action research study. It discusses the most common validity threats and how to reduce them. Finally, Chap. 11 describes how to document and report action research studies.

I hope that this book will encourage researchers and practitioners to work together and to use research projects as a means of advancing the field of software engineering.

Gothenburg, Sweden   Miroslaw Staron
August 2019

Acknowledgments

This book is a work based on years of experience with industrial research. This experience has been shaped by many collaborators, far too many to thank all of them individually. I am enormously grateful to work with my industrial colleagues.

I would like to thank my colleagues from Ericsson, which is the company where I started my journey with action research. In particular, I would like to thank Wilhelm Meding for the support and encouragement throughout the years, in particular, for the encouragement after my failures. There would be no book if it was not for Wilhelm's encouragement.

I would also like to thank Micael Caiman, who supported me throughout all the years. Micael has always been kind enough to provide me with guidance and ideas, as well as with access to the physical infrastructure at Ericsson. I'm extremely thankful for this, and I hope that Micael knows it.

Ericsson is only one of many companies that supported me. I am indebted to my colleagues at Volvo Cars, who provided me with directions, ideas, and access to their infrastructure, including the possibility to be part of their research efforts. In particular, I would like to thank Kent Niesel, Hans Alminger, Darko Durisic, Martin Nilsson, and Anna Sandberg. They have helped me more than I could have expected and, most probably, more than they realize.

I pitched the idea of this book to some of my colleagues at the department (IT Faculty, Department of Computer Science and Engineering, Software Engineering Division—yes, that is a long name) during a lunch. I got mixed reactions, but some of my colleagues supported and encouraged me, in particular, Agneta Nilsson, Miroslaw Ochodek, and Imed Hammouda. Thank you all for this. I really appreciate that. I would also like to thank Richard Berntsson Svensson, who engaged in discussions about the content of the book and pointed me to several publications in this area.

I'm also indebted to my publisher—Ralf Gerstner—who supported me during the process and who bootstrapped my writing process. If you ever need a publisher, I sincerely recommend Ralf. It's difficult to find a more skilled professional.

Finally, I would like to thank my family for the support, encouragement, and kindness during the writing process. The book is an investment of their time, which I hope I can repay one day.

Contents

Chapter 1
Introduction

If you can't describe what you are doing as a process, you don't know what you're doing.

—W.E. Deming

Abstract In the introduction chapter, we provide an overview of software engineering both as an engineering discipline and a scientific one. We provide an overview of action research origin and its historical perspective and describe how action research is used currently in the disciplines related to software engineering. The review of usage of action research in the related disciplines shows that there is a need for describing action research focusing on the specifics of software engineering research.

1.1 Introduction

Decades ago, when humanity was divided into classes and when knowledge was a privilege of the few, conducting research was reserved to scientists. The times, however, changed. Research education has been part of many university curricula, and conducting research projects is a popular activity in high-skill industries. Software engineering is an example of such an industry. It's an industry where research and development are interconnected, and it's often difficult to distinguish when software research ends, innovation begins, and software development continues.

Modern software engineering companies provide every interested employee with a possibility to spend a percentage of their work time on research projects. These research projects can be individual or team efforts, short and long, curiosity driven or applied.

All scientific disciplines use research methods which are the most appropriate for the study at hand. It is also the case that the nature of the discipline makes certain studies more important than others and, by implication, certain research methodologies more important than others.

© Springer Nature Switzerland AG 2020
M. Staron, *Action Research in Software Engineering*,
https://doi.org/10.1007/978-3-030-32610-4_1

Software engineering is an applied engineering science. We base our theories on empirical observations and, increasingly often, on ethnography. However, we also apply our new methods in industrial projects, learning and improving the methods during the application. Thus, we often apply action research as our favorite research methodology.

At the same time, action research methodology has been developed to combine learning, researching, and making actions. Therefore, it seems that the application of action research to software engineering is rather straightforward.

1.2   What Action Research Is

Action research is one of the research methodologies that gained popularity in the second part of the twentieth century [BMGM03]. The reason for its popularity is that action research focuses on organizational learning as part of the process of research.

Action research is defined by Sagor as *is a disciplined process of inquiry conducted by and for those taking the action. The primary reason for engaging in action research is to assist the actor in improving and/or refining his or her actions*, [Sag00]. As the definition indicates, it is focused on improving the work of the actors taking the action.

Another definition is presented by Reason and Bradbury as *a participatory, democratic process concerned with developing practical knowing in the pursuit of worthwhile human purposes, grounded in a participatory worldview which we believe is emerging at this historical moment. It seeks to bring together action and reflection, theory and practice, in participation with others, in the pursuit of practical solutions to issues of pressing concern to people, and more generally the flourishing of individual persons and their communities* [RB01]. In this definition, Reason and Bradbury emphasize the aspect of participation and the aspect of practical solutions—creating new practices and new products.

Baskerville describes action research as an important example of modern research method in the area of information systems: "It is empirical, yet interpretive. It is experimental, yet multivariate. It is observational, yet interventionist." These characteristics make it perfect for software engineering research.

Many of the sources defining action research introduce the cyclic dependency between its iterative elements. Action research projects are iterative and organized in action research cycles. Each cycle starts with the diagnosis of a problem and ends with documented reflections on learning.

An example of an action research cycle is presented in Fig. 1.1, which is adopted from Baskerville [Bas99]. Each cycle starts with the diagnosing of the problem, which is done either by exploring the problem provided by the company's context or by exploring the outcome of the learning activity from the previous cycle.

For software engineers, these kinds of cycles are familiar from other contexts. For a software developer, diagnosing can be seen as requirements engineering; this cycle resembles iterative software development, e.g., in a V-model or Agile [Rup10]. For a

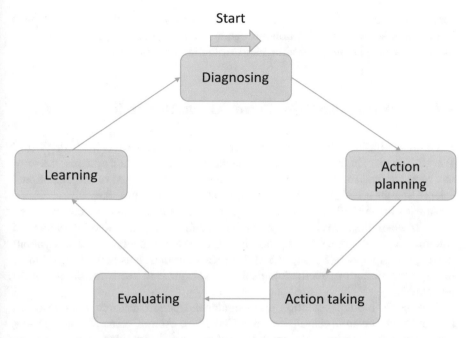

Fig. 1.1 An action research cycle

quality manager, the cycle resembles Deming's quality cycle (Plan-Do-Check-Act, [Dem81]).

1.3   The Concept of Action

McNiff [McN13] defined action as "anything you do" and you reflect on. As action research comes from the disciplines where researchers and practitioners are the same persons (e.g., teachers in schools, nurses), this kind of definition that action is "anything you do" and the evaluation is the reflection is quite straightforward as it separates doing/acting from thinking/reflecting.

However, in software engineering, the action teams consist of both practitioners and researchers (but often different persons); therefore, this definition would be confusing, for example, conducting or "doing" an analysis by a research would count as an action, which is not correct. Therefore, we use the following definition of action:

> An action is an activity done by or in collaboration with practitioners, which includes an intervention in the practice of the collaborating practitioners or their organization.

According to this definition, therefore, an analysis does not intervene with the practice and therefore is not an action. However, a presentation of results of a study for a team, where the team has to take a decision if they change their practice or not, is an action. We use this definition throughout the book, because for the purpose of discussions and planning, executing, and evaluating actions, it suits us well.

1.4   Short Historical Timeline of Action Research

According to Baskerville [BWH96], the term action research was coined after World War II. However, in the area of computer science, or information systems, the term has been adopted in 1978. Susman and Evered [SE78] focused on organizational science and the crisis of research focused on changing organizations.

Already in the 1980s, action research gained more attention as one of the research methods where the focus is on combination of empirical studies and interventional studies, i.e., recognizing the science is not only about studying but also about making things happen [Sus83, EC93]. It was also criticized as being "consultancy in disguise," despite its methodological merits, rigor, and needs to follow ethical guidelines.

The 1990s brought attention and popularized action research as a research methodology for information systems [BWH98]. Action research was getting popular mainly as empirical research entered the area of computer science.

In 2000, Wohlin et al. [WRH+00] published the first book about empirical software engineering, focused on experimentation. The book established an important foundation and has been cited widely, followed by books on case studies [RHRR12].

However, as a community, we recognized the need for action research only recently. Ferrario et al. [FSN+14] have recognized the need to use action research to study the social impact of software engineering. Finally, Petersen et al. [PGA+14] proposed a thesis that action research can increase the pace of technology development in academia and in industry.

1.5   Software Engineering and Its Context

Action research has been applied in many different disciplines, and there exist guidelines on how to conduct action research studies in education [Cor54] or information systems [BWH96]. Although software engineering is close to information systems in many ways, it is also different in the sense that it studies the process of developing software rather than process of using software to improve other disciplines.

Software engineering is defined by ISO/IEC/IEEE [ISO10] as "1. the systematic application of scientific and technological knowledge, methods, and experience to the design, implementation, testing, and documentation of software. 2. the application of a systematic, disciplined, quantifiable approach to the development, operation, and maintenance of software; that is, the application of engineering to software."

This definition shows that software engineering is focused on the aspect of being **systematic** in the ways of developing, designing, testing, and maintaining software products. In this way, we can see that action research should play an important role in providing us with this systematic applications.

Although this definition is widely accepted, it's a challenge when discussing software engineering in start-ups. Since start-ups are known to focus on establishing their business on the market and focus on customer needs and increasing the flow of revenue, they need to balance engineering practices with quick addressing of customer needs.

One way of introducing structured research in start-ups is to use experiment systems [LM15, Bos12]. A software experiment system is a systematic way of differentiating features deployed to customers and collecting feedback from the usage of these features to further drive the development of the software product. Software experiment systems are often organized in cycles, just like action research projects. One example of such a cycle is the build-measure-learn cycle as described by Ries [Rie11] (Fig. 1.2).

Action research is all about feedback, and using software experiment systems, we can expand our research activities to involve customers too. We can learn about which features are the best from the perspective of customers and see what they like best.

We explore the details of software experiment systems and their role in modern action research in the next chapter.

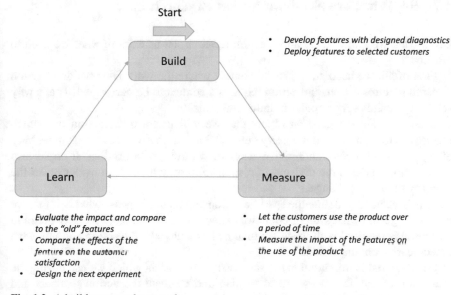

Fig. 1.2   A build-measure-learn cycle

1.6   Action Research in Software Engineering

Action research, as a research methodology, entered software engineering from the field of information systems. A study by Santos and Travassos [ST09] and [ST11] found that the number of action research studies in software engineering is on the rise. Since the studies were conducted in 2009 and 2011, the number of action research studies has since increased even more.

The nature of software engineering, which is a mix of technology and social sciences, makes action research nicely applicable and helps to increase the impact of academic research and impact of new technology development. Petersen et al. [PGA+14] identify the action research methodology as one of the models of research transfer.

We can see the action research methodology as a means of transfer of research results. However, it is much more than that—it is a method for co-development of research results, where academia and industry can work together. Through this co-development, the researchers and practitioners learn from each other, and thus they develop research results which contribute to both the industrial practice and academic theories, tools, methods, and knowledge development.

This co-development and collaboration is one of the reasons why I chose to call the research teams in action research as *action teams*. They are focused on action and intervention in the first hand. They complement that with theory development as a secondary goal of the research.

1.7   So, What We Need for Action Research Is...

Given what we know so far about action research, let us explore what we need to practice it.

First of all, we need an industrial context where the work is embedded. Action research requires action, and action requires a context to be performed. That's why action research is very popular in industrial projects.

Second of all, we need an object that we will perform the action on, which requires us to explore, and precisely define, what is it that we want to change. Very often, this is a process, an activity, ways of working, or a product. It could also be a specific role and the division of responsibilities, which we consider under the category of process change.

Third, we need to define the specific action and its outcomes—what is it that we try to change and what kind of effect we expect from the change. Precisely defining the action is required both when we plan and execute/take the action and when we reflect/learn from the action.

Finally, what is important is the success/failure criteria which we use during the evaluation of the action—we need to plan and evaluate the action's impact and prepare for learning from it. We also need to understand how to diagnose for the next action research cycle or how to wrap up the action research project.

However, we also need to understand that action research is not a methodology for everyone. It is not a good methodology where we need to study a problem outside of its context, e.g., when we need to experiment with different technologies to understand their differences. For this kind of projects, it's better to choose experiments. If we chose action research, our industrial partners can be discouraged by the fact that we need to set up formal experiments, which is a time- and effort-consuming activity. The action research is also not a good method when we want to study a problem, without the need to make an intervention. Then it is better to design a full-fledged case study, or we risk that our industrial partners get discouraged by the fact that "we do not do anything" at the company because we do not make any intervention.

1.8   Outline of This Book

This book is organized in a similar way as action research project is organized. We go through each phase of the project and discuss it. We combine the theory of action research with a number of examples or practical cases. Each chapter provides new insights into the details of action research and provides the readers with better understanding on how to apply it.

Each chapter contains the description of a number of practical cases, or example, of how this application can be done. These examples come from my experience of working as a researcher at a number of companies during my career. Although I was never employed by any of these companies, I usually organized my research as action research projects, design science research projects, case studies, or experiments. Action research allowed me to make impact in industry, for example, by designing measurement systems or dashboards [SM18].

The examples presented in the book come from my experience, but they have been changed to fit the purpose of the book. Whenever possible, I provide references to the original publications for reference. I found it easier to convey the points by changing the existing experiences rather than creating an imaginary project and describe it gradually throughout the book. I hope that the readers understand this and disregard the inconsistency between the reality and my examples. I sometimes use imaginary cases, diagrams, and data sets to illustrate points in this book. The goal of all examples is strictly illustrative and should not be taken as findings as they are not designed with this in mind; for this, I refer the reader to relevant publications whenever these are cited.

An Example of a Practical Case
In all the chapters of this book, these kinds of boxes include examples, illustrations, and practical cases. They show how the theoretical points are applied. They include tables and illustrations, references to original texts, and explanations of what the examples mean.

1.8.1 Chapter 2: Action Research as Research Methodology in Software Engineering

Although action research methodology has been introduced for over 40 years ago, it has not been used in software engineering until the last decade, at least not that much. This means that we need to understand the background of action research and understand why it was designed and introduced. This helps us to understand how to apply the methodology in practice. It also helps us to understand its strengths and weaknesses. Therefore, we elaborate on the principles of software engineering as an applied branch of science to show how it combines social and technical research cultures. We show that because its applied nature, it needs to combine both theoretical research methods and applied ones. Then we provide a description of action research as a methodology, based on the canonical action research presented by Baskerville [Bas99]. We use the same cycle as Baskerville, but we focus on more modern techniques of interacting with the context—software experiment systems. We introduce each element of an action research cycle and describe its purpose.

1.8.2 Chapter 3: Diagnosing

Every action research project, and every action research cycle in the project, starts with the diagnosing phase. The action research methodology recognizes the fact that every research study starts with an exploration on the initial research problem and identifies more tangible and actionable research problems to address. As a researcher and as an action team, we need to recognize that one of the most important elements of all kinds of research studies is the precise and unambiguous problem formulation. Action research, being applied and problem oriented, has an entire phase devoted to just that activity—diagnosing. This chapter describes the diagnosing activity of action research. In particular, we can read a description of the techniques for understanding the problem—interviews, analysis of log files, and focus group workshops.

1.8.3 Chapter 4: Action Planning

Action research is a methodology which advocates actions taken by individuals and reflecting on them. This means that there are inherent biases. For example, as humans, we are always less critical to our own actions than to actions of others. Therefore, we need to make a good plan for the action taking. We need to identify which actions are taken, how, when, and why. After the diagnosing phase, we need to divide the research problem into a set of actions, and this set of actions needs to take us to the solution of the diagnosed problem. The action planning chapter describes the way in which we plan the studies in action research. It draws on the experiences of designing case studies and experiments. However, it provides more comprehensive description on how to include software engineering tools and techniques in the design.

1.8.4   Chapter 5: Action Taking

When conducting an action research project, the key part is the action taking phase. In this phase, we make an intervention in the company's operation and therefore cause some effect on the organization. The action taking, however, is much more than a simple intervention, and it requires us to prepare with the measurement setup, a framework on how to capture the effects of the change. In this chapter, we describe the principles of executing studies by starting to examine the principles of setting up experiments—running trials, collecting the data, storing the data, and defining the veracity of the measurements used and the associated measurement error. In this chapter, we show how to prepare for the data collection and how to conduct it. This chapter also describes how to set up an infrastructure for software experiment systems to be used in software engineering.

1.8.5   Chapter 6: Evaluating

Making an intervention or taking the action leads to effects on the organization, the team, and the individual practitioners and researchers. Being part of the action team, each individual has some attitude toward the actions taken and observes the effects of the action. These observations are important, but it is even more important to be able to objectively assess these effects, reduce the bias in the observations, and increase the transparency in research activities. Therefore, the action team needs to conduct formal evaluations of their action and the effects of these actions. This chapter describes the methods and tools used to analyze the data from action research studies. It provides the description of the main statistical methods, machine learning methods, for continuous data analysis. We also discuss the methods for visualizing the data in order to make the impact on the learning process.

1.8.6   Chapter 7: Learning

One of the most important characteristics of action research is that it is a methodology designed for learning. It helps to elevate the competence of the collaborating organizations and researchers to the same extent as it is aimed to make improvements. Therefore, identifying, specifying, and disseminating learning are crucial in any action research project. In this chapter, we describe methods used to increase the learning in the organization and how to identify learning important for theory development. We focus on the role of the researchers in this process and the need to reduce the bias introduced by them. We base this chapter on the theories and practices from software process improvement field. However, we focus on identifying learning outcomes from studies, organizing them in categories and packaging for the next action research cycle.

1.8.7   Chapter 8: Action Research vs. Design Science Research

Until this point, we have learned about what action research is and how to practice it. It is, nevertheless, not the only research methodology aimed at improving industrial practice by proposing changes. A methodology which is the closest one is the design science research. In this chapter, we contrast action research methodology with constructive research, which shares some of the commonalities (creation of new artifacts during the research process). We go into depth of what design science research is and how it differs from the action research. We discuss these two methodologies with a help of a number of examples, finishing the chapter with guidelines when to choose each methodology.

1.8.8   Chapter 9: Ensuring Sustainability of Knowledge

It is straightforward to design one study and to conduct it. However, it is not easy to make the results "stick" in the industrial practices, and it is not straightforward how to ensure that the results are long-lasting. In this chapter, we focus on the question of how to assure that the knowledge from an action research cycle is institutionalized. We discuss the methods for documenting the knowledge and for making sure that they become practices. We do this in form of checklists, aimed at the action teams and their organizations. These checklists help to quickly identify gaps in the execution of studies and help to improve the industrial collaboration. They also help the action teams to understand each other better, which is (in my opinion) one of the cornerstones of developing long-lasting results.

1.8.9   Chapter 10: Validity Evaluation of Action Research Studies

Conducting a research project includes making choices. By selecting a team, an organization, and a measurement method, we make a choice. These choices, the setup, and the execution of the study can lead to problems with validity. In this chapter, we list and discuss threats to validity of action research studies. We combine the known threats to validity of empirical studies with the known threats to validity of constructive studies. This chapter helps to understand what we need to do in order to minimize problems that certain choices can bring.

1.8.10   Chapter 11: Reporting Action Research Studies

The goal of every research study is to contribute to the body of knowledge. This means that reporting and documenting research studies are almost as important as the studies themselves. There are many ways in which this can be done, and each way has a different goal. In this chapter, we describe how to report on action research studies. We discuss and elaborate on elements of a research report and the goals of the report; we do it in a generic way, and then we explore two different ways of reporting studies. We present how to document the studies from two perspectives—focused on the results and focused on the story of the action research.

1.9   Let's Go!

The goal of this book is to help everyone interested in industry-academia collaboration to conduct research in collaboration. It's for those academics who are not afraid to step out of the comfort zone and enter industry, where we can meet experts from all kinds of areas of software engineering. It is also for the industrial researchers who know that they want to do more than just develop software that they want to contribute to the development of knowledge. It is also for the stakeholders in research projects, who want to understand how to manage industrial research projects, and the stakeholders who search for guidelines on their role and expectations.

I hope that this book will help everyone interested in research in industrial contexts. I hope that the book will help my future students to conduct research that has impact on their industrial partners, which leads to innovation and to the great satisfaction that the innovation brings.

I hope that the book will help my industrial colleagues and practitioners, who are interested in a structured way of improving their work and interested in learning about how to improve and how to develop their businesses and their career.

I also hope that this book will help to develop the field of software engineering to include more aspects of industrial validation of research results. From my experience, such evaluation does not need to be difficult. On the contrary, it can be much more fun than one may think if it is done with the involvement of industrial partners from the beginning.

Therefore, without further ado, let's dive into the details of action research and its applications!

References

[Bas99] Richard L Baskerville.   Investigating information systems with action research. *Communications of the AIS*, 2(3es):4, 1999.

[BMGM03] Mary Brydon-Miller, Davydd Greenwood, and Patricia Maguire.   Why action research? 2003.

[Bos12] Jan Bosch. Building products as innovation experiment systems. In *International Conference of Software Business*, pages 27–39. Springer, 2012.

[BWH96] Richard L Baskerville and A Trevor Wood-Harper. A critical perspective on action research as a method for information systems research.   *Journal of information Technology*, 11(3):235–246, 1996.

[BWH98] Richard Baskerville and A Trevor Wood-Harper. Diversity in information systems action research methods. *European Journal of information systems*, 7(2):90–107, 1998.

[Cor54] Stephen M Corey. Action research in education. *The journal of educational research*, 47(5):375–380, 1954.

[Dem81] W Edwards Deming. Improvement of quality and productivity through action by management. *National productivity review*, 1(1):12–22, 1981.

[EC93] Max Elden and Rupert F Chisholm. Emerging varieties of action research: Introduction to the special issue. *Human relations*, 46(2):121–142, 1993.

[FSN+14] Maria Angela Ferrario, Will Simm, Peter Newman, Stephen Forshaw, and Jon Whittle. Software engineering for'social good': integrating action research, participatory design, and agile development. In *Companion Proceedings of the 36th International Conference on Software Engineering*, pages 520–523. ACM, 2014.

[ISO10] ISO ISO. Iec/ieee 24765: 2010 systems and software engineering – vocabulary. Technical report, Technical report, Institute of Electrical and Electronics Engineers, Inc, 2010.

[LM15] Eveliina Lindgren and Jürgen Münch. Software development as an experiment system: a qualitative survey on the state of the practice. In *International Conference on Agile Software Development*, pages 117–128. Springer, 2015.

[McN13] Jean McNiff. *Action research: Principles and practice*. Routledge, 2013.

[PGA+14] Kai Petersen, Cigdem Gencel, Negin Asghari, Dejan Baca, and Stefanie Betz. Action research as a model for industry-academia collaboration in the software engineering context. In *Proceedings of the 2014 international workshop on Long-term industrial collaboration on software engineering*, pages 55–62. ACM, 2014.

[RB01] Peter Reason and Hilary Bradbury. *Handbook of action research: Participative inquiry and practice*. Sage, 2001.

[RHRR12] Per Runeson, Martin Host, Austen Rainer, and Bjorn Regnell. *Case study research in software engineering: Guidelines and examples*. John Wiley & Sons, 2012.

[Rie11] Eric Ries. *The lean startup: How today's entrepreneurs use continuous innovation to create radically successful businesses*. Crown Books, 2011.

[Rup10] Nayan B Ruparelia. Software development lifecycle models. *ACM SIGSOFT Software Engineering Notes*, 35(3):8–13, 2010.

[Sag00] Richard Sagor. *Guiding school improvement with action research*. Ascd, 2000.

[SE78] Gerald I Susman and Roger D Evered. An assessment of the scientific merits of action research. *Administrative science quarterly*, pages 582–603, 1978.

[SM18] Miroslaw Staron and Wilhelm Meding. *Software Development Measurement Programs: Development, Management and Evolution*. Springer, 2018.

[ST09] Paulo Sergio Medeiros dos Santos and Guilherme Horta Travassos. Action research use in software engineering: An initial survey. In *Proceedings of the 2009 3rd International Symposium on Empirical Software Engineering and Measurement*, pages 414–417. IEEE Computer Society, 2009.

[ST11] Paulo Sergio Medeiros dos Santos and Guilherme Horta Travassos. Action research can swing the balance in experimental software engineering. In *Advances in computers*, volume 83, pages 205–276. Elsevier, 2011.

[Sus83] Gerald I Susman. Action research: a sociotechnical systems perspective. *Beyond method: Strategies for social research*, 95:113, 1983.

[WRH+00] Claes Wohlin, Per Runeson, Martin Höst, Magnus C Ohlsson, Björn Regnell, and Anders Wesslén. *Experimentation in software engineering*. Springer, 2000.

Chapter 2
Action Research as Research Methodology in Software Engineering

If we knew what it was we were doing, it would not be called research, would it?

—A. Einstein

Abstract Compared to other research methodologies, action research is probably the youngest one. It's been introduced in the middle of the twentieth century and has gained attention ever since. It became popular because it appeals to both researchers and organizations who seek impact and utilization of scientific results in practice. In this chapter, we present the principles of action research and provide concrete guidelines on how to propose an action research project. We elaborate on the main parts of the action research methodology and exemplify them. We show how we can use experiment systems to involve customers in action research, and we finish the chapter by presenting how to manage action research projects.

2.1 Introduction

Empirical methods in software engineering have a long tradition. The advances in the last two decades, started by the book of Wohlin et al. [WRH+12] and its popularity, are just one of the indications. Experiments, case studies, and surveys became very popular as methods for collecting data about software engineering practices and increased the collaborations between academia and industry. Research studies conducted according to these methodologies were conducted in increasingly orderly fashion, and software engineering journals became increasingly varied about the quality of the empirical research.

Today, action research is believed to swing the balance in software engineering toward industrial practices [DST11], mainly because it focuses on improvement of the practice, learning and emphasis on what practitioners do rather than what they say they do [ALMN99]. Compared to other research methodologies, where the focus is either on the observation and learning or the evaluation, action research

© Springer Nature Switzerland AG 2020
M. Staron, *Action Research in Software Engineering*,
https://doi.org/10.1007/978-3-030-32610-4_2

places more focus on the intervention (like in experiments), the context (like in case studies and observations), and learning.

For example, some of the major problems with experimentation in software engineering, which stop the experimentation from addressing really important problems, are:

- finding participants with industry experience,
- finding experiment objects which scale to industrial context, and
- isolation of treatments which results in nonrepresentative contexts.

These problems often result in experimenting with students and toy problems and therefore make it difficult to transfer the results of experiments to industry. This means that the experiments are perceived as of limited use when collaboration with industry. Examples of successful industry experiments are rather scarce [SHH+05].

On the other hand, research methods based on the principles of observation, e.g., case studies, are more realistic and often conducted in industrial settings. However, they are burdened with the fact that case studies are most often about observing practices, analyzing them, and, in the end, improving them. Therefore, these methods cannot introduce changes to software engineering practices, and studying them is very much needed to increase the rate of introducing improvements to software engineering practices.

Action research can change this. It can scale to larger problems than experiments because it addresses industrial contexts. It can introduce changes to its context and at the same time contribute to theory-building.

In order for the action research project to be successful, both the researchers and the practitioners need to have a respect to each other. Melin and Axelsson [MA07] recognized this problem and discussed its implications. One should not engage in action research collaborations if the academics see the industry as "case study objects" nor when the industry sees academics as "cheap consultants."

In this chapter, I introduce action research as a research methodology, by exploring the following:

- what each phase of action research is and why we need it,
- who can conduct action research, when, and why,
- how many cycles should an action research project have,
- how to collect data and make project decisions based on it,
- how to visualize the data using modern tools, and
- how to involve customers by designing experiment systems.

In this chapter, I provide an example of how a research proposal for an action research project can look like. I also explain what each part of this proposal aims at and what it should contain. The chapter ends with guidelines on how to manage action research projects, which is intended for managers at the collaborating organizations.

2.2   Phases of Action Research Cycles

There are a number of different ways of describing action research, which often differ in the number of phases of an action research project or the focus of it. The basic description contains only two phases, situation assessment and problem intervention, as presented in Fig. 2.1 after [Bas07] and [DST11].

The basic principle behind this simplified cycle is the separation between the observation part (situation assessment) and the intervention part (problem intervention). This view is naturally oversimplistic as it does not prescribe the necessary rigor and systematic manner of conducting research. It does not emphasize the part of reflection, learning, and theory-building needed in action research projects.

Therefore, there is a more familiar way of describing action research cycles, so-called canonical action research [RGN, SE78], which is presented in Fig. 2.2.

Throughout this book, I refer to the canonical action research as the action research unless explicitly specified otherwise.

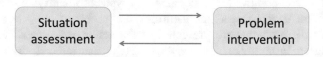

Fig. 2.1 Simplified action research cycle

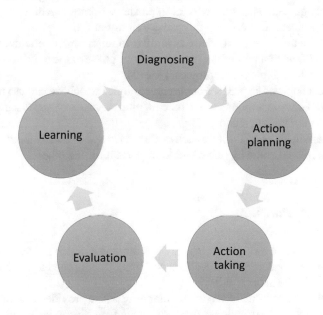

Fig. 2.2 Canonical action research cycle

2.2.1 Diagnosing

Every action research cycle starts with addressing the question of *What is the real problem?* Although the question is often partially answered when initiating the project, it's important to specify which part of the problem should be addressed in each cycle.

The first phase of each action research cycle—diagnosing—is unique for action research. Instead of starting a project with a detailed problem formulation, action research recognizes the fact that one needs to be embedded in the context in order to elicit the problem correctly. Therefore, every action research cycle starts with a precise diagnosis of which problem should be solved.

Action researchers should start by collecting opinions and symptoms which they need to explore in order to decide which challenge to address during the action research cycle. It's important that the researchers focus on discussions with the practitioners when exploring the context and deciding what to do. The problem to be solved in each cycle should be limited in scope, and its effects should be measurable.

Melin and Axelsson [MA07] recognize two types of identifying research problems: when an action researcher identifies the problems, i.e., research-driven initiation, or the problems are presented to the action researcher, i.e., problem-driven initiation. From my experience, the first type, i.e., research-driven initiation, is more common for the diagnosing part, whereas the problem-driven initiation is more common for the overall definition of the research project. Avison et al. [ABM01] recognize the possibility of both parties working together in recognizing the research problem, i.e., collaborative research initiation.

We could see the diagnosing phase as similar to requirements elicitation phase in agile projects of the first part of the market analysis phase of the build-measure-learn cycle of continuous deployment projects [Rie11].

In the next chapter, Chap. 3, we explore techniques which we can use to diagnose the problem. These techniques are a mix of interviews, surveys, discussions, and requirements engineering techniques.

In this chapter, let us go through each of the phase and overview them, explaining how they are related and why one phase is important for the others.

2.2.2 Action Planning

Planning of actions in a single cycle is always done in a collaborative manner. Academic researchers, industrial researchers, and practitioners need to work together to decide who does the actions and when.

The collaborative nature of the action planning phase provides a unique opportunity for both practitioners and researchers to engage in discussions. The discussion are often aimed at finding ways to solve the problem diagnosed in the first phase and identify resources, products, and processes to be investigated and adjusted.

In the action planning activity, the action team (which is how I call the research team) discusses their plans with the reference groups and needs to get approval for the required resources from the management team. The plans need to be aligned with theoretical foundations of the work, i.e., the action team needs to identify theoretical or empirical work relevant for the diagnosed problem and plan the actions accordingly.

In this phase, the action team, together with the reference team, makes the plans for which data should be collected, from which objects, using which tools. The team also plans for which analysis methods should be employed to assess whether their actions lead to solving the diagnosed problem.

Often, although far from always, the action team plans their actions using standard project planning tools, like Gantt charts and work breakdown structures. However, these are often lightweight and documented only internally for the action team to follow and use as a communication tool to management.

2.2.3   Action Taking

The action taking phase is dedicated to making changes in the context— interventions. The phase is executed according to the plans laid out in the previous phase and is conducted by the action team. The reference group is involved on a regular basis to provide feedback and to help the action team to solve the challenges that they encounter [ASSH16].

The action taking phase is specific for action research as it is one of the research methodologies where making changes are allowed, midst in the operations. It's called a flexible research design methodology [Rob11]. For example, the action team is allowed to change the ways of working for software development teams and observe these changes.

It is important to note that the action taking phase is both about making the change and observing its effect. As action research is a quantitative methodology, the data collection activities provide the possibility to reduce the bias of subjective observations and provide quantitative evidence. This quantitative evidence is used in the next phase—action evaluation—to assess the effects of the actions and is used as the input to the next cycle's diagnosing phase.

2.2.4   Evaluation

In the evaluation phase, the action team analyzes the data collected from the previous phase. The team uses statistical methods to make the analyses and presents the results to the reference team and the management.

In case when the data shows that the diagnosed problem is indeed solved using the actions taken, the outcome is straightforward. If the data is inconclusive, the action team either needs to plan for additional analyses and additional data to be collected or needs to pivot, i.e., finalize the current cycle, specify learning, and find a new diagnosis of the problem given the new data collected. Then the action team continues with the next cycle to address this diagnosed problem.

In the evaluation section, the action team usually uses the same statistical methods as experimentation, i.e., descriptive and inferential statistics.

The action team also needs to assure that the analysis of their data is aligned with the theories used in the cycle. This is important in order to make the contribution to the theory-building in the next phase.

2.2.5 *Learning*

The final part of the action research cycle is the specification of learning. It is done both as practical guidelines for the involved organizations and contexts and as theory-building for the research community.

The practical guidelines are often specified in terms of guidebooks, white papers, and instructions at the company's web. For example, software development teams often use wiki-s to specify good practices and document good examples. That's often when the results of action research cycles can be found.

The contribution to the theory-building is often specified as scientific papers, with the scientific rigor and relevance. It is often the case that these are documented as experience reports from industrial studies, e.g., [Med17].

2.3 Action Research Cycles in Software Engineering Organizations

The canonical action research is an established, general research method. The experience of my team, however, shows that the action research is best described and defined when we provide the context of it.

Figure 2.3 shows the context of action research in terms of inputs and outputs. Throughout the book, I come back to this cycle and add new elements to it, e.g., stakeholders, customers, actors, and theories.

The important aspect of the figure is the input to the action research projects. Practitioners often bring the needs to improve their organizations, products, or operations. The researchers often bring in the needs to evaluate or validate methods and tools in the new context of the collaborating organization. The different colors of these two inputs indicate that the two parties—industry and academia—often come from different directions and bring these inputs independently of each other. The mixed colors of the phases of action research and the outputs show that the rest of action research is done collaboratively and that it impacts both industry and academia.

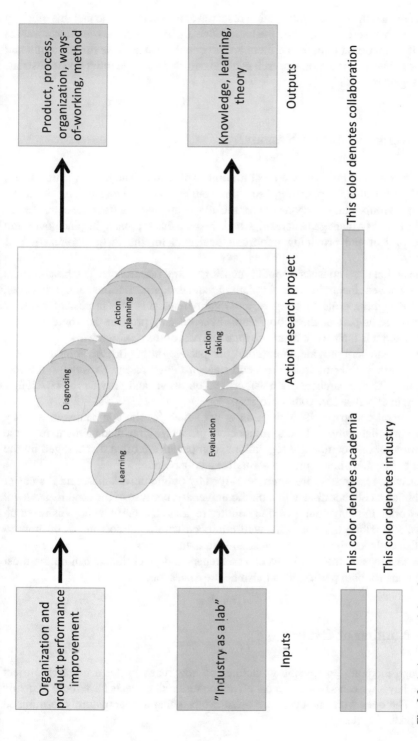

Fig. 2.3 Action research in software engineering

The main point of successful action research collaboration is the fact that industry and academia work together and the knowledge, theories, methods, and tools impact both. It is important to note that there are no double cycles—one for academia and one for industry. The action research cycle is one, and the academics and industrials work together.

2.4 Actors in Action Research

In action research projects, we meet a number of actors. There is an action team, who is responsible for planning, executing, and evaluating the research. There is a reference group, who is responsible for the advice and feedback for the action team. Finally, there is a management team, who is responsible for managing and governing of the project and providing important decisions for the institutionalization of change.

The action team consists of both practitioners and researchers. The practitioners are software engineers involved in planning and executing actions, e.g., architects, testers, designers, project managers, and quality managers. It is important that they are involved as part of the action team, because they provide the context of the actions, and it is their work that is changed as part of the research work.

The researchers provide an external perspective on the organizational change, and their role is to bring in theories and state-of-the-art research results to the collaboration. The researchers often ask critical questions and provide the possibility to bring in expertise from other projects.

In several countries, the legislation is not suited for the companies to directly engage in collaborations. Due to intellectual property rights management, resource allocation, or anti-competitor regulations, companies are often discouraged by the amount of legal work required to formalize a collaboration.

However, researchers are often employed by public universities, and it's easier to establish a collaboration with a public university, because of the established legal frameworks. In many countries, the country regulators specify who owns research results, and public financiers are well equipped with legal documents on how to establish collaborations between academia in industry.

For that reason, the mix between researchers and practitioners can be the most fruitful one for both parties; it can also be the easiest one.

2.5 Number of Cycles

Although there are no specific guidelines on how many cycles a research project should have, we can say that almost all action research projects have more than one cycle. The ones with one cycle are often projects that are prematurely terminated after the first cycle.

From my experience, each action research cycle should last for at least 1 month, as it requires preparations and time for reflection. In order to prepare for the shortest cycle, for example, introducing something during a 2-week sprint in agile software development, we still need time to prepare (diagnose and plan) and the time to reflect (evaluate and learn). This means that these activities add up to the time and even the 2-week sprint will require at least 1 month of time as a research cycle.

From my experience, a good action research cycle is somewhere between 3 and 6 months long. It is linked to the schedule of the project or organization (its context) and results in a research paper. For example, please take a look at the work of Antinyan et al. on validating measures using action research [ASSH16].

2.6 Collecting the Data

In the process of collecting data in action research projects, many contemporary researchers rely on tools used for software development. These tools provide different interfaces to get the data and, often, provide a description of the data model used to store information internally.

2.7 Visualizing the Data

Visualizations, diagrams, and charts are very popular in modern dashboards. Besides the standard charts like the bar chart, boxplot, or histogram, we can use more advanced visualizations to make our dashboards visually more appealing. They also help to understand and diagnose the problem.

An example of a diagram which is often used in visualizations is a scatter plot, as shown in Fig. 2.4. The diagram is used to explore dependencies between two variables. In Fig. 2.4, we visualize the dependency between the lines of code and number of methods of one version of eclipse projects. The data set is available openly from http://bug.inf.usi.ch/index.php.

In the scatter plot, we can see how two variables are dependent on one another. This simple diagram helps us to identify whether dependencies occur when they should not, to find missing dependencies, or simply to find data points which are outliers. We can use this kind of diagram to raise awareness about a specific dependency in the action team and communicate them to the management team and to the reference team.

However, we can explore more than two variables, which means that we need to use more advanced types of scatter plots. For example, Fig. 2.5 presents the dependency between three variables.

Although 3D visualizations are interesting and provide the possibility to nicely interact by zooming in or rotating the diagrams along their axes, they cannot visualize dependencies between more than three variables. For that, we need

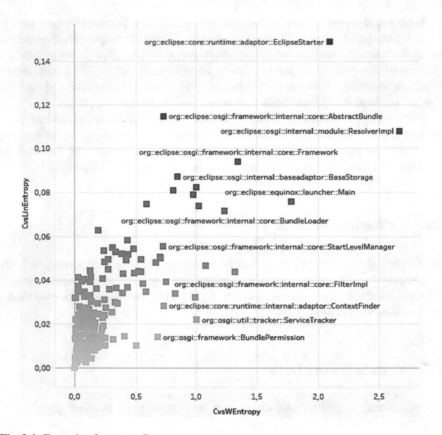

Fig. 2.4 Example of a scatter diagram

another type of chart—correlogram. A correlogram consists of a number of scatter plots, which visualize dependencies between multiple variables pairwise. Figure 2.6 provides such a visualization.

Correlograms provide us with the possibility to capture collinearity between variables and therefore reduce the number of measures. It allows us also to observe deviations from the expected trend in collinearity.

From my experience, using visualizations is a very powerful tool to make an impact on the industrial partners and to lead the discussion to the data rather than toward speculative statements and so-called gut feeling. There is nothing wrong with speculations and "gut feelings," but they can be misleading, and they can lead to unnecessary effort and costs in the action research projects.

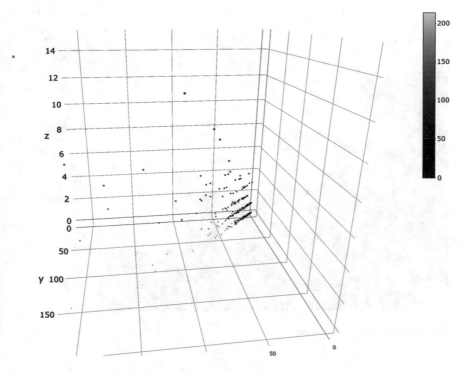

Fig. 2.5 Example of a 3D scatter plot

2.8 Software Experiment Systems

Action research projects are done at industrial partners and usually focus on the data available at the company. However, the companies do not possess all knowledge of their products, as they do not control how their products are used. Sometimes in the action research projects, this knowledge of how the customers use the product is very important to avoid suboptimizations and to increase the business value of the action research project. Luckily, there is a modern way of getting the insight from the customers' use of the products—software experiment systems.

Software experiment systems are often used to collect the data from customers in an organized manner. Recent studies, e.g., by Fabijan et al. [FDOB17], show that these studies are organized around learning and therefore are suitable to be used as part of action research. Companies like Microsoft [KLSH09], Facebook [BEB14], and Google [TAOM10] are known to use this type of customer involvement.

Software experiment systems are based on simultaneously deploying different types of features to customers and measuring the interactions of the customers with these features. The differentiation between features deployed to customers is often referred to as A/B testing [SK13]. The data collected from the customers is based on measures such as retention, activation, and recommendation. However, the

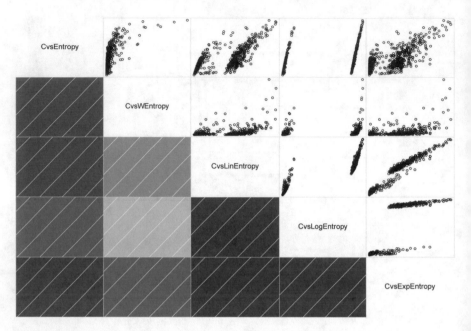

Fig. 2.6 Example of a correlogram

measurements can be of any type, depending on what the actual feature is about and how to measure the success of the interaction of the feature.

The software experiment system is similar to action research; therefore, it can be very useful for action research scientists:

- diagnosing phase of action research is similar to hypothesis formulation in experiment systems,
- action taking phase is similar to feature deployment,
- evaluation phase is similar to the hypothesis testing phase, and
- both experiment systems and action research focus on learning from the results.

The software experiment systems are based on the same principles as experiments in software engineering in general:

- we have two or more groups of customers in the experiment—one control group and one or more test groups,
- each group gets a different treatment at each trial, and
- we measure the same characteristics for the control group and the test group.

The main advantage of the experiment systems comes when we can deploy different features to customers in a flexible way. For example, if we have a web application which is used by many customers—a search engine, a social media platform, or a similar one—the goal is to have as many experiment subjects (customers) as possible to use the product.

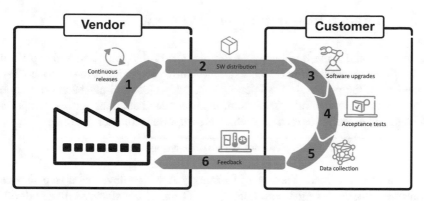

Fig. 2.7   Conceptual overview of experiment systems setup

Figure 2.7 presents a conceptual overview of an experiment system setup with the vendor providing software to the customers, collecting the data from them, analyzing the data, and improving the software based on that. It comes from one of my research partners and shows how they work with the data collection.

The important part of this cycle, which involves the customers, is the extended partnership between the vendors and customers. They need to have a very different level of trust than before as the vendors can have access to the data of the customer's customers (e.g., cloud providers can have data from the customers of companies providing storage services).

In my experience, I've encountered this kind of partnerships a few times, and I had the privilege to work with one of these setups. It was not easy to enter this kind of collaboration, but it provided me and my research team with a completely different set of experience. Instead of relying on our partner to tell us how they work with the customers, we got the firsthand experience about how the customers work with our partners. Since we come from a public university, the customers were very open about the aspects of the collaborations. We, as researchers, were trusted to be objective in reporting of this collaboration.

The experiment systems provide a great way of extending action research to involve customers, as we show in this book.

2.9   An Action Research Project Proposal

In this section, let me introduce an example of a project proposal and explain the parts of this proposal based on this example. The example helps to illustrate what is necessary in the proposal for an action research project and makes the subsequent explanation more concrete. The example introduces headlines for each important element and exemplifies elements which are important for each headline.

Title: Product Downtime Measurement

Context

Software development **Team A** of **Company A** which develops **a web service for checking car's registration numbers**. The team consists of software developers, testers, and architects. All team members are involved in the research.

Goal

The team needs to **improve the quality of their product** by minimizing the number of times the product restarts. They need to **understand how to measure the downtime** of their product during the development to forecast the downtime at the customer's site. They need to find or develop a new measure to quantify downtime during development. This measurement needs to be representative for the downtime for the product in field, i.e., once the product is deployed at the customer.

Actors

Team A is the main actor in the project as they are working on the introduction of the measurement. The **role of the university researcher** is to review existing, documented, and published experiences with downtime measurements. The **role of a quality manager and release manager** is to provide reference whether the measurement leads to the expected quality increase. The **role of the product manager** is to provide the evaluation of the final outcome, and the **role of the line manager** is to sponsor the research.

Intended Outcome

We plan to introduce the found or defined measure for product downtime and to define and introduce ways of using this measure in the software development process at Company A. We expect the downtime at the customer side to **decrease by 30%** as a result of using this measure to guide design decisions during development.

Actions

First, we plan to run a review of existing experiences with product downtime measurement at the company and in literature. We also plan to identify and document problems related to downtime that the company wants to remove. Second, we plan to find the measure, use it in a pilot project, and discuss experiences with the reference group. Then we plan to use it in a pilot project deployed to the customers. Based on the results of this deployment, we plan to define measurement methods for the measures, indicators, stakeholders, and actions related to different levels of the indicator.

Data Collection and Measurements

We plan to collect the data from two or three internal releases of the product. The exact measurement methods are defined based on the results of the first action research cycle. For the first cycle, we plan to collect the following measures:

- the number of software failures for regression test run for ten builds,
- the McCabe cyclomatic complexity of the source per each build,
- the number of software exceptions thrown per each regression test run,
- the number of "try" blocks per software module.

Evaluation

The evaluation of the new method is planned by **measuring whether the downtime of the product decreased over time (i.e., over two or three releases)**. The reference group and the quality and product managers provide their opinion whether the reduction of the downtime is satisfactory, and, therefore, they define the stop criteria.

What we want to learn:

- how to set up the internal development environment so that we can use prerelease measurements and in-development measurements to assess the post-release values of the same measures,
- what kind of internal product structure has the lowest impact on post-release downtime, and
- how to use product diagnostics from the field in terms of customer data protection and how to set up the legal framework regarding the collection of data from the customers.

Ethical Considerations

We need to prepare **an informed consent** for everyone in the team; we also need to make an initial presentation about **which actions (interventions)** we plan in this project; we also need to stress what is expected from each project member and ask **how they want the project to benefit them**.

The presented proposal is rather detailed and rich in concrete plans. This is quite common as industrial partners and practitioners in the action team need to present these proposals to their management. So, the proposal can "live" its own life in the company, and, therefore, it has to be detailed.

Here comes the strength of the action research and its flexible research design nature. Instead of using abstract terms to describe the project in order to leave room for potential adaptations in the project, we embrace the change, and we are open to adjustments. We make a plan, and our industrial partners know that the plan can change depending on the situation in the company, the availability of data, or external factors. However, the detailed plan provides them with the ability to make a more informed decision about the project.

In the subsequent sections, we look into the details of each part of this proposal.

2.9.1   Context

In action research, the context of the research project defines what and how we plan and act in the project. The context is important for defining the goals and actors, as they need to be part of the context when they are part of the actions or outside when they are part of the evaluation.

The context can change as the action research project progresses. It can change from one cycle to another when we identify that we need to change the context in order to succeed in the project. Typical contexts in software engineering are (the list is not exclusive):

- Development team: a team of different software engineers (often with different roles) that have a common goal to develop a specific piece of functionality (usually a feature, a component).
- Software product: an offering to a customer which can be sold or licensed.
- Service: work which is defined and sold to customers as a service, i.e., not a web service, which can be seen as a product.
- Software deployment: an offering or a product which is installed or licensed to a specific customer. It is important that this deployment has a client or a customer that can be involved in either the actions or evaluation part of the action research project.
- Software process: a set of activities that are performed in order to specify, develop, and deploy a software product. Processes are often company specific, but they need to be documented and thus systematic and organized.
- Company: a complete software development environment, where software engineers need to interact with other roles. The typical other roles are sales, purchasing/procurement, legal, and infrastructure providers (e.g., IT support).

The list of potential contexts can be much longer, but it is important that software engineers, their products, and practices are in the center of the action research. If they are not, the project may still be characterized as action research, but they make the contribution to other fields of sciences, and it's better to follow the guidelines for these fields.

A counterexample of the context is a procurement teams which buy components from automotive tier 1 suppliers for an automotive OEM (original equipment manufacturer) [Sta17]. Since these components include software, but are mainly mechanical, the procurement specialists are often non-software engineers, and, therefore, the context of the project is not within software engineering.

2.9.2 Goal

The goals of action research should be focused on developing software engineering practices in their context.

The primary goals are to improve the practices and the products relevant for the context (e.g., a software development team), as they should be in the focus of the project. It is important that the goal defines what the purpose is and why we do this project. I recommend to use the goal specification template from GQM [CR94].

One of the reasons why we write the proposal for research is to communicate it to the industrial partners and their management. Therefore, we need to be able to link the goal specification to the problem that is important for the context of the proposed action research project.

The secondary goals are to build theories and universal practices that can be generalized to other software engineering contexts. However, per definition, this is a secondary goal and is part of the documentation and learning for the organization.

2.9.3 Actors

The role of describing the actors is to provide a description of what is expected from different persons and roles in the proposal. As the action research projects often compete for resources with software development projects (which are bread and butter of the companies), the proposal must show clearly who are and how they are expected to participate in the project.

The management of the industrial partner needs to be able to assess the resource and staffing possibilities for the proposed project. The more specific the description of the actors is, the better.

It is also important that the industrial partners are involved in performing the actions, not just observing or providing feedback. It is also important that the actors are part of the operations of the company and not solely additional staff allocated for the research project.

Researchers can and should be involved in these projects. However, they must be embedded in the company context—they need to be part of the context on a daily basis, spending time at the company premises, and they need to be accepted by the company as "one of their own."

2.9.4   Intended Outcome

The expected outcomes of an action research project should be in the form of concrete, measurable improvements. Since this research methodology is a positivistic, quantitative way of conducting research, it should provide observable and objective intended outcomes.

It is often better to state the intended outcome quantitatively and then refine these objectives during the project than being vague and subjective. It's important that these outcomes can be validated by the management of the company and organization that is the context of this research.

Stating clear goals, from my experience, always starts a good discussion about the value of the project and leads to the improvements of the intended project proposal. Some managers want to refine the goals, which leads to the refinement of the intended outcomes. Some other managers, however, like the goals and would like to refine the resources to match the intentions.

2.9.5   Actions

Although it could seem that this is the most important part of the proposal, this section should detail the first cycle and outline the potential follow-up cycles. It should be clear on how many cycles we plan, but it does not have to be specific about the details of all cycles.

We do not need to detail all the cycles as the action research cycles are often dependent on one another. The results of one cycle lead to learning and diagnosing in the next cycle. Therefore, the proposal should detail one cycle and delineate the subsequent ones.

2.9.6   Data Collection and Measurements

Collecting the data and measuring are important parts of any action research project. It should also be specified in the proposal, with details for the first cycle. Listing specific measures is important, but defining their precise measurement methods and functions is not necessary [SM18].

2.9.7   Evaluation

Evaluation is important for every research project, and in some cases, like in the experiments, it is straightforward and based on established statistical methods.

In action research, the evaluation part can be based on statistics, as this research methodology falls under the category of quantitative research methods. However, it needs to be complemented with the observation of the context of the study, as action research projects are done in the context of software development companies and organizations. Being part of an organization means that the quantitative evidence can (and should) be complemented with the opinions of the stakeholders or surveys in the company. Sometimes, these opinions can outweigh the statistical evidence.

It is important to note that action research projects require specific planning of evaluations. As compared to experiments, the action research projects include actions in the evaluated entity, the evaluation needs to take the changing context into account. In many cases, the action research projects involve external stakeholders to evaluate or even customers. The external stakeholders are persons who have relevant roles in the company, but they are not involved in the actions. The customers can be involved if we consider using software experiment systems as part of the evaluation [FGMM14, Bos12].

2.9.8 What We Want to Learn

Organization's learning is crucial in action research projects. In many cases, the action research projects fail to achieve their intended outcomes and goals but leave the company with precious knowledge. It can be knowledge about new technologies, limitations that cannot be overcome, or just the understanding of the details of a specific phenomenon, like a product, service, or ways of working.

Therefore, it is important to describe what we intend to learn from the specific project—both in terms of the context and in terms of the theories used in the project.

For the theories applied in this project, we can specify how we advance the state of the art in that area, whether we provide the evidence supporting or rejecting the theory.

2.9.9 Ethical Considerations

Since action research projects are based on interactions with its context and software engineers, we need to provide ethical considerations for the project, in particular, how we will select the participants, how we will store their personal data, and how we will anonymize the data so that it does not lead to any harm to individuals and companies.

An interesting aspect is the legal part of the collaborations with the companies. We need to make sure that we have all the agreements in place and that all intellectual property rights are handled according to the regulations specific to the countries where the research is conducted. Avison et al. [ABM01] refer to this as a *formalization* of the research project.

2.10 Managing Action Research Projects

So far, we discussed the actors and practitioners in action research projects. However, the role of management is equally important, so we should also understand the ways in which action research projects are managed. Colleagues from the University of Gothenburg and Chalmers studied the collaborations which my action team was involved in, which we use as the basis for this section [SPA11, SC17].

Figure 2.8 shows an example organizational chart of an action research project. The figure contains three parts: (1) the action team, (2) the reference group, and (3) the management.

The role of the action team is to plan and execute the research project. They are responsible for diagnosing, planning, taking, and evaluating the action. They also need to ensure that learnings are specified and disseminated in the organization.

The role of the reference group is to provide the possibility to get feedback on the progress of the project and to reduce biases. The reference group also helps the action team to diagnose the problems and therefore steers the project in the right direction. As the action team is conducting the research, they are biased toward a positive outcome of the project. The reference team is responsible to provide the action team with the feedback on how to reduce this bias and identify when the bias is jeopardizing the outcome of the study.

Finally, the management of the company is important as they decide upon the resources needed for the project. The resources, in turn, determine the scope of the project. The product and process management are important as they help to support the project in making the right impact of the results of their actions.

Fig. 2.8 Organizational chart of action research projects

2.11 Summary and Conclusions

Action research is believed to bring in new ways of interactions between research and practice in software engineering. The action research methodology can help to make the academic results more applied and practitioner's research more rigorous and strict. However, conducting the research project needs to be carefully planned and executed.

In this chapter, we show the main elements of action research and describe it as a methodology. We show who can do action research and how to visualize or analyze the data from the action research projects. We also introduced software experimentation systems as a way of extending action research to customers. We showed how a project proposal can look like for action research projects and how to use different types of actors in the course of the project.

In the next chapter of the book, we dive into details of how to diagnose problems for each cycle in the action research. In the subsequent chapters, we go into detail of the other phases.

References

[ABM01] David Avison, Richard Baskerville, and Michael Myers. Controlling action research projects. *Information technology & people*, 14(1):28–45, 2001.

[ALMN99] David E. Avison, Francis Lau, Michael D. Myers, and Peter Axel Nielsen. Action research. *Commun. ACM*, 42(1):94–97, January 1999.

[ASSH16] Vard Antinyan, Miroslaw Staron, Anna Sandberg, and Jörgen Hansson. Validating software measures using action research a method and industrial experiences. In *Proceedings of the 20th International Conference on Evaluation and Assessment in Software Engineering*, page 23. ACM, 2016.

[Bas07] Richard Baskerville. *Educing Theory from Practice*, pages 313–326. Springer US, Boston, MA, 2007.

[BEB14] Eytan Bakshy, Dean Eckles, and Michael S Bernstein. Designing and deploying online field experiments. In *Proceedings of the 23rd international conference on World wide web*, pages 283–292. ACM, 2014.

[Bos12] Jan Bosch. Building products as innovation experiment systems. In *Software Business*, pages 27–39. Springer, 2012.

[CR94] Victor R Basili-Gianluigi Caldiera and H Dieter Rombach. Goal question metric paradigm. *Encyclopedia of software engineering*, 1:528–532, 1994.

[DST11] Paulo Sergio Medeiros Dos Santos and Guilherme Horta Travassos. Action research can swing the balance in experimental software engineering. In *Advances in computers*, volume 83, pages 205–276. Elsevier, 2011.

[FDOB17] Aleksander Fabijan, Pavel Dmitriev, Helena Holmström Olsson, and Jan Bosch. The benefits of controlled experimentation at scale. In *Software Engineering and Advanced Applications (SEAA), 2017 43rd Euromicro Conference on*, pages 18–26. IEEE, 2017.

[FGMM14] Fabian Fagerholm, Alejandro Sanchez Guinea, Hanna Mäenpää, and Jürgen Münch. Building blocks for continuous experimentation. In *Proceedings of the 1st international workshop on rapid continuous software engineering*, pages 26–35. ACM, 2014.

[KLSH09] Ron Kohavi, Roger Longbotham, Dan Sommerfield, and Randal M Henne. Controlled experiments on the web: survey and practical guide. *Data mining and knowledge discovery*, 18(1):140–181, 2009.

[MA07] Ulf Melin and Karin Axelsson. Action in action research–illustrations of what, who, why, where, and when from an e-government project. In *International Conference on Electronic Government*, pages 44–55. Springer, 2007.

[Med17] Wilhelm Meding. Effective monitoring of progress of agile software development teams in modern software companies: an industrial case study. In *Proceedings of the 27th International Workshop on Software Measurement and 12th International Conference on Software Process and Product Measurement*, pages 23–32. ACM, 2017.

[RGN] Davison Robert, Martinsons Maris G., and Kock Ned. Principles of canonical action research. *Information Systems Journal*, 14(1):65–86.

[Rie11] Eric Ries. *The lean startup: How today's entrepreneurs use continuous innovation to create radically successful businesses*. Crown Books, 2011.

[Rob11] Colin Robson. *Real world research*, volume 3. Wiley Chichester, 2011.

[SC17] Anna Börjesson Sandberg and Ivica Crnkovic. Meeting industry: Academia research collaboration challenges with agile methodologies. In *Proceedings of the 39th International Conference on Software Engineering: Software Engineering in Practice Track*, pages 73–82. IEEE Press, 2017.

[SE78] Gerald I Susman and Roger D Evered. An assessment of the scientific merits of action research. *Administrative science quarterly*, pages 582–603, 1978.

[SHH+05] Dag IK Sjøberg, Jo Erskine Hannay, Ove Hansen, Vigdis By Kampenes, Amela Karahasanovic, N-K Liborg, and Anette C Rekdal. A survey of controlled experiments in software engineering. *IEEE transactions on software engineering*, 31(9):733–753, 2005.

[SK13] Dan Siroker and Pete Koomen. *A/B testing: The most powerful way to turn clicks into customers*. John Wiley & Sons, 2013.

[SM18] Miroslaw Staron and Wilhelm Meding. *Software Development Measurement Programs: Development, Management and Evolution*. Springer, 2018.

[SPA11] Anna Sandberg, Lars Pareto, and Thomas Arts. Agile collaborative research: Action principles for industry-academia collaboration. *IEEE software*, 28(4):74–83, 2011.

[Sta17] Miroslaw Staron. *Automotive Software Architectures: An Introduction*. Springer, 2017.

[TAOM10] Diane Tang, Ashish Agarwal, Deirdre O'Brien, and Mike Meyer. Overlapping experiment infrastructure: More, better, faster experimentation. In *Proceedings of the 16th ACM SIGKDD international conference on Knowledge discovery and data mining*, pages 17–26. ACM, 2010.

[WRH+12] Claes Wohlin, Per Runeson, Martin Höst, Magnus C Ohlsson, Björn Regnell, and Anders Wesslén. *Experimentation in software engineering*. Springer, 2012.

Chapter 3
Diagnosing

The noblest pleasure is the joy of understanding.

—Leonardo da Vinci

Abstract The first phase of action research is diagnosing the problem to be addressed. Although it seems to be a straightforward task, diagnosing can be difficult as we need to understand the context of the project and the theories needed to take action. In this chapter, we explore different ways of diagnosing the problem—starting from observational ones like interviews and finishing up with analytical ones like statistical data analysis from experiment systems.

3.1 Introduction

Diagnosing in action research can take multiple forms, and therefore it's quite interesting. Many researchers perceive this phase as a literature search or interview phase, but diagnosing the problem is much more than that. In its essence, diagnosing is the phase where we collect information about the problem expressed by practitioners and identify the root cause of this problem that we can solve. We collect the data by conducting literature reviews when we need to learn about the state of the art in that particular area. However, diagnosing is primarily based on "walking the floor," i.e., getting to understand the product, the organization, and the context of the action research project.

From experience, I have observed that it takes about 2 to 6 months for the diagnosing phase of the first cycle. Researchers need to make mistakes, and learn from them, in order to understand the context. They need to be seen as part of the practitioners' teams in order to get accepted by the industrial partners. Practitioners, on the other hand, need to understand what research is about. They need to find the way of looking beyond the symptoms and need to have patience for the structure and rigor of research studies.

© Springer Nature Switzerland AG 2020

M. Staron, *Action Research in Software Engineering*,

https://doi.org/10.1007/978-3-030-32610-4_3

In this chapter, we go through a number of methods for diagnosing the research problem. We start with interviews, both structured and unstructured (so-called by the coffee machine). We continue with observations and focus group meetings and workshops. Finally, we get back to the concept of experiment systems and look into how we can use the data from the field in the diagnosing phase.

In the end of the chapter, we discuss the roles involved in the diagnosing, we provide an example, and we show how diagnosing can differ from one cycle to another.

3.2   Role of Theory in Diagnosing

When designing our diagnosing phase, we need to start from the theory which is used as the basis for this action research cycle. Theory, in this context, does not need to be an explicitly established theory like a set theory or a theory of relativity. The theory, in this context, is the description of the phenomena that need to be studied, theoretical relationships between elements of that phenomenon, and the rationale behind them.

The theory is important as it guides the design of our diagnosing methods, e.g., which questions we can ask during our interviews or what we observe in the organization.

Theory   Defects are a symptom of ways of working in a project.

Rationale   This theory describes our understanding how defects inflow can show different ways that a software team work, i.e., differences between Agile and Waterfall.

Definition   Defect inflow is a number of defects reported per week in a development project.

Theoretical Model   The defect inflow from waterfall projects is characterized by the peak, which is caused by the fact that gradually integrated functionality leads to gradually increased number of tests executed. The increased number of tests executed leads to higher number of reported defects; see Fig. 3.1.

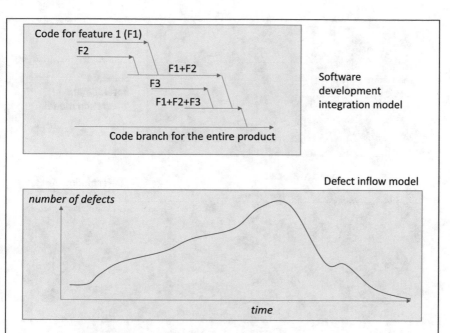

Fig. 3.1 Defect inflow related to waterfall development

The defect inflow from continuous integration projects [DMG07], usually Agile, is characterized by sequences of increased and decreased number of defects reported. As code is integrated to the main branch continuously, the trend line oscillates, and the amplitude is not as high as in the waterfall projects. As testing is done continuously on the main branch, the trend line is rather flat as shown in Fig. 3.2.

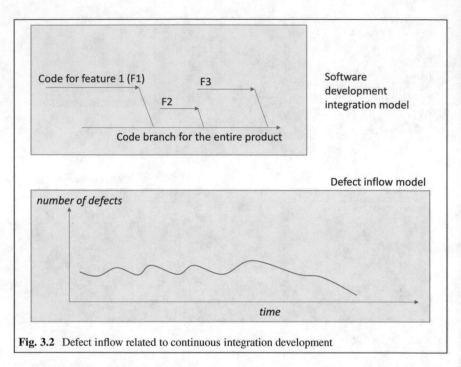

Fig. 3.2 Defect inflow related to continuous integration development

The example of defect inflow shows that the theory in action research does not need to be formally defined using mathematics. The important part of the theory is that it is explicitly specified, and, therefore, it can be used to the following.

3.3 Interviews

The basic way of getting information for diagnosing a research problem is to use interviews. We use interviews in many forms. We use open-ended interviews where we basically ask questions based on a predefined protocol with the possibility to change the questions as the conversation goes. We use close-ended interviews where we follow the interview protocol to the letter and do not change the questions.

In the context of action research, interviews are often mixed with other types of information sources. Formal interviews are often complemented with the informal discussions, e.g., the so-called coffee machine discussions, where we talk to software engineers during meetings, ask questions, and get information without the prior plan for that.

The topic of interviews is a wide topic, and there are great guides on how to conduct them. Therefore, let us only go through the most essential parts, i.e., how to prepare and document them. I recommend the guide by Foddy and Foddy [FF94] to explore this topic in more depth. I also recommend the website of social research methods as a great source of information about interviews (http://www.socialresearchmethods.net).

3.3.1   Preparing for Interviews

Preparing for interviews is a bit more than just preparing questions. It includes also preparing the actual interview occasion. We need to prepare the documentation of the consent for all respondents, we need to prepare ourselves by rehearsing, and we need to prepare the technical equipment for recording the interview.

When designing the questions, we need to ensure that the questions are linked to the theory which we use in diagnosing. Quite often, we seek to understand how valid our theoretical model is, and therefore we need to ask about elements of that theoretical model.

The example below shows example questions linked to the theoretical model presented in the previous section.

Questions About the Process Model
- How can you characterize (and why) your process model—waterfall, agile, continuous integration?
- Do you integrate features with each other, or do you integrate each feature to the main branch?
- If the above is not true, please describe your feature integration process.

Questions About Test Process
- How often do you execute your test scope, e.g., every day, once a week, after every build?
- How often do you add new tests to the scope, e.g., every execution, every week, after every commit?
- Which of the two development models from Figs. 3.1 or 3.2 better characterizes your company's software development model?

Questions About the Defect Inflow
- Do you report defects found during all test phases?
- What is the difference between defects found by different types of test cases (e.g., integration tests, unit tests, feature tests) in terms of severity of frequency?
- Which of the two defect inflows from Figs. 3.1 or 3.2 better characterizes your company's defect inflow?

This example set of questions[1] shows that they are connected to the theory presented earlier in Sect. 3.2. Once we have both the theoretical frames and the questions, it is easier to validate that our questions indeed ask about the right phenomena.

These questions help us to diagnose whether the theoretical assumptions are indeed valid for the studied context. They allow us to understand whether the action planning phase is done correctly or even how to plan our actions in the next phase.

3.3.2 Documenting Interviews

Today, we have many more technical solutions to document interviews. In the "old days," the main solution was to tape the interviews, transcribe them, and then use them as input to qualitative data analysis methods like the Grounded theory [SC90]. Today, we often use smartphones and other tools to record the interviews, and we can use voice recognition programs to transcribe them. Regardless of the form, however, we always need to obtain the informed consent from the respondent. The consent should, at least, provide the following information:

- the purpose of the interview,
- description of where the data from the interview will be stored,
- description of who has access to the data,
- description of how we will use the data and whether it will be anonymous (if so, how the anonymity will be preserved), and
- note on how to withdraw the consent given during the interview (in case the respondent changes her/his mind about the interview).

Sometimes, researchers are afraid that regulations about data protection can stop them from engaging in this practices, which is not accurate. Often, the data protection regulations require us to be clear about how we will handle the data, and as long as we are, the respondents can make a conscious decision about their participation and whether they agree to our policies.

Interviews should be documented in detail regarding the participants, time, place, and the other necessary information to assure the quality of the analysis.

---

[1] For the sake of simplicity, I use the same figures again, but this introduces a bias as the respondents see both the defect inflow and the development model. For the real interview protocol, we should paste the relevant part of Figs. 3.1 and 3.2 here—either with the development model or the defect inflow.

3.3.3   Appreciative Inquiry

Appreciative inquiry [CS87] is a specific way of conducting interviews. It is based on the principle that conducting a dialogue or a conversation leads to a change in the context where this dialogue and conversation are conducted. The format for conducting and documenting is the same as for other forms of interviews. The difference is in the way the questions are formulated and posed.

The main idea behind the appreciative inquiry is that we can influence the attitude to our actions by positive dialogues, appreciation of the action of the context, and presenting a positive view of the future.

Cooperrider et al. [CW+01] have established five principles of appreciative inquiry:

- The Constructionist Principle: conversation leads to the perception of the real world around us.
- The Principle of Simultaneity: inquiry and change are interchangeable, and, therefore, asking questions can, by itself, cause a change.
- The Poetic Principle: we choose what we study, and this choice is reflected in the results of our studies.
- The Anticipatory Principle: by focusing the conversation on positive views on the future, we create positive actions in the present.
- The Positive Principle: sustaining a change requires a lot of positive energy, e.g., social interactions, raising hope, inspiration, and motivation.

The above principles indicate that in the diagnosing phase of action research, we can already create a positive ground for the success of the later phases. When we plan for action taking, we can also include significant amount of communication activities in order to motivate and inspire our context when conducting action research.

Since the appreciative inquiry is a means to drive the change by itself, it needs to be used with caution. In most cases, this way of interviews works best in later cycles of the action research, when the research team is familiar with the context, the organization. The research team, then, has the first-hand experience and therefore can refer to the relevant practices directly.

3.4   Observations

Observations are very popular in psychology, and they have been adopted in software engineering together with the popularization of the usage of ethnographic methods in software engineering [HKRA94]. There are many types of observations, but for action research, participatory observations are the most popular ones. They allow the researchers to be part of the team and observe the team at the same time.

3.4.1   Preparing for Observations

Before an observation takes place, we need to decide upon what and when it is going to be observed. To our help, we have the theoretical frames which we establish during the diagnosing phase.

The frame below shows an example of an observation protocol, where we explore the relation between the defect inflow and the development style. In particular, we focus on the activities of the tester in the context of software integration and build.

Purpose of the Observation To document how the test process is conducted at Company A

Information

Role of the observed person	
Time of the observation	
Duration of the observation	

Observation of Events

Item	Observed	Not observed	Details
Tester conducts root cause analysis directly after the failed test case			
Tester writes a defect report directly after the failed test case			
Tester runs all test cases every time a build has finished			

Observer's Notes

....
....
....
....

The protocol is derived from the theory described in this phase. It also shows that the observation is a complement to an interview. It contains both specific elements what to observe (yes/no questions) and information about the context of the observation.

It is quite common that there is a dedicated place for unstructured observer notes. These notes, however, are often long, and, therefore, the space only shows that it is possible to keep them, while most researchers keep a separate diary for these kinds of notes.

3.4.2 Documenting Observations

Observations are documented in two ways: notes of the observer and recordings of the observations. Although the latter is very popular in psychology and sociology when studying social processes, the former is very popular in software engineering.

The observer should make notes of everything that he or she finds important during the observation. The theoretical frames established in the diagnosing help the observer to make decisions on what to note/record. However, the observer should also be aware that too much focus on the theory can lead to omission of important information; therefore, the observation protocol should be reflected in the documentation. There are three main ways of documenting the observations (http://www.simplypsychology.org): event sampling, time sampling, and instantaneous sampling.

Event sampling is based on the predefined events that trigger the documentation. For example, a researcher may decide to take note of the behavior of the practitioner when he/she starts the testing process.

Time sampling is based on the predefined time periods when the documentation occurs. For example, the researcher can decide to take notes of the first 10 min of every software integration meeting during the software development.

Instantaneous sampling is based on the observer deciding when the observation takes place and takes note only of what happens at that instant, ignoring everything that happens before or after. For example, the researcher can decide to note what happens when a test case fails.

Seaman [Sea99] advocated that "The observer's notes should not be visible to any of the meeting participants. In fact, the notes should be kept confidential throughout the study. This gives the researcher complete freedom to write down any impressions, opinions, or thoughts without the fear that they may be read by someone who will be offended by them." This shows the importance of the independence between the research team and the rest of the team; at the same time, it illustrates how transparent the researcher needs to be when discussing the consent with the observed practitioners.

3.4.3 Participatory Observations

Since action research requires the presence of researchers in their context, often the organizations where the research is conducted, pure observations are often not practical. Action researchers engage often in participatory observations (also known as participant observations, [Jor89, Jor15]), where they can naturally be among the observed groups. This type of observation is defined by the SAGE Encyclopedia of Communication Research Methods as "Participant observation is the process of entering a group of people with a shared identity to gain an understanding of their community" [All17]. Seaman [Sea99] recognized the participatory observations as one of the ways of exemplary qualitative methods in software engineering already in 1999.

However, being part of the observed group means that researchers can influence the group and therefore bias the results. The participant observation method has been discussed in the research community extensively, exactly because of this fact—the potential risk of bias. Therefore, researchers engaging in participant observations need to pay special attention to this, prepare the protocol beforehand, and turn to other researchers when analyzing the results (using analysis method triangulation).

From my personal experience, this type of diagnosing and data collection is the most fruitful one for action researchers. Being part of the environment over a period of time provides the possibility to get accustomed with the collaborating company and understand their daily routines. Oftentimes, it is impossible to understand the real challenges just by interviewing the practitioners. Becoming part of the environment provides the possibility to understand the meaning of the answers obtained during interviews. It provides the researcher with the possibility to assess the importance of different statements and to prioritize them when making analyses.

Finally, the participant observations are important for the researchers to personally develop their skills. University professors need to be up to date with the industrial practices and industrial problems in order to prepare their students to fully engage in their professional life.

3.5   Focus Group Workshops

Focus groups are one more way of including multiple stakeholders in the study. According to Conklin and Hayhoe [CH10] focus groups are "group interviews," so in addition to the participants who are the subjects of the research, this technique requires one or two experienced interviewers or facilitators, who pose questions, follow up short answers that may not be clear, and draw out a variety of perspectives in the group to questions posed.

Focus groups are used extensively in research when the researchers want to gather opinions from multiple stakeholders at the same time. This type of group interview requires preparations in order to avoid group drifting (e.g., discussions off-topic) or domination (e.g., by one person or one idea).

Kontio et al. [KLB04] discussed the need, opportunities, and threats of focus groups in software engineering, including more modern evolutions of this method—online focus group meetings. The experiences documented by Kontio and his team included positive aspects such as aided recall (when one participant's recollection of an event triggers others to recall either a similar or opposite events) or negative aspects as social acceptability (when social participants can feel the need to be part of the group and therefore can omit important facts).

In the example of the box below, I show an example from experience on how we used a focus group workshop to find the formula for calculating release readiness in one organization; the research is described in our of our papers [SMP12].

Focus Group Workshop to Find Formula for Release Readiness

A manager solicited a study to find a formula for release readiness of his organization's software product. The manager suspected that it is possible to find a formula which could predict how many weeks the organization needs to finish up the testing and defect removal of the software, i.e., when the software is ready for release. In order to diagnose the problem and start to identify measures to construct the formula, we conducted a focus group meeting.

Participants

The participants of the meeting were the quality manager of the product in question, the measurement program leader for the organization in question, the line manager soliciting the formula, and the test leader of the product.

The quality manager brought expertise in the defect discovery and removal process. The measurement program leader provided the knowledge about which measures are available, how they are collected, where they are stored, and what the frequency of their collection is. The line manager provided the expertise in the context of the formula and the needs of the organization. The test leader helped us with the understanding of how the test process was designed and executed at the organization. My role was to develop the formula and to assure that no mathematical problems were present in the formula (e.g., no collinearity exists).

The Meeting

The meeting lasted for ca. 1 h. It started with the presentation of the needs of the organization from the line manager. Then each participant could provide the input on what can be measured and how. The group discussed different options and, in the end, settled for a formula (similar to the one published in [SMP12]).

Outcome

The outcome of the meeting was a proposal of a formula that would include the number of defects, divided by the average defect removal ratio.

The Next Step

After the meeting, the researcher (I) would develop the formula together with the measurement program leader. We would discuss the draft with the test leader to understand how to quantify the test progress and with the quality manager to understand which defects should be included in the calculations. This was part of the next step of the study, i.e., action planning.

This example of the focus group meeting illustrates that it is important with the right set of competence to explore and understand the topic, especially important in the context of the diagnosing phase.

3.5.1 Preparing for Focus Group Workshops

In order to sufficiently prepare for the meeting, we need to set the goal of the meeting, identify and invite the relevant participants, and prepare adequate form of the meeting.

In the preparations for the focus group workshops, one of the crucial aspects is the precise definition of the problem to discuss. The topic needs to be clear, and there should be at least one person in the workshop who knows the "why" behind this problem. Understanding the reason for discussing the problem leads to the right focus of the meeting and keeps the group "on track." If the group lacks this understanding, time can be spent on discussing "what do we mean by <the problem>".[2]

The focus group workshops are particularly suitable for those types of problems where we need to construct a common understanding, for example:

- creating a mind map, a conceptual, or a domain model for the study at hand,
- defining dependencies between entities in order to find measures and check the dependency between these measures,
- finding the most important requirements for the developed prototype, or
- assessing whether the results from the previous action research cycle are to be explored further in the current cycle.

Once we defined the problem, it's important to identify the relevant roles and then the relevant individuals who represent these roles. Although every problem requires different competence and roles, there are a few guiding principles which I've used:

- perform a stakeholder analysis and then choose roles from different stakeholder groups, in particular, the stakeholders that are directly affected by the action research project,
- find roles that have different perspective on the same problem, e.g., quality managers who require extra activities and project managers who organize the resources in the project,
- find individuals who get along well with each other but represent different perspectives, in particular, I choose persons whose job would be affected by different outcomes of the action research project, and
- find individuals who have the real saying in their organization and, if they are willing, include them in the reference group of the action research project.

Quite often, or almost always, I also talk to the participants before the actual meeting—most often for a few minutes only. Firstly, to introduce the goal of the focus group meeting to the participants. Secondly, and foremost, to get their feedback on the goal and setup. It happens almost always that the participants have

---

[2]If this kind of discussion occurs, my advice is to pause the meeting, clarify the definition of the problem, and then continue with the focus group workshop.

Table 3.1 Example forms of focus group meetings and their applicability

Form	Applicability
Brainstorming	Provides the ability for everyone to express their opinion while initiating discussions at the same time. Works best when we want to identify the most important or burning issues
Brainwriting (post-its)	Starts with the participants' individual preparations of ideas and writing them on post-its. Then the moderator prepares a summary and moderates the discussion. Works best if we want to list as many ideas as possible and group them. Grouping, however, can draw attention away from single, most important, issues and ideas identified
Moderated discussion	The group discusses a set of predefined ideas and issues, and the moderator assures that all opinions are heard. Works best when the focus group is to find a common understanding or common view on a topics, for example, deciding on the formula on release readiness from our example
Panel	Participants can sit in the panel and present different opinions on the predefined ideas and issues. Works best when the focus group needs to explore advantages and disadvantages of the ideas and issues
Real-time survey	Providing the participants with the possibility to rate the answers or post questions online (e.g., similar to webinar) lets the discussion continue at the same time as letting the participants steer the discussion and include all participants. It is useful in focus groups where there are many participants and we need to document all ideas—similar to brainstorming but with focus on discussions

their own view on the problem, often posing questions that make me rethink the setup, e.g., "Will we discuss the resource allocation on this meeting?"

Once we identified the participants, we need to set up the meeting and choose the right form for the meeting. Table 3.1 summarizes some of the most popular forms of the focus group meetings linked to when they work best.

Conducting the meeting depends on the form of the meeting, but there are a few generic principles which all kinds of focus group meetings should respect. First of all, the moderator should be passive and oriented on listening to the participants. It is important that the moderator's view on the topic does not bias the group, but the moderator should be able to bring the focus of the meeting on the problem at hand. The moderator is also responsible to assure the quality of the meeting in terms of facts, i.e., when the group makes their conclusions based on false premises (e.g., false assumptions or missing facts), the moderator should provide these facts or correct the premises whenever possible.

3.5.2 Documenting Focus Group Workshops

Interviews are often documented in form of transcripts and analyzed using qualitative methods. Focus groups are often documented depending on the form but
very seldom with a full transcript or even a recording of the group. Instead, the
results of the focus group are often documented using bullet points summarizing the
discussion and/or mind maps of ideas, issues, and their grouping.

A common technique is to use card sorting, i.e., grouping post-its prepared by the
participants into categories or themes. The categories or themes can be predefined
or can emerge during the analysis, depending on the need. If the need is to find the
most important topics, then no predefined categories are better, whereas if the need
is to find subtopics within specific themes, then we should prepare the list of themes
upfront.

3.6 Collecting Quantitative Data

Modern software development companies use tools that allow to collect data directly
from development environments, which are sometimes called "source systems" in
this context.

Example tools used in contemporary companies, which are often used to
diagnose the problems, are:

- Software build tools, which are tools for automatically built software binaries
  from source code; Jenkins (http://jenkins.io) is an example of these tools.
- Requirement tools, which are tools for structured management of software
  requirements and variants; IBM Rational Reqpro and IBM Rational Doors
  (http://www-03.ibm.com/software/products/en/ratidoor) are two examples of
  such tools.
- SW development tools, which are tools for organizing the process of programming, building, debugging, and testing of software; Eclipse (http://www.eclipse.
  org) and MS Visual Studio (http://www.visualstudio.com) are the two most
  popular software environments in this category.
- SW repositories, which are tools for organizing collaborative software
  development activities, in particular parallel programming and integration of
  source code; Git (https://git-scm.com/), SVN (https://subversion.apache.org/),
  and IBM Rational ClearCase (http://www-03.ibm.com/software/products/en/
  clearcase) are some of the most popular tools in the market today.
- Defect databases, which are tools for structured management of problem
  reports in software; Atlassian Jira (https://www.atlassian.com/software/jira) and
  BugZilla (https://www.bugzilla.org/) are the most common open source tools in
  this category.

The above categories of tools cover the most common categories of source systems. They can be complemented with more proprietary systems for collecting field data from the product usage, customer feedback, financial status, and employee satisfaction. The main feature of any source system is the ability to access the data in an automated, programmatic manner. This ability is important when we use the data from the source systems as input to the measurement instruments (and measurement tools) [SM18].

An additional source of information is the software experiment platforms [KT17], which help to augment the code and collect the data from the field. They are particularly useful when the action research is done on systems already in field and/or during later cycles of action research.

An example of software experimentation platform is the Wasabi platform (https:// github.com/intuit/wasabi). The platform allows to augment the code and execute feature experiments. The experiments provide the data to understand and diagnose the problems in the diagnosing phase. They also allow the experiment to validate hypothesis during the evaluation phase of the action research cycle.

3.7   What Each Role Does in This Phase

In this phase of the cycle, all groups involved in the action research have a role crucial to the success of the project.

Action Team
The action team is the main group involved in data collection and analysis. It needs to prepare presentations to the reference team and to the management team about the outcomes and to get their feedback on the validity of their findings.

As the action team is focused on the preparation of the materials and collecting the data and analyzing it, they need the help of the reference team for finding the right data sources, informants, and documents.

Reference Team
The reference team plays a role of advisors for the study. Since the reference team consists of practitioners from the company where the research is conducted, they need to ensure that the researchers examine the right products and documents and talk to the right stakeholders. As a reference group, they also need to be the "sounding board" for the researchers, which means that they can provide the first, initial, validation of the findings. They are the group that can indicate that the diagnosis needs to be refined by further inquiries or whether it is complete.

However, the reference team needs to be aware that they can also bias the course of the study as they can dismiss diagnoses that are not aligned with their opinions. For that, they need to be open-minded for the findings of the research team and critical toward their own opinions.

Management Team

Finally, the management team needs to help the research team in providing the access to the right informants, documents, and products. The access can be physical (e.g., time of an architect for the interview, access to a defect database) or organizational (e.g., informing that the study conducted is sanctioned by the management and that it is aligned with the company's policy). The management team also needs to ensure that the research team has the ability to collect the data without the need to report individual findings to the management. The principle of anonymity of the informants is important for the openness and veracity of the information collected during the diagnosis.

The management team also needs to be informed about the diagnosis at the end of the cycle, and they need to have the ability to help the researchers to validate the diagnosis. As the management team sponsors the research project (often), they need to be able to scope the project.

As the management team also has direct links to employees through their daily duties, they need to be able to present the opinions of their employees in case they hear feedback about the research study.

3.8   Example of Results from the Diagnosis Phase

The result of the diagnosing phase is a set of research questions, problems, or hypothesis to address in the action research cycle at hand.

An example of the result comes from the study of release readiness indicator, presented in [SMP12].

Formula to Calculate the Release Readiness, the First Draft

$$\text{Release Readiness} = \frac{\text{number of known defects}}{\text{defect removal rate} - \text{defect discovery rate}}$$

This formula sounds logical, but after a short investigation, we can spot a number of mathematical problems, e.g., what happens if the *defect discovery rate* is larger than the *defect removal rate* is that the formula given negative number of release readiness. However, as a result of a diagnosing phase, the result was very good to start the next phase—action planning.

3.9   Formulating Research Questions

The diagnosing phase should finish with the set of research goals and questions that need to be addressed in the cycle. The research questions help the action team to keep increased focus in their planning. The action team can always go back to the research question and critically evaluate their plan—*Will this plan lead us to answering the research question?*

There are many different types of research questions, depending on the type of the study and the goal of the study. A good summary of types of studies and the related research questions, targeted toward software engineering, can be found in the article of Shaw [Sha02]. Shaw identifies five types of research questions and exemplifies them:

1. Method or means of development, e.g., "How can we automate X?",
2. Method for analysis, e.g., "How can I evaluate the quality of X?",
3. Design, evaluation, or analysis of a particular instance, e.g., "What is a (better) design or implementation for application X?",
4. Generalization or characterization, e.g., "What are the important characteristics of X?", and
5. Feasibility, e.g., "Is it possible to accomplish X?"

The first type of questions, which concern method or means of development, is the most common ones in action research. Questions of this type allow to focus on the improvements in the collaborating company and, therefore, provide the best guidance for the action teams. The questions of the second type, methods for analysis, are also pretty common in action research as they help to focus on the activities of software engineering. The same is true for the third type as well.

The fourth type, generalization and characterization, is not that common in action research, but it can be used. Questions of this type are related to the generalization of knowledge and are often addressed best by case studies and observations. It's difficult to address them by introducing the change in the organization and observe the effects of that change.

The last type, feasibility questions, is also quite common in action research. It can be seen as a subtype of the questions related to the methods and means of development. Although they are common in action research studies, I strongly recommend to use the first type instead, because the first type is constructive in nature and addressing the first type of question is a method or a process. The answer to the last type of question is a simple "yes" or "no."

Research Question for the Action Research About Release Readiness: Different Variations of the Question

Means of Development How can we assess release readiness of a software product using defects and test plans?

Method for Analysis How can we analyze test plans and defects to calculate release readiness?

Evaluation of a Particular Instance How can we improve the calculation of release readiness?

Characterization Which are the main indicators in the area of release readiness?

Feasibility Can we calculate release readiness of a software product using defect inflow and test progress?

3.10 Diagnosing Phase in Second, Third, and the Subsequent Cycles

For the first iteration, the diagnosing phase takes as the input the information from practice and theory (see Fig. 3.3). In the first phase, the input is mostly from the outside of the project, and in the second cycle, these two sources are complemented with the input from the project itself—the learning phase of the previous cycle.

The balance changes over time, and, as the project progresses, the input from the learning of the previous cycle becomes increasingly important. The consequence of that is the increased importance of the reference team, the focus group workshops with the reference team and the research team, as well as the quantitative data collection from the project's previous cycle.

There are primarily two reasons why focus groups are getting more importance during the later cycles. The first one is the fact that the reference group and the research team get more understanding of the project, get more familiar with each other, and therefore can discuss the problems more effectively. Both groups get objective data from the previous cycles, and the results of their discussions are more "to the point."

The second reason is caused by the fact that the progress of the project means that the topics discussed as increasingly more detailed and less external input can be helpful in deciding the new course of action. The external academic input is secondary in terms that instead of using "industry-as-a-lab" model, the research team actively searches for literature relevant to solve the problem identified by the focus group (research team + reference group).

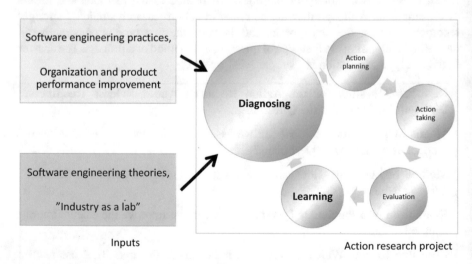

Fig. 3.3 Diagnosing in the first phase has different input as in other phases

3.11 Software Experiment Systems and Diagnosing

When using the experiment systems, the diagnosing phase is about finding which hypothesis to test and which experiments can be potentially executed. In this phase, we need to find what we are interested in testing any why. We also need to balance the costs and benefits for each hypothesis. This balancing is important as making an experiment means that we need to have at least two versions of the product (one for the control and the test group) and the development of these feature costs.

A good source of the inspiration for starting the diagnosing phase is the customer feedback [MDF+18]. The customers often provide feedback on what to improve in the product, and this feedback can be used to define what kind of modifications we can do and how. However, since the customers provide the feedback from their perspective, we still need to work a lot in order to operationalize the feedback into a hypothesis which can be used in an experiment.

Turning Customer Feedback into a Hypothesis

Feedback The search function in the program provides irrelevant search results.

Hypotheses Since the customer's feedback can be interpreted in different ways, the action team decided that they need to explore a number of hypotheses:

1. change the ranking algorithm from textual similarity ranking to most frequently used features ranking,
2. change the number of displayed results from 100 to 10 most relevant ones, and
3. change the algorithm for searching from textual search to metadata-based search.

Identifying a number of hypotheses helps the action team to direct their next phase, i.e., choosing the hypothesis to run in the planning phase.

3.12 Summary

The diagnosing phase of each action research cycle provides answers to the most important question of every research project—"What is the problem that we need to solve?" The process of seeking these answers is equally important as the answers themselves—especially in action research.

In action research, the process of diagnosing has the secondary role of understanding the context—the organization, the product, and the team that works with them. This process provides the ability to the research team to understand each other and to find a common language.

Once the diagnosing is done, the team knows what the problem is, and they need to move to planning what actions to take. The team needs to find methods and tools to be used to solve the problem, and that is the topic of the next chapter.

References

[All17] Mike Allen. *The SAGE encyclopedia of communication research methods.* SAGE Publications, 2017.

[CH10] J. Conklin and G. Hayhoe. Focus group workshop. In *2010 IEEE International Professional Comunication Conference*, pages 273–274, July 2010.

[CS87] David L Cooperrider and Suresh Srivastva. Appreciative inquiry in organizational life. *Research in organizational change and development*, 1(1):129–169, 1987.

[CW+01] David L Cooperrider, Diana Whitney, et al. A positive revolution in change: Appreciative inquiry. *Public administration and public policy*, 87:611–630, 2001.

[DMG07] Paul M Duvall, Steve Matyas, and Andrew Glover. *Continuous integration: improving software quality and reducing risk.* Pearson Education, 2007.

[FF94] William Foddy and William H Foddy. *Constructing questions for interviews and questionnaires: Theory and practice in social research.* Cambridge university press, 1994.

[HKRA94] John Hughes, Val King, Tom Rodden, and Hans Andersen. Moving out from the control room: ethnography in system design. In *Proceedings of the 1994 ACM conference on Computer supported cooperative work*, pages 429–439. ACM, 1994.

[Jor89] Danny L Jorgensen. The methodology of participant observation. *Thousand Oaks: SAGE*, pages 12–26, 1989.

[Jor15] Danny L Jorgensen. Participant observation. *Emerging trends in the social and behavioral sciences: An interdisciplinary, searchable, and linkable resource*, pages 1–15, 2015.

[KLB04] J. Kontio, L. Lehtola, and J. Bragge. Using the focus group method in software engineering: obtaining practitioner and user experiences. In *Proceedings. 2004 International Symposium on Empirical Software Engineering, 2004. ISESE '04.*, pages 271–280, Aug 2004.

[KT17] Ron Kohavi and Stefan Thomke. The surprising power of online experiments. *Harvard Business Review*, 95(5):74, 2017.

[MDF+18] David Issa Mattos, Pavel Dmitriev, Aleksander Fabijan, Jan Bosch, and Helena Holmström Olsson. An activity and metric model for online controlled experiments. In *International Conference on Product-Focused Software Process Improvement*, pages 182–198. Springer, 2018.

[SC90] Anselm Strauss and Juliet M Corbin. *Basics of qualitative research: Grounded theory procedures and techniques.* Sage Publications, Inc, 1990.

[Sea99] Carolyn B Seaman. Qualitative methods in empirical studies of software engineering. *IEEE Transactions on software engineering*, (4):557–572, 1999.

[Sha02] Mary Shaw. What makes good research in software engineering? *International Journal on Software Tools for Technology Transfer*, 4(1):1–7, 2002.

[SM18] Miroslaw Staron and Wilhelm Meding. *Software Development Measurement Programs: Development, Management and Evolution.* Springer, 2018.

[SMP12] Miroslaw Staron, Wilhelm Meding, and Klas Palm. Release readiness indicator for mature agile and lean software development projects. In *International Conference on Agile Software Development*, pages 93–107. Springer, 2012.

Chapter 4
Action Planning

A goal without a plan is just a wish.

—Antoine de Saint-Exupéry

Abstract The diagnosing phase, described in the previous chapter, leads us to understanding what we need to do in the current action cycle. It shows what kind of problem needs to be solved. Simply put, it provides us with the basis to start planning of our actions. The action planning chapter describes the way in which we plan the studies in action research. It draws on the experiences of designing case studies and experiments but focuses on the co-creation of the plan by the action team.

4.1 Introduction

So, the diagnosing phase is done, and everyone understands what the problem is and can get to work. Sounds simple, but there is more to it that than. Action planning is the phase where we need to break the problem down into manageable pieces, discuss who in the action team does what, and prepare for it. We need to understand the constraints of the collaborating company, its infrastructure and resources. We also need to assure that we have the right access—both to the competence from the company (someone needs to explain to the action team how things work) and to the infrastructure (the action team needs to access systems and data, which usually requires appropriate access rights).

Since the access to the competence and infrastructure requires costs, the action team needs to be very specific about the goals and expected outcomes—they need to repackage the diagnosed problem into a description of the potential solution and what impact the solution has on the company (Fig. 4.1).

Although these different types of access are important, it is also important what we need to include in the plan, which is:

- activities and participants—what we do and whom we interact with, during the planned cycle,

© Springer Nature Switzerland AG 2020

M. Staron, *Action Research in Software Engineering*,
https://doi.org/10.1007/978-3-030-32610-4_4

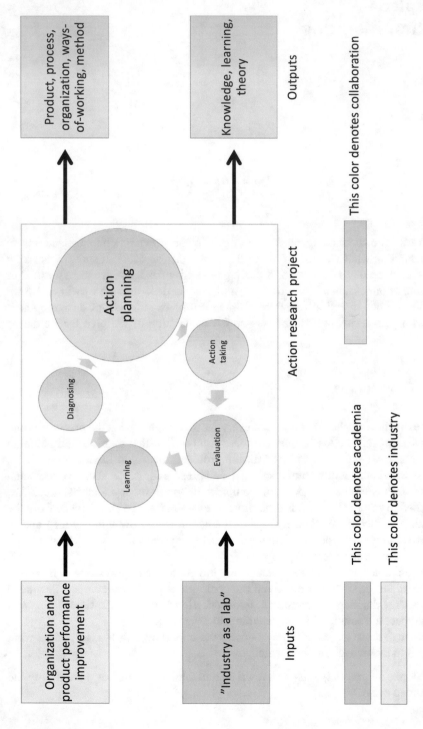

Fig. 4.1 Action research cycle focused on planning

- milestones in the cycle—when we reach measurable objectives (e.g., finish all interviews),
- deliverables—what we deliver at each milestone (e.g., transcripts of the interviews),
- status/planning meetings with the action team—when we meet and discuss the ongoing progress,
- meetings with the reference group—when we report and discuss the intermediate results with the reference team (e.g., summary of the first interview),
- presentations to the stakeholders—when we present the intermediate results to our stakeholders (e.g., present analyses of the first interviews to the management), and
- writing up the results in reports—when we document the results.

Each of the above planning items is logical, and we need to assure that we include them in the plan. The plan itself does not need to be extensive. The main purpose is to define these elements, not to overly document them. Let us explore these elements in the upcoming sections.

4.2 Access to Competence

The action team consists of both practitioners and researchers. However, the practitioners, who are part of the team, are focused on solving the problem and often need to ask their colleagues to help solve specific problems in each cycle. Therefore, we need to plan for the access to the right competence to obtain the right information and to provide the solution which is used in industry.

For example, a quality manager can be part of the action team, with the goal to find new measures for internal software quality; he needs to find software developers who can inform the action team about how they judge what makes software complex [ASS17, ADSS18]. It is also the software designers who can provide the right feedback when the action team identifies the measures.

To identify the right competence, we need to start from the problem diagnosing and address the following questions:

1. Who is affected by the problem that was diagnosed? These roles/persons can be asked to provide requirements for the solution; they can also be part of the reference group.
2. Who can provide us with the complementary view compared to the roles affected by the problem? These roles/persons can provide us with the information necessary to design the solution to the problem.
3. Who can be affected by the solution outlines in the diagnosing phase? These roles/persons can be used in the reference group for the evaluation phase of this cycle.

Some of these roles and person were present during the diagnosing phase. For example, the persons who participated in the focus group workshops can participate in the reference group.

We need the access to the competence as the practitioners working at the organization, where we conduct our action research, know their products and practices best. It is also important to identify this competence, these roles and persons, as we need to include meetings with our plan. We also need to assure that the management (both of the action team and these additional practitioners) agrees to taking the time of these practitioners in the study.

Failure to identify the right competence can lead to either failure in solving the problem (because of lack of understanding of the problem) or the lack of impact of the solution (because we do not align the solution with the organizational context).

4.3   Access to Infrastructure

In the action research study, we need to remember that we need to study real projects, products, and organizations. Therefore, it is important that we have access to the company's product and premises in order to be able to study them.

The access to the premises is important as the action researchers need to be part of the organization, teams, and groups. Being part of the organization allows the action team to experience the formal and informal structures in the organization. It allows to identify the right persons to obtain information and to understand how the company works. This understanding cannot be obtained by interviews only as the interviews are only as good as the questions asked. The access to the company premises gives the action team the possibility to ask the right questions. It also gives them the possibility to ask them to the right persons and at the right time.

From experience, I could say that if we do not have access to the company premises, and we cannot spend time at the company premises, the action research becomes quickly a case study in which we need to rely on practitioners to obtain the necessary information. The planning for the access to the infrastructure requires:

- planning when we spend the time at the company premises,
- planning whom we meet during the visits, and
- understanding what needs to be done during these visits.

We need to plan for storing the company's information at the company's premises. We should not take the information outside carelessly as we cannot guarantee that the infrastructure to store information outside of the company's premises has the same security levels as the company requires. If we keep the information and data from the company at the company's premises and plan for spending time at the company, we can monitor the effort we spend on the action research project.

However, sometimes we work with organizations that are remote to our locations. This means that we cannot spend time regularly and frequently due to travel restrictions. In such cases, we need to ensure that the practitioners who are part of the action team can conduct research activities on our behalf. We need to plan for regular status reports and remote videoconference meetings in order to secure efficient communication within the action team.

4.4 Planning of Actions, Activities, and Participants

In all empirical studies, planning for data collection and analysis is the main part of the research plan.

In the action research, the plan needs to circle around the actions done in the cycle—the action taking part. This is more similar to the design of experiments, where we have both the control and test group, and one of the test groups gets a different treatment from the control group. In action research, however, there are no groups, and we make one action, which we can see as a change of treatment. So in the essence, we have the control group before the action is taken and the test group after the action is taken.

The action itself can be any kind of intervention that is done at the studied context. It can be as complex as making a change in the way of working or as simple as making an analysis off-line and presenting the results to the reference team to compare the results with the online operations of the company. An example of this off-line action taking is when we collect data from the company's test system, create a recommender, and execute the recommender without orchestrating the testing process; we compare the results of the recommended tests with the results of the actually executed tests.

From experience, the following types of actions are the most common:

1. making changes to processes—when the action team causes a change,
2. making analysis off-line alongside the online processes—when the action team makes an analysis, compares the results, and presents the results to their stakeholders
3. creating input to the organization to change—when the action team prepares the new material and the stakeholders decide whether to adopt it.

The major characteristics of the actions are that:

- they are done based on the data of the context—not on the example data or data from other companies,
- they are done in close collaboration between researchers and practitioners, i.e., done by the action team,
- they are aligned with the diagnosed problem, i.e., the action has to have solved the identified problem, and
- the design of the action is based on some theoretical foundation, i.e., it has the potential to contribute to the theory building.

Therefore, we need to be very specific when the actual action happens and what the impact should be. This means that in the action planning phase, we need to specifically plan which action is taken, when it is taken, and how to measure the impact of it. This measurement of impact should take into consideration the status before the action is taken and after it is taken, as in this way, we can objectively assess the impact of the action.

In action research projects, we also need to plan for how to maximize the impact of our activities, i.e., maximize the value of the work for our industrial partners. The focus on the maximal value is important because it provides us with the constant reminder about why we conduct this action research project.

Therefore, we need to plan for both the data collection activities, which we need in theory building and constructing the solution to the problem diagnosed in the previous phase. We also need to plan for activities that collect the data from the organization after the introduction of the solution (evaluation activities). Then we also need to plan for the action activities, which are intended to introduce the solution to the company operations and solve the problem.

4.5   Planning of Milestones

Normally, when we plan the projects in software engineering, we create a work breakdown structure (WBS), and based on it, we define which activities are needed to deliver these items from the WBS. Research projects can be designed in the same way. Figure 4.2 shows we can design the beginning of an interview study based on it.

The figure shows when we start and when we finish the activities. If the activities are mapped directly to the deliverables and milestone, it is easy to monitor the progress of the project. However, this is not always the case. The iterative nature of action research makes it sometimes difficult to link the activities to deliverables and milestones directly. Therefore, we can also design the study with the focus on deliverables and/or milestones. Figure 4.3 shows an example of it.

These two plans are oriented on the data collection but do not show what action is taken and when. Figure 4.4 shows which action and when it is taken in the form of a star in the plan. The interviews are also divided into pre-action and post-action

Activity	2019-01-01	2019-01-08	2019-01-15	2019-01-22	2019-01-29	2019-02-05	2019-02-12	2019-02-19	2019-02-26	2019-03-05
Interview design										
Intervew material preparation										
Conducting interviews										

Fig. 4.2 Standard, software development project-based planning of activities

Activity/deliverable	2019-01-01	2019-01-08	2019-01-15	2019-01-22	2019-01-29	2019-02-05	2019-02-12	2019-02-19	2019-02-26	2019-03-05
Questions prepared				▓						
Materials online							▓			
Interviews conducted										▓

Fig. 4.3 Delivery-oriented planning of activities

Activity/deliverable	2019-01-15	2019-01-22	2019-01-29	2019-02-05	2019-02-12	2019-02-19	2019-02-26	2019-03-05	2019-03-12	2019-03-19	2019-03-26	2019-04-02	2019-04-09	2019-04-16	2019-04-23
Questions prepared		▓													
Materials online				▓											
Pre-action interviews conducted						▓									
Changing the process										*					
Post-action interviews conducted												▓			
Analysis prepared													▓		
Presentation to reference team															▓

Fig. 4.4 Delivery-oriented planning of activities including the action taken

interviews, in order to show the assessment of the action's impact and the relation of it to the pre-action status.

The frame below shows an example of how the delivery-oriented plan for one cycle can be organized with the focus on actions taken and the measurement of their impact.

Action Plan for the Introduction of the Release Readiness

In the diagnosing phase, the action team found that the release readiness can be assessed using the formula presented in Sect. 3.8.

The action in this example is the presentation of the calculated release readiness to the stakeholder. It is the action as this presentation can have an impact on the stakeholder's decisions. The measurement of this impact is the interview with the stakeholder as part of the presentation, when we ask for his opinion about the veracity of the calculated value and ask for his interpretation of the situation or value of the release readiness indicator.

In this example, the period for the action taking and evaluation is limited to 5 weeks for the sake of simplicity (Fig. 4.5).

Activity/deliverable	week 1	week 2	week 3	week 4	week 5	week 6
RR (Release Readiness) calculated						
Presentation to stakeholder	*					
RR (Release Readiness) calculated						
Presentation to stakeholder		*				
RR (Release Readiness) calculated						
Presentation to stakeholder			*			
RR (Release Readiness) calculated						
Presentation to stakeholder				*		
Analysis of feedback						
Presentation to reference team						

Fig. 4.5 Planning of the release readiness assessment cycle

This example illustrates also that we can plan for several actions in the same cycle, given that the actions are of the same kind. In this example, it makes little sense to present the results to the reference team after every action taking (presentation to and feedback from the stakeholder), as we need to understand the dynamics of how the stakeholder interprets the information. We also need to understand whether the stakeholder decided to make any changes in his organization based on these calculations.

This way of organizing a cycle within an action research shows when the deliverables are to be ready. We can develop them iteratively and create pilot studies to validate the deliverables. In the case of this example, we can even conduct a pilot interview before the materials are fully developed to validate the quality of the materials.

4.6 Planning of Deliverables

The plan for deliverables and milestones specifies when we need to deliver, but it does not specify in detail what we should deliver. We need to complement this with the plan of what should be delivered, or a kind of "requirements specification" for each deliverable. We need to specify what we expect from each deliverable, which provides us with the flexibility on what kind of rigor we must have for each activity.

For example, we can describe what kind of information we need from the interviews and link the questions which we ask to the research goals and research questions, which we formulated in the diagnosing phase, described in Sect. 3.9.

This link is important as we need to plan also what kind of action is needed to observe the effects.

Linking the Deliverables to Research Goals and Questions
In the diagnosing phase, we identified the need to understand whether defects are symptoms of the ways of working. In particular, we posed a hypothesis that changes in ways of working, such as transformation from a V-model to Agile, can be observed in changed defect inflow. We specified that in Sect. 3.2.

Therefore, the research question posed was: *To which extent do defect inflow profiles reflect the ways of working?*

The deliverables are organized into three categories:

1. perceptions of the development team: describing whether the software development team recognizes using defect inflow profile as a good symptom,
2. quantitative data: quantifying whether there is causal relationship between changed ways of working and the shape of the defect inflow profile, and
3. assessment of the quantitative data: evaluation whether the quantitative data shows the right causality.

In the first category, the perceptions, we need to make a list of possible factors that affect the defect inflow. We should also understand whether each factor causes the defect inflow to increase or to decrease. Therefore, the deliverable is **the list of factors, linked to their impact on the defect inflow**.

In the second category, the quantitative data, we need to check whether these factors affect the defect inflow as prescribed by the development team. We need to collect the data that quantifies the factors and links that to the defect inflow. Depending on the factors, this link can be either a correlation coefficient or identified period in the project where the factor changes.

Therefore, the deliverable is:

- **correlation table:** for the factors that can be quantified, for example, the increased number of executed test cases correlated to defect inflow,
- **evidence table:** for the factors which cannot be quantified, for example, we need to identify the vacation periods and observe whether the average the defect inflow in these periods differs from the non-vacation periods.

In the third category, the assessment of the evidence, we need to evaluate whether these causality relationships are indeed causal relationship. Therefore, we need to collect the evidence from the software development team. Thus, the deliverable is **the list of factors' impact (either correlation or evidence) weighted by the software development team; if more than one person is the assessor, the appropriate statistics are provided.**

4.7 Planning of Status/Planning Meetings

Action research projects have one more type of planning that is important but does not exist in the other types of research methods—status meetings and status reports. Industrial partners, the action team, and the reference team need to understand the status in order to plan further activities. The goal of these meetings is to resolve potential issues in the project and to obtain feedback on the project progress from the reference team.

In the canonical action research approach, this planning is done mostly in the learning phase where the action team reflects upon the outcome of the research activities. In the action research projects in software engineering, however, this status reporting needs to be more frequent than that. In particular, we need to describe the status, present it, and reflect on it at least biweekly. The biweekly frequency is the right one as it allows us to spend 1 week on the research activities and then a day to prepare the status report and distribute it to the reference team a few days in advance. It also allows us to capture the feedback from the status meeting and then adjust the plan.

Typical Agenda for the Status Meeting

The goal of the meetings with the reference group is to discuss the status of the project and to get feedback on the preliminary results. Therefore, the agenda should reflect this:

1. Short presentation of the goals of the cycle (to remind the group of what we want to achieve).
2. Short presentation of the findings since the beginning of this cycle.
3. Presentation of the actions taken since the last status meeting.
4. Questions and feedback on the actions.
5. Presentations of the deliverables, analyses, and results since the last status meeting.
6. Questions and feedback on the deliverables, analysis, and results since the last status meeting.
7. Presentation of open issues and questions that the action team has and needs feedback from the reference team.
8. Discussion about the open issues and questions.
9. Short presentation of the plan until the end of the cycle and until the next status meeting.

4.7.1   Planning of Presentations to the Stakeholders

The stakeholders need to be informed about the progress of the project and the intermediate findings but not as frequently as the reference team. The goal of the presentations to the stakeholders is to initiate actions on their side and to assure that the project's goals are aligned with the goals of the organization. Therefore, we need to assure that the stakeholders are informed at least once per action research cycle.

These meetings require that we focus on the findings from the practical perspective, i.e., what kind of impact our findings have on the organization. The action research projects are often of limited scope, e.g., one team or one product, since we need to assure that we control the context of the actions performed by the action teams. Thus, it is the meetings with the stakeholders where we can cause the change to have impact beyond the scope of the project.

4.8   Planning of Writing Up the Results

We need to remember that the action research projects are indeed a kind of research projects, where the publication of the results is very important. It helps others to build upon our results, and it helps us to reflect upon our findings in the light of the existing research.

Therefore, we should always plan for writing a research report or a research paper based on the results in every cycle. If the cycle does not solve a problem large enough for a research paper, we should write the part of the paper that the cycle contributes to. We need to set aside sufficient time to write and to reflect. We also need to set aside enough time for the literature studies to compare the results of the cycle with the existing body of knowledge.

The presentations of the results for the stakeholders provide a good starting point for the reflection on the results. We start from these results and complement them with the findings from literature and with the reflection on the theories used in this cycle. In this way, we build theories or validated existing ones.

4.9   Planning in the Second and Subsequent Cycles

In the first cycle, the planning phase takes longer compared to the subsequent phases, simply because we need to plan for getting the access to the infrastructure, people, and set up the first research deliverables. This is often the largest focus of the first action research cycle planning. It is also the cause of uncertainty in the cycle.

In the subsequent cycles, we focus mostly on the research goals and deliverables. Since the diagnosing phase changes in the subsequent cycles, the planning phase needs to adjust too. Examples of the adjustments are:

- analyses need to take into account evidence from the previous cycles,
- presentations need to take into account the results from the previous cycles,
- there may be changes in the reference groups or the action teams, which require extra planning, and
- the goals of the research project evolve since the first cycle.

In particular, the evolution of the goals is very important, a fact that is unfrequently admitted. Only a few papers discuss this kind of need of evolution of research goals, e.g., Prudhomme [PBC+05].

We should be prepared for that as this evolution is an integral part of action research. As we progress in the project, we learn new things and therefore adjust the goals, and we also establish new theories [BR12]. Sometimes, the goals become more specific as we learn exactly what the solved problem is. Other times, the organizational context changes, and we need to adjust the goals to align the project with the organization. Finally, the goals can change as we discover new theoretical frameworks as we know more about the studied problems and organizations.

4.10   Roles in Action Planning and the Process of Creating the Plan

The development of the action plan starts with the breakdown of the research goal and research questions into deliverables. This provides us with the list of deliverables which we put as milestones in the plan.

Once we know the deliverables, we find which actions need to be taken in order for us to obtain the data necessary to create the deliverables. We link the actions to the appropriate analyses and add them to the action plan.

Finally, once we know the actions, we create the plan for the access to infrastructure and competence. Based on this access, we establish the timeline, and then we can plan for the meetings with the stakeholders and presentations to the reference team.

The action team is responsible for the development of the action plan. However, the reference team must support the action team with the input on what kind of access is required, which products and processes must be evaluated, and which persons within the company must be involved in the study and when.

The project stakeholders and line managers need to be involved in helping the action team to get access. As they usually are the roles with the right authority, they must be involved in the planning phase. They also need to be involved in the planning phase by providing feedback, in particular, on the feasibility of the plan.

4.11   Example of an Action Plan

In order to illustrate a simple action plan, let us continue on the example of the release readiness, where the goal of the action research study was to investigate whether it is possible to calculate the release readiness date from project status parameters rather than by looking at the project plan.

Release Readiness Action Plan
In this plan, we plan the actions and deliverables in the first cycle, which has been diagnosed in the previous phase.

Research Goals and Deliverables
The goal of this cycle is to explore how well we can calculate the release readiness date based on the test progress and defect status. The formula for the calculation has been developed as part of the diagnosing phase.

The deliverables in the cycle are:

1. raw data used for calculation of release readiness
2. calculated release readiness, updated on a weekly basis
3. diagram showing the release readiness for the product per week
4. summary of the feedback from the release manager who assessed how well the release readiness number reflects the current status
5. summary of the impact, in particular, whether the stakeholder's feedback resulted in changes at the company (e.g., resource reallocation) or the formula (if it does not provide the correct value)

Actions
In this cycle, we plan to conduct the following actions:

• calculation of the formula
• presentation to the stakeholder and observation of the effect of the stake-holder's actions (e.g., resource reallocation).

These two actions are to be done at least three times during this cycle.

Access to Infrastructure and Competence
In order to take the above actions, we need to have access to:

1. database with the test planning,
2. database with the defect reports,
3. database with the test results,
4. a tester who can validate the data from the databases, and
5. a quality manager who can validate the data from the defect reports database

---

Release Readiness Action Plan, Cont.

Meetings and Presentations

We plan for biweekly status report meetings with the reference team, biweekly evaluation meetings with the release manager, and monthly meetings with the stakeholders.

Timeplan

Activity/deliverable	week 1	week 2	week 3	week 4	week 5	week 6	week 7	week 8	week 9	week 10	week 11
Access to databases obtained											
Weekly evaluation meetings booked											
RR (Release Readiness) calculated											
Presentation to release manager				*							
Status meeting											
RR (Release Readiness) calculated											
Presentation to release manager						*					
RR (Release Readiness) calculated											
Presentation to release manager							*				
Status meeting											
RR (Release Readiness) calculated											
Presentation to release manager								*			
Analysis of feedback											
Status meeting											
Presentation to stakeholder											
Results documented/published											

4.12   Action Planning in Experiment Systems

Action planning in experiment systems is about choosing the right hypothesis to be tested and designing the experiment that can test them. Our plan needs to include the following (as a minimum):

- which hypothesis to test in the experiment
- how many groups (and thus treatments) we include in the experiment
- how we measure the difference between the groups in the experiment, we call it the dependent variable or the success metric and
- how do we define the success of the experiment, i.e., which level of the dependent variable we can associate with the success.

The most common success metrics in online experiments are often related to user engagement, retention, and recommendations. The user engagement is measured in the number of users who used the feature for a specific period of time after the experiment initiation. The retention is the number of users who used the feature several times after being exposed to the feature. The recommendation is a measure of how many times the users recommended the product to others. These rudimentary metrics provide the first step to understand which of the features is better for the product—the feature that was provided to the control group or the one that was provided to the test group.

Experiment for Improving Search Function in a Measurement Systems Web Portal

Diagnosed Problem After reviewing the customer feedback, in particular, the complaints about the low relevance of the results of the search, the action team focused on the search function of their measurement web portal. They diagnosed the problem to be related to the display of results, which was based on text similarity. The current algorithm ranked the measurement systems based on whether the searched text was close to the beginning of the name of the measurement system.

Hypothesis Changing the algorithm to rankings, the most frequently used measurement systems higher, increases the relevance of the search.

In the experiment, the action team decided to have two groups: a control group, which would be exposed to the same ranking algorithm as previously, and the test group, which would be exposed to the new ranking algorithm. The groups would be selected randomly, and the experiment system would track assignment of users to groups, so that the same user is not provided with two treatments when using the search function twice. The measure of success was the time it took for the user to click on a search result (counting from the beginning of the search).

The experiment was planned to be done during a period of 2 weeks, so that the team could capture the behavior of the users at any work time and that it would allow the users to get familiar with the new algorithm.

The planning of the experiment is concluded when the setup of the experiment is decided. In the next phase, the action execution phase, the treatment levels need to be implemented, and the experiment test bed needs to be prepared.

4.13 Summary

The action planning phase of each action research cycle is an important milestone for the research. It provides the action team with the ability to establish the required access to the infrastructure, access to competence, and ensure that they can take actions in the next phase.

What is specific for the action research, compared to other types of research, is that the plan is often action oriented and deliverable oriented. This focus is needed as the action team needs to plan for status reporting and meetings with the stakeholders. In these presentations and meetings, the team needs to show concrete deliverables and results from the actions taken and discuss the impact of the actions taken.

In this chapter, we showed how an action plan can look like and how to create one. We discussed the main parts and provided examples. The next step is to take the actions and observe their impact on the studied organizations.

References

[ADSS18] Vard Antinyan, Jesper Derehag, Anna Sandberg, and Miroslaw Staron. Mythical unit test coverage. *IEEE Software*, 35(3):73–79, 2018.

[ASS17] Vard Antinyan, Miroslaw Staron, and Anna Sandberg. Evaluating code complexity triggers, use of complexity measures and the influence of code complexity on maintenance time. *Empirical Software Engineering*, 22(6):3057–3087, 2017.

[BR12] Nicolai Bodemer and Azzurra Ruggeri. Finding a good research question, in theory. *Science*, 335(6075):1439–1439, 2012.

[PBC⁺05] Guy Prudhomme, Daniel Brissaud, Denis Choulier, et al. Clustering engineering design research: A methodological framework. In *ICED 05: 15th International Conference on Engineering Design: Engineering Design and the Global Economy*, page 3949. Engineers Australia, 2005.

Chapter 5
Action Taking

The journey of a thousand miles begins with a single step.

—Lao Tzu

Abstract Once we make a plan for the actions, we need to execute them, and we need to execute them correctly and efficiently and with a lot of respect to the host organization—our context. In this chapter, we explore the types of actions in action research in software engineering. We look deeper into what it means to execute these specific actions. We also describe how to prepare before action taking, e.g., what data to collect and how to collect the data for the later usage in the evaluation phase. We focus on actions taken in the company with the focus on company's employees, and we explore customer experiment systems, i.e., when customer data is involved.

5.1 Introduction

Taking action is the core of action research. Compared to design research, it is the actions that we study and evaluate in action research. We prepare to act in the planning phase, and in this phase, we prepare the actions, and we execute them. Before we take the actions, we need to prepare the setup so that we can later evaluate the actions and learn from them.

I remember the first time that my research team conducted an action research project and, in particular, the first time that the team took the first action. In the diagnosing phase, we identified the problem of project performance reporting at our partner company. The main problem was that the performance reporting was focused on manual collection of data from multiple sources, quantifying the data, analyzing it, and presenting in form of a PowerPoint presentation. The summary of the presentation was a slide with "smileys" showing which project parameters were satisfactory and which were not. In the planning phase, we decided to develop another way of performance reporting—using MS Excel files with VBA (Visual Basic for Applications, built-in Excel scripting language) to collect, analyze, and visualize the data. We planned to take up to ten indicators and report them in Excel

© Springer Nature Switzerland AG 2020
M. Staron, *Action Research in Software Engineering*,
https://doi.org/10.1007/978-3-030-32610-4_5

instead of PowerPoint. We called this Excel file a "measurement system." The action that we took was that one of our colleagues, a quality manager responsible for performance reporting, used a screenshot of the MS Excel during his meeting with the product manager, whose information needs were whether the project is on time and within quality limits. We prepared for this action by preparing a set of questions that we asked during the meeting, e.g., discussing the "freshness" of the data. The action taking took place during a number of meetings where the quality manager used Excel instead of PowerPoint, and we evaluated the action after this series of meetings. The outcome was that the product manager wanted to use only Excel, as it was updated daily and had predefined criteria. We learned which indicators could be calculated and visualized automatically, and the impact was that the organization changed their measurement program to be fully automated, based on this concept of measurement systems [SM18].

The above action taking helped me to understand the power of action research and the ability to learn from the organization. We never talked about "research transfer" after this action taking, simply because there was no research to transfer; the action taking was so embedded in the organization's operation that either it got adopted directly or it evolved, over several action research cycles, until it got adopted.

In the example above, this sounds like a very simple and exciting activity, and to some extent it is. If prepared carefully, the action taking phase is the most exciting phase as that when the "fun" is. Thus, in this chapter, we describe and discuss the following:

- running trials—describing how to rigorously prepare before the action is taking, e.g., setting hypotheses and research questions, defining the evaluation criteria,
- collecting the data—describing how we collect the data during action taking, both qualitatively and quantitatively,
- storing the data—discussing how to secure that the data stored does not reveal any sensitive information about our partners, at the same time providing possibilities to replicate our study,
- defining the veracity of the measurements used and the associated measurement error—discussing whether what we observe is something we can actually trust,
- preparing data collection for continuous data analysis using machine learning— discussing the most common challenges toward collecting high-quality data that we can use as input for machine learning, and
- setting up an infrastructure for software experiment systems to be used in software engineering—describing how we can involve feedback from customers in our action research projects.

Let us, therefore, go through the necessary elements before we take the actions and then when we take the action, as seen in Fig. 5.1. What happens after the action taking is the actual analysis and evaluation, which is the part of the next phase.

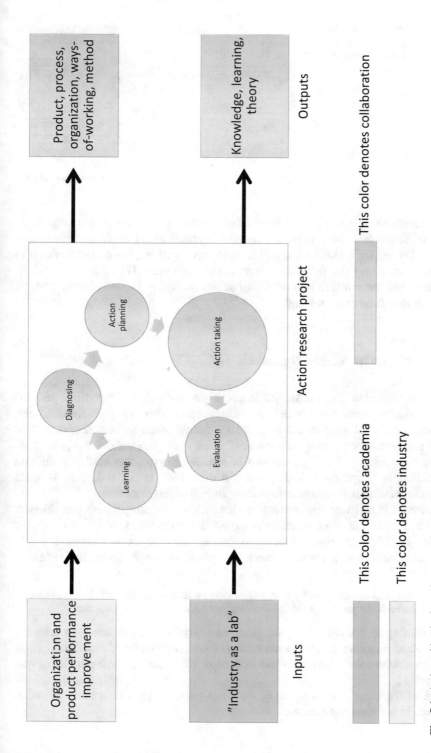

Fig. 5.1 Action taking in the action research cycle

Fig. 5.2 Three elements of action taking: preparation, action, and data collection

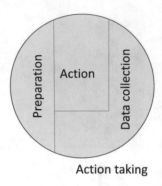

Action taking

The preparation is when we prepare all we need to take the action. In the example from my first action, the preparation was the development of the first measurement system. During the action taking and after the action taking, we collect the data to be able to evaluate the effects of the action in the next phase (Fig. 5.2).

But before we can dive into details of action taking, let us also discuss what an action is in software engineering.

5.2   Actions in Action Research

As we mentioned in Chap. 1, McNiff [McN13] defined action as "anything you do" in the action research study, which one reflects upon. This is a good starting point for consideration of what an action is, but it is not sufficient for our context.

As action research comes from the disciplines where researchers and practitioners are the same persons (e.g., teachers in schools, nurses), this kind of definition that action is "anything you do" and the evaluation is the reflection is quite straightforward as it separates doing/acting from thinking/reflecting.

However, in software engineering, the action teams consist of both practitioners and researchers (but often different persons), and therefore this definition would be confusing, for example, conducting or "doing" an analysis by a research would count as an action, which is not correct. Therefore, we use the following definition of action:

> An action is an activity done by or in collaboration with practitioners, which includes an intervention in the practice of the collaborating practitioners or their organization.

According to this definition, therefore, an analysis does not intervene with the practice and therefore is not an action. However, a presentation of results of a study for a team, where the team has to take a decision if they change their practice or not, is an action.

Let us therefore discuss some of the most popular types of actions in action research in software engineering.

Direct interventions introduce changes to the company's operations directly. The practitioners change their ways of working as the action, and they collect the data to evaluate the change. These kinds of actions are the most similar ones to the actions defined in other social research literature. Examples of such actions are:

- replacing manual reporting of effort with automated extraction of MS Outlook calendar,
- adding one additional reporting step to report which team should resolve a newly detected defect, and
- removing manual quality assessment of each commit in continuous integration pipeline.

Indirect interventions influence practitioners to make the change themselves. The researchers and practitioners present new results, analysis, and solutions to practitioners who decide whether they adopt them or not. This kind of research is more specific to software engineering where the researchers are embedded in software development organizations, although they are not part of the software development team, i.e., their work is not part of the company's operations. Examples of such actions are:

- presenting results from complexity analyses showing that the McCabe complexity should be replaced by "nesting depth" of the code; the practitioners are presented with the results and will make the decision to adopt the results or not,
- presenting results from analysis of clones in source code calling for action to measure and monitor cloning practices; the architects decide whether to adopt this new measures and monitoring tools, e.g., [SME+15], and
- conducting a cross company workshop to identify factors that impact the speed of code reviews; the practitioners exchange ideas and learn from each other, and they can decide which practices to adopt.

Both types of actions intervene with the normal ways of working at the collaborating company, just to a different degree. The indirect interventions make a change, whereas the indirect ones cause the change to happen (or a reflection to happen, sometimes the change is actually rejected).

Nevertheless, regardless if the intervention is direct or indirect, we need to remember about a number of principles that help us to evaluate the actions.

5.3   Principles of Action Taking: Similarity to Experiment Trials

In the discussion of the principles, we start with the understanding of the principles of experimentation. These principles are important because they establish the necessary foundation for taking actions—two treatment levels or two factors.

In software engineering, the most recognized work in the area of experimentation is the Wohlin et al.'s "Experimentation in Software Engineering: An Introduction" [WRH+12]. Contemporary experimental scientists know a number of different kinds of experiment designs, both in software engineering and in other disciplines. We recognize simple two-factor experiments, as well as repeated measures multifactorial designs. However, for an action researcher, the main principles of the simplest, two-factor designs are more than sufficient.

The two factors or two treatment levels are important in experimentation as they provide the basis for analysis. One treatment level or factor can be recognized as the control group and the other treatment level or factor as the test group. If, after the experiment's trial, we can observe a difference between the output of the control group and the test group, then we can say that there is a difference between the factors.

This can be illustrated in the Fig. 5.3, with the single trial experiment operation. There are a few principles that are worth highlighting:

1. There is a distinguishable difference between two different factors or treatment levels. For example, in a requirements understandability, one treatment level can be use case format of requirements, and the other treatment level can be textual format of requirements.
2. The two groups are rather equal in number and characteristics, i.e., they come from the same population and do now have a bias. For example, in the requirements experiment, the groups are students from the same class, assigned randomly.
3. The measurements of the output are related to the input, i.e., there is a chance that we can quantify the difference. For example, in the requirements understandability experiment, we ask each experiment subject to fill in a test for understanding; if one of the requirement's specification format is superior to the

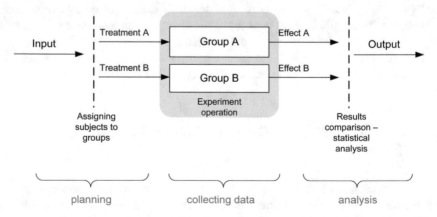

Fig. 5.3 The most basic principle of the experimentation—two groups and two factors in one experiment trial with two groups—A (control) and B (test)

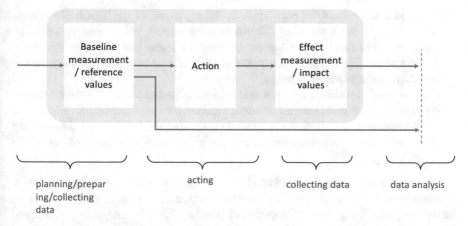

Fig. 5.4 Principles of the action research design, showing that the comparison is between the baseline and effect measurements

other, we can expect that one of the groups will have much higher score on this understandability test.

In action research, the above principles are also valid. However, the design of action research often differs a bit from the design of experiments. In particular, there are no test and control groups but pre- and post-trial measurements. The design of the action, in the same framework as the design of the experiment from Fig. 5.3, is presented in Fig. 5.4.

The main difference between the experimentation and action research, in this context, is the fact that we compare the values of the measures before and after (or during) the action is taken. Therefore, we need to use exactly the same measurement framework for both cases. In particular, we need to use the same (or equivalent) measurement instruments where we know that these measurement instruments do not introduce any systematic error (measurement bias).

The other difference between action research and the experiments is that experimentation is done in an isolated environment where the influence of external (confounding) factors is minimal. In action research, the action team is embedded in the organization, influences the organization, and intervenes with its operations. Therefore, the action team needs to ensure that the analysis is done in a broader context than in the experiments.

Therefore, we complement the principles with new ones:

1. The measurement and evaluation framework is defined á priori. The action research team defines a set of criteria for how to evaluate the impact of the action. For example, when evaluating the introduction of the Excel-based measurement systems, we used the criterion of information timeliness (how "fresh" the measurement value is).

2. The action team does not participate in the provision of the qualitative assessments/data. If the evaluation criteria rely on expert assessment or usability analyses, these should be done on external subjects. For example, the introduction of the Excel-based measurement system relied on the evaluation of the usability by the product manager.
3. If the action introduces changes that require adjustments of the measurement instruments (or criteria), then we should measure the systematic errors introduced by the measurement instruments before and after the action, and these errors should be taken into account when comparing the results from before and after action taking.

These principles mention the last element which is important in the context of defining actions—instruments. Almost every action taking requires some sort of instrument, which can be new PowerPoint presentation, piece of software (script), or another artifact. The instrument is used when we take the action, for example, the instrument used in action taking when introducing the new way of reporting project performance was the Excel-based measurement system.

5.4   Before Taking the Action

When preparing for taking the action, we need to remember about two aspects: preparing the evaluation framework (and collect the reference, benchmark data) and preparing the access to the infrastructure.

5.4.1   Preparing the Evaluation Framework

To prepare the evaluation framework, we need to start with the goals defined in the diagnosing and planning phases. There, we defined the goals and linked the deliverables to these goals. Here, we define how we will evaluate the impact of the action, e.g., whether a change in a process was successful or not.

There are multiple ways of organizing such a framework. One of them, one of the most popular ones, is the Goal-Question-Metric framework, or shortly GQM, [CR94]. The GQM framework is based on three major concepts—the goal of the measurement, questions which need to be addressed to attain the goal, and the metrics which need to be used in order to answer the questions. Conceptually, it can be defined as in Fig. 5.5.

Figure 5.5 contains also an example of how the definition can be used. The important part is the elaborate definition of the goal in this example. It is written in the same format as the original GQM framework creators recommend.

Although the graphical format presents well in the presentations (e.g., for the stakeholders), in practice, we can use a textual format. In the example below, we provide a simple measurement framework to assess the results of the introduction of measurement systems in a textual format.

Example of the Measurement Framework for Introducing Measurement Systems

Before introducing the measurement systems to the organization, the action team needs to decide how the success of the introduction is measured.

Goal: The purpose is to evaluate the effect of using measurement systems on performance measurement from the point of view of product managers in the context of large software projects.

Question 1: What is the timeliness of the measures?

Metric 1: Information retrieval time—the minimum time from the request for information until the measurement is visualized.

Question 2: What is the usability of the measurement systems?

Metric 2: Time to get overview—the time taken for the stakeholder to answer the question, *What is the current status of my product development?*

The example illustrates the team's ability to operationalize their research goals into measures. It can be done is a simple way, such as above, or it can be more elaborate. GQM is quite flexible, so the goals can be defined at all levels of the organization and all kinds of studies or even to link the goals to the organization's business strategies (e.g., [BLR+10]).

Before we take the action, we need to collect the data for the metrics defined in our evaluation framework.

5.4.2   Preparing the Access to the Infrastructure

Once we define the measurement framework to evaluation the action taking, we need to ensure that we have the access to the infrastructure, just as we planned. Collecting the reference measures before the action is taken gets very useful in this context. We can use it to validate our access rights and our ability to measure the variables needed to assess the effect to our actions.

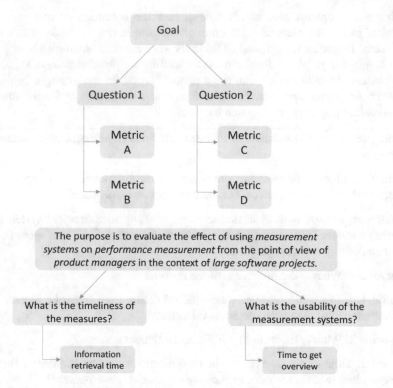

Fig. 5.5 Elements of the GQM framework alongside an example

In order to collect the data, we need to set up instruments for data collection. These instruments vary depending on the type of data collection, e.g.:

- interview protocols for the interviews,
- survey materials and the corresponding analysis methods,
- software to extract data from documents,
- scripts to analyze artifacts like source code and extract data from these, and
- scripts to extract data from software that analyzes artifacts for further analysis.

The data collection from interviews is similar to what we described for the diagnosing phase. Preparing for the quantitative data collection, however, requires a preparation of a database, which is, frequently, called a measurement database [SM15].

Toolchain of Measurement Instruments to Extract Data from Source Systems for Source Code (Git)

In order to understand the impact on software quality, the action team decided to set up a measurement instrument for analyzing the number of designers who contribute to source code development.

The measurement instrument extracts data from a primary system used to support software development—Git version control. The measurement instruments analyze who commits source code to the main repository and therefore provide data to analyze whether the changed reporting of quality had an effect on the developer's commit frequency; see Fig. 5.6.

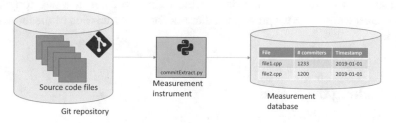

Fig. 5.6 Design of a measurement instrument to extract the data about source code committers

This measurement instrument extracts the information about how many committers a specific file had on a given day. The data is stored for further analysis in the measurement database. The collection is in line with the way in which modern organizations design and govern their measurement programs [SM18].

Most of the modern organizations which I've studied prioritize openness of these measurement instruments and the entire evaluation framework very high. It is important that the action team shares the code for measurement instruments as it shows how the measurements are done, which increases the transparency of the research and allows to comment on or improve the data collection. If the measurement instruments are often institutionalized after action research projects (or adopted by the organization), the ability to maintain and modify these instruments is appreciated.

If the instruments are institutionalized, then it is important that they are version controlled. Since the instruments evolve, the collected data evolve, and it's important to be able to trace back how the data was collected over time or how the changes in the measurement instruments impacted the data.

We also need to prepare the data storage, i.e., the measurement database from Fig. 5.6. The database should be structured in such a way as it follows all the principles related to research ethics, privacy, and security. It is important that we store the consent from the subjects who participated in the study alongside with their data, so that we can check whether a given analysis is allowed. We also need to assure that no personal data is stored or collected if we do not have the consent from the subjects. For example, in the Git commit measurement database from Fig. 5.6, we store the number of committers but not the individual information about who made a commit. Neither do we store the data per committer, i.e., data like the number of commits that a particular person made. Although this data is available in the source system, since we do not have the consent, nor have we applied for ethical approval for the study, we cannot collect this data.

When we have the ethical approvals, we need to assure the privacy of the stored information. We need to assure that the access to the personal information is only provided for the action team and not for the stakeholders or the reference team. In case we need to present the data to the reference team in a raw format, the individuals whose data we present need to ask for the permission of the individuals again.

5.5 Taking the Action

When the preparations are done, it's time to start taking the action. Depending on the action team's composition, the action can be taken a bit differently. If the action team is composed of practitioners who change their own ways of working, action taking tends to be more focused on the reflection, and when the action team comprises both practitioners and academics, the focus shifts to impact on the industrial practice. In the former, since the practitioners are part of the organization, it's easier to make the change, but it's more difficult to be objective in the observation of the effects— as humans, we are intrinsically biased toward our own actions. In the latter, it is easier to be objective (although the objectivity is never a given thing), but as the team includes outsiders, the host organization may have difficulty to change their operations based on the advice from the academics.

To increase the objectivity, we use the assessment framework defined in the preparations. In action taking, it is important that we collect the data in parallel, just as prescribed by the assessment framework defined in the preparations. The reflection comes naturally when we have the data collected and when we can conduct analyses of the data.

To increase the impact, the action team should combine the strengths of its individual members and their roles. The introduction of changes into the organization can be led by the practitioners in the action team, whereas the analysis and discussions can be led by the academics. Both roles should be present both when making changes and when analyzing, but the organization's internal cultures often accept their peers a bit more than the outsiders—the organizations tend to avoid the so-called non-invented here syndrome.

The action which we take can involve more than just individuals, and therefore we need to act differently in these three situations:

1. Action requiring the change in our own work or the work of one individual in the host organization.
2. Action introducing changes to the work of a team or a part of the organization.
3. Action requiring the change of the entire organization and/or including its customers.

5.5.1 Individual Actions

For the actions involving only the individuals or only the action team, we should ensure that we collect the data while we make the change. A bit like the old-fashioned PSP (Personal Software Process), where logging activities is of essence [Hum95], [JKA+03]. These notes are important when presenting the results to the reference group.

An important part of individual action taking is keeping the journal. In the journal, we keep the important design decisions about our study, results, and reflections. Keeping the journal is like keeping a research diary where we note down important events and results. The journal is a complement to all the measurement instruments that are used to collect the data according to our assessment framework.

It is also important to be able to keep objectivity. There are two threats to the objectivity, in addition to the ones common for other studies:

1. Fear of losing the credibility if the study, or action, is unsuccessful.
2. The hype factor, or the initial positiveness to change.

As researchers, the action team needs to be aware of both of the above. The team should focus on the understanding of the organizational hurdles and hinders. They are important when the scalability of the results is discussed.

The second threat, the hype factor, is specific to action research studies. The action team is by definition a bit more aligned to make the change since they are part of the research. The team has diagnosed the problem, has designed and planned the action, and is now in the midst of executing on the plan. Since it is the team that devised the solution to the diagnosed problem, they want the solution to be successful. Therefore, the action team needs to be transparent about this and needs to get external opinion about the solution—in the first hand from the reference team.

An example of a study where an action researcher reflected on their study is presented by Mathiassen and Börjesson [MS13]. In that paper, the authors focused on the transparency of the researcher when reflecting upon the actions taken.

5.5.2 Actions Involving Others, Like Teams of Organizations

In the action taking which involves teams and organizations, the action team becomes participatory observers [Jor15]. They are part of the operations of the team, and, at the same time, they observe what the team does. This means that many of the ethnographical of observations apply. In particular, the action team needs to consider the threats to validity of such studies. In particular, the action team needs to observe whether the effects of their actions can be attributed to action itself or whether they are attributed to the setup of the study. For example, the action team's meetings taking place "first thing in the morning" can make the team more positive because of the generally good moods in the morning, not because of the positive effect of the action. Here, again, a good measurement framework helps a lot. Setting the right goals and the right measures helps to minimize the problem of introducing bias when conducting the study.

For the actions introducing the changes to teams and organizations, the change needs to be agreed upon beforehand. We need to prepare introduction sessions where we explain how the action should essentially be done. In our research, for example, when we introduced a new metric to the team, we need to ensure that the team understands the implications and that they are on-board with this change [ASSH16]. We achieved that by frequent meetings with the team and with the reference group, combined with individual meetings with the designers when we needed extra information or when they needed to understand how our measurement "really" works.

Data collection from a team is also different as it requires interviews and interaction with the team, in addition to quantitative data from the software products and tools. We need to remember that the team's attitude to change is an important factor in the success or failure of the adoption of the change [GKA+82], [LTF17]. Although trying to intervene and change the attitude of the team to the change would be seen as a bias in other types of research, it is not necessarily a bias in action research. Since in action research we make the intervention, we need to be transparent about the interventions when reporting and take them into consideration for theory building. In order to take these into consideration, we need to keep the research log where we note the reactions of others and their questions, comments, and feedback. In the log, we also note the interventions that the action research takes.

Finally, we need to make sure that we do not cause the so-called Hawthorne's effect, which is the effect when the participating team adjusts their behavior in order to please the action team. In order to minimize the effect, we need to assure that we use the reference team and ask for their help in identifying the behavior in the team which is not aligned with their observations. Since the reference team is not part of the action team, they can get different feedback from the team than the action team.

5.5.3   Actions Involving Customers

For the actions requiring a change in the organizations that affect the customers, we need to ensure that the company's leaders and managers are aware of our actions and approve them—the stakeholders need to be fully aware of the consequences. We also encourage the use of experiment systems, where we use controlled experimentation methods as part of action taking and evaluating phases [BE12].

5.5.4   Knowing When to Pivot

Although the action team's goal is to succeed with the improvements, sometimes not everything goes according to their plan. Sometimes, when taking the action, the action makes matters worse rather than better. For the sake of the completeness of the research, the team could continue, but it's better to stop the action and revert to the old ways of working.

The action team should do it when they reflect upon the result and observe these negative results. It could be either during the action taking or during evaluation.

In the case of the pivot, the action team should ensure that they analyze the causes of that, compare it with the expected results or planned effects, and document their observations during the learning phase of the cycle.

5.6   Collecting the Data

During, and after, action taking, we need to collect the data according to the assessment frameworks prepared at the beginning.

Depending on the data, we can collect it during the action taking or after. The data which can be collected after the action taking is such a data that is extracted from source systems. In Fig. 5.7, the script in Python collects the data from Git source code repository after the action was taken. The data is there so the timestamp of the data collection is not important.

Measurement Instrument for Collecting the Number of Committers in Git

In the assessment framework, the action team defined the need to understand whether their action changes the pattern of how many committers per file and per date the software development team makes. Below is the Python script which collects that data. The repository is an example, an open source repository of the Genivi development platform from the automotive domain [Sta17].

```python
#
# This measurement instrument counts the number of committers per file for a given repository
#
import os
import pandas as pd

# get the committers to a file
#os.chdir("C:/Users/miros/source/repos/genivi-dev-platform")
#os.popen('git log --pretty=format:"%f;%cn;%ci" > ../revisions2.csv')

# read the file into a pandas data frame
allRevisions = pd.read_csv('C:/Users/miros/source/repos/revisions2.csv', sep=';')

# add column names
allRevisions.columns = ['filename','user','date_long']

# convert date time into two separate columns
datesRevs = pd.DataFrame(allRevisions.date_long.str.split(' ', 1).tolist(), columns = ['date','time'])

allRevisionsDates = pd.concat([allRevisions, datesRevs], axis=1, join_axes=[allRevisions.index])

# group by user name
byUser = allRevisionsDates.groupby('date')

# count how many times per user (and print to screen)
resultCommitters = byUser['user'].agg(np.size)

# name the columns
resultCommitters.columns =['date','committers']
```

Fig. 5.7 Measurement instrument to extract the data about source code committers Source code in Python

This measurement instrument extracts the information about how many committers a specific file had on a given day. The data is stored for further analysis in the measurement database. The collection is in line with the way in which modern organizations design and govern their measurement programs [SM18].

Git is one of the systems where it is not possible to manipulate the data. Once a file is committed and pushed to the main repository, there is always a trace of that. An administrator cannot change the data, and therefore it is possible to collect reliable data about the pre-action situations even after the action taking.

However, many source systems provide the ability for the administrators to correct mistakes in the data. For example, most defect management systems, like IBM's ClearQuest or the open source BugZilla, provide the possibility to manipulate their underlying databases to correct mistakes. Administrators can, for example, adjust date of events in case of mistakes or errors, and they can also change properties of the reported defects to correct mistakes. While such actions contribute to the quality of the data collected, they introduce bias to the collected data—data collected during the action taking may therefore differ from the data collected after the action taking.

For the systems where it is possible to make changes to the data reported, it is better to collect the data periodically: before, during, and after the action taking. Even if we can collect data of lower quality, it is still important to capture these events and log them as part of the research log. These events provide the information about how well the organization understands actions (Fig. 5.8).

Result From the Data Collection: A Table with Committers Per File and Per Date

Using the measurement instrument implemented in Fig. 5.7 results in a table of committers per date.

Fig. 5.8 Results from executing the Python script extracting information about the committers

	A	B
1	Date	Committers
2	2015-02-05	4
3	2015-02-12	2
4	2015-02-13	1
5	2015-02-16	2
6	2015-02-20	12
7	2015-03-04	1
8	2015-03-09	1
9	2015-03-27	2
10	2015-04-01	3
11	2015-04-07	1
12	2015-04-09	2
13	2015-04-14	2
14	2015-04-15	1
15	2015-04-16	4
16	2015-04-17	2
17	2015-04-29	2
18	2015-07-23	6
19	2015-08-03	5
20	2015-08-04	2

This table is needed for further analysis and evaluation of the action taking. We can observe whether the action taken caused changes in the number of committers per date. However, this raw data needs to be analyzed properly as it does not show a number of important aspects, e.g., frequency of commits (as the time span between the commits is not normalized).

For the qualitative data collection, we use the same methods as we described in the diagnosing phase—interviews, observations, and focus group meetings. The methods are used in the same way, and the results are analyzed in the same way.

5.7   Using Experiment Systems to Collect the Data: A Special Case of Action Taking

Data collection through the experiment systems is similar to the quantitative data collection from the organization. To be effective in the data collection, we need to establish an experiment framework, or experiment platform, for the experimentation. This platform must include the ways of randomizing the users who get different treatments, keeping track of which group each user belongs to, and it needs to the able to collect the success metrics.

One example of such a platform is the platform used for online experiments at Microsoft—Microsoft ExP [KCL+09]. The platform provides the developers of online systems (e.g., a search engine) to take advantage of the experimentation system without the need to redesign the entire infrastructure. This kind of platforms provides the basic functionality of experiment systems, like the assignment of users to group and collecting metrics. However, we need to extend these platforms with the metrics that are relevant for the experiment at hand.

Experiment for Improving Search Function in a Measurement Systems Web Portal

For the experiment, the action team prepared two dedicated releases of the portal. The first release with the same search algorithm as before, but with the augmented code to collect the success metric—time from search to click. The second release with the modified algorithm and the same augmented code to collect the success metric. They released the website during a Saturday to be able to capture the increased workload during the Monday morning. The previous release of the website was reinstalled after 2 weeks of operation.

The action team collected data from over 5000 searches distributed almost evenly. The number of data points was sufficient for the next step—inferential statistics.

Although software experiment systems are predominantly quantitative, there are applications where customers are asked about their perceptions by augmented applications. A study by Mayer et al. [MBM+17] is an example of such an experiment system prepared at Microsoft. The data collected from the computers of 20 developers was complemented with a tool that collected their perceptions. This kind of research opens up for new directions and a link between the quantitative data and qualitative data analyses in software experiment systems. However, we should remember about the ethical aspects of this kind of studies and ensure that they have been scrutinized by ethical review boards relevant for our country, university, or company.

The main difference between the software experiment systems and the data collection in the action research projects is the ability to interpret the data. Dmitriev et al. [DGKV17] identified a number of problems with interpretation of the data. They point out, in particular, that there are tangible risks of confounding factors when conducting the experiments. An example of such a factor is the introduction of a bug when implementing the new feature for the test group.

5.8 Summary

Action taking phase of the action research cycles is presumably the central component of this kind of research. It is the phase when we actually make an intervention and collect the data to be able to assess the impact of the intervention. However, it is also much more than that. Before taking the action, we need to prepare for measuring its effects. We need to establish the measurement framework. We also need to prepare the place for data collection.

This chapter introduced and discussed techniques, methods, and tools for preparing for action taking and for action taking itself. We started with establishing the principles of action taking, which are similar to the principles of experimentation. In the course of the chapter, we discussed the types of actions that can be taken and how to collect the data from them. We also provided the pointers on how to collect the data. Finally, toward the end of the chapter, we discussed how experiment systems can be used in the data collection phase.

Now that we have taken the action and collected the data, we need to evaluate the effects. We need to understand how to analyze the data and how to draw conclusions from it.

References

[ASSH16] Vard Antinyan, Miroslaw Staron, Anna Sandberg, and Jörgen Hansson. Validating software measures using action research a method and industrial experiences. In *Proceedings of the 20th International Conference on Evaluation and Assessment in Software Engineering*, page 23. ACM, 2016.

[BE12] Jan Bosch and Ulrik Eklund. Eternal embedded software: Towards innovation experiment systems. In *International Symposium On Leveraging Applications of Formal Methods, Verification and Validation*, pages 19–31. Springer, 2012.

[BLR+10] Victor R Basili, Mikael Lindvall, Myrna Regardie, Carolyn Seaman, Jens Heidrich, Jürgen Münch, Dieter Rombach, and Adam Trendowicz. Linking software development and business strategy through measurement. *Computer*, 43(4):57–65, 2010.

[CR94] Victor R Basili-Gianluigi Caldiera and H Dieter Rombach. Goal question metric paradigm. *Encyclopedia of software engineering*, 1:528–532, 1994.

[DGKV17] Pavel Dmitriev, Somit Gupta, Dong Woo Kim, and Garnet Vaz. A dirty dozen: Twelve common metric interpretation pitfalls in online controlled experiments. In *Proceedings of the 23rd ACM SIGKDD International Conference on Knowledge*

Discovery and Data Mining, KDD '17, pages 1427–1436, New York, NY, USA, 2017. ACM.

[GKA+82] Paul S Goodman, Lance B Kurke, Chris Argyris, Barry M Staw, and Clayton P Alderfer. Change in organizations. Technical report, CARNEGIE-MELLON UNIV PITTSBURGH PA GRADUATE SCHOOL OF INDUSTRIAL ADMINISTRATION, 1982.

[Hum95] Watts S Humphrey. *A discipline for software engineering*. Addison-Wesley Longman Publishing Co., Inc., 1995.

[JKA+03] Philip M Johnson, Hongbing Kou, Joy Agustin, Christopher Chan, Carleton Moore, Jitender Miglani, Shenyan Zhen, and William EJ Doane. Beyond the personal software process: Metrics collection and analysis for the differently disciplined. In *Software Engineering, 2003. Proceedings. 25th International Conference on*, pages 641–646. IEEE, 2003.

[Jor15] Danny L Jorgensen. Participant observation. *Emerging trends in the social and behavioral sciences: An interdisciplinary, searchable, and linkable resource*, pages 1–15, 2015.

[KCL+09] Ronny Kohavi, Thomas Crook, Roger Longbotham, Brian Frasca, Randy Henne, Juan Lavista Ferres, and Tamir Melamed. Online experimentation at Microsoft. *Data Mining Case Studies*, 11:39, 2009.

[LTF17] Per Lenberg, Lars Göran Wallgren Tengberg, and Robert Feldt. An initial analysis of software engineers' attitudes towards organizational change. *Empirical Software Engineering*, 22(4):2179–2205, 2017.

[MBM+17] André N Meyer, Laura E Barton, Gail C Murphy, Thomas Zimmermann, and Thomas Fritz. The work life of developers: Activities, switches and perceived productivity. *IEEE Transactions on Software Engineering*, 43(12):1178–1193, 2017.

[McN13] Jean McNiff. *Action research: Principles and practice*. Routledge, 2013.

[MS13] Lars Mathiassen and Anna Sandberg. How a professionally qualified doctoral student bridged the practice-research gap: a confessional account of collaborative practice research. *European Journal of Information Systems*, 22(4):475–492, 2013.

[SM15] Miroslaw Staron and Wilhelm Meding. Measurement-as-a-service–a new way of organizing measurement programs in large software development companies. In *Software Measurement*, pages 144–159. Springer, 2015.

[SM18] Miroslaw Staron and Wilhelm Meding. *Software Development Measurement Programs: Development, Management and Evolution*. Springer, 2018.

[SME+15] Miroslaw Staron, Wilhelm Meding, Peter Eriksson, Jimmy Nilsson, Nils Lövgren, and Per Österström. Classifying obstructive and nonobstructive code clones of type I using simplified classification scheme: a case study. *Advances in Software Engineering*, 2015:5, 2015.

[Sta17] Miroslaw Staron. *Automotive Software Architectures: An Introduction*. Springer, 2017.

[WRH+12] Claes Wohlin, Per Runeson, Martin Höst, Magnus C Ohlsson, Björn Regnell, and Anders Wesslén. *Experimentation in software engineering*. Springer, 2012.

Chapter 6
Evaluation

If your experiment needs a statistician, you need a better experiment.

—Ernest Rutherford

Abstract Once we plan and take actions, we need to understand the impact of the action on the organization. Since we are part of the action, and our actions cause effects, we need objective data to analyze the impact of these actions. In this chapter, we describe a selection of data analysis techniques, which are used often as part of action research studies in software engineering. We provide a selection of data visualization methods, statistics, and machine learning to show how to assess the impact of our actions. We also discuss qualitative data analysis methods that can be helpful in analyzing data collected in our research logs or through interviews and workshops.

6.1 Introduction

Understanding the impact of the action taken is a crucial phase of any action research cycle. By collecting data before, during, and after action taking, we can explore the impact of our action and thus evaluate it.

The evaluation is crucial as we base the decisions on the next steps in the study on the outcomes of it. The typical way of working in the evaluation phase of an action research cycle is as follows:

1. Clear and prepare the data.
2. Visualize and explore the data.
3. Run inferential statistics to check for the effect of the action.
4. Interpret and validate the finding with the action team and the reference team.

The cleaning of the data is an important step in every study. During the collection of the data, our focus is on obtaining data points, finding relevant measurement

© Springer Nature Switzerland AG 2020

M. Staron, *Action Research in Software Engineering*,
https://doi.org/10.1007/978-3-030-32610-4_6

entities, and applying measurement instruments. We only look at the quality of the data once it is collected, either at the end or once we collect groups of data points. In the process of quality assessment, we often find that the data needs to be cleaned—it can be noisy because of the measurement instruments, and it can contain unbalanced data (e.g., defective modules are fewer than the non-defective modules which need balancing when we use machine learning to analyze the data).

Cleaning of the data is often intertwined with the visualization of the data. We explore the data visually using diagrams and charts, and at the same time, we can identify outliers, missing values, or unexpected dependencies. Visualizing the data focuses on providing the awareness of the data, not so much on analyses, for that we use inferential statistics and machine learning. However, the visualization needs to be objective and thorough as it can be misleading. It can happen that we unintentionally trigger wrong chain of decisions if the data is not visualized correctly (Fig. 6.1).

We also need to use the inferential statistics to ensure that we know how significant (statistically) the observed effect is. There are many different statistical tests to be used in different circumstances, and I recommend to read a book about statistical methods to dive deeper into how to use them. In this chapter, we focus on the most popular ones to illustrate the usage of the inferential statistics.

Finally, in our workflow with the data, we need to interpret the results of statistical testing, and we need to validate these findings by discussing them with the reference team and the stakeholders. Here, the workflow differs a bit from case studies, experiments, and design science research, as the action team explicitly discusses the results with the reference team. This discussion can lead to the change in the diagnosing phase for the upcoming cycle, e.g., by designing additional actions.

In this chapter, we explain what each workflow phase means and how to work with it. We discuss the most fundamental techniques which the action team can use.

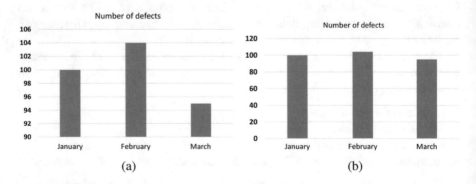

Fig. 6.1 Example of two diagrams (**a**) misleading with the scale starting at 90 (**b**) objective

6.2 Cleaning and Preparing the Data

In all data collection procedures, we risk getting data which requires cleaning or filtering. It's normal that data collection does not always go according to the plan. Our scripts may stop working, or our respondents may be sick when we need to ask for their opinion. Therefore, before we start exploring the data, we need to clean it from missing values, corrupted data points, or incomplete data points.

We also need to prepare the data for the analysis. We need to reshape the data so that we can apply the statistical methods appropriate to the analysis at hand.

Data Collected Before and After the Action Taking

In the action research project introducing a new framework for database handling, the action team posed a hypothesis that the number of defects changed as a result of that action. The measurement was the number of defects reported per day. Figure 6.2 shows the defects collected 10 days before and after the action taking.

Fig. 6.2 The number of defects reported before and after the action taking. The data is shown as displayed in Microsoft Excel. The data is only for the first 10 days of measurement and the first 10 days after the action taking

	A	B
1	Defects before	Defects after
2	40	31
3	40	29
4	41	32
5	41	32
6	39	32
7	42	26
8	41	28
9	38	30
10	40	31
11	40	30

The data series does not contain any missing data, and therefore we can use the data as is for the visualizations and statistical analyses.

One of the most common problems with data collection is missing data points. The measurement instruments which are used to collect the data can malfunction, and thus our data set can be incomplete. If this happens, we can use several data imputation techniques to add the point to the data set. We can also remove the data point. The latter is recommended if we have a sufficient number of data points, while the former is recommended when our data points are scarce.

Data Imputation Using Mean Values

In the action research project introducing a new framework for database handling, the action team posed a hypothesis that the number of defects changed as a result of that action. The measurement was the number of defects reported per day. Figure 6.3 shows the defects collected 10 days before and after the action taking. One of the data points was missing.

Fig. 6.3 Imputed data point (5), which is a mean value of the points before and after

	A	B
1	Defects before	Defects after
2	40	31
3	40	29
4	41	32
5	**40**	32
6	39	32
7	42	26
8	41	28
9	38	30
10	40	31
11	40	30

The data series with the imputed data point is larger than if the data was removed. However, if we use inferential statistics and compare mean values, the results of the imputation can bias the test. This should be discussed as a threat to the validity of our conclusions.

Other methods used for data cleaning are:

- removal of outliers [BFM11],
- balancing data sets for machine learning [BPM04],
- removal of duplicate items,
- removal of irrelevant data (e.g., defects reported before and after the project),
- reformatting (e.g. "Defect" should be replaced by "defect"), and
- scaling, normalization, and standardization.

Using these techniques provides us with the data which leads to more correct results when used in statistical tests.

6.3   Data Visualization

The first step in visualizing the data is to plot all data points on a relevant diagram. In most cases, we can use the basic statistical diagrams like bar charts, line charts, or scatter plots. These diagrams give the first understanding of how the data looks like.

Visualization of the Data About Defect Inflow

In the action research project introducing a new framework for database handling, the action team posed a hypothesis that the number of defects changed as a result of that action. The measurement was the number of defects reported per day. Figure 6.4 shows the defects before and after the action taking.

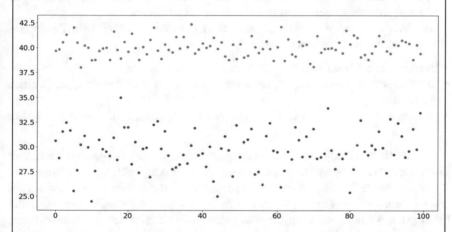

Fig. 6.4 Defects reported before (green) and after (blue) the action taking. The data is artificial. The data is ordered per day—100 days before the action taking and 100 days after the action taking

The figure shows that the number of defects changed. The number of defects reported after the action taking is lower than before the action taking.

However, we can use more advanced visualization techniques for more advanced data exploration, such as:

- heatmaps to explore the frequency of three dimensional data sets, e.g., [SHF+13],
- circular heatmap to explore the frequency in seasonal data, e.g., [BRE13]
- bipartite graph to show dependencies between two data sets, e.g., [ÇSM18], and
- circle packing to show inheritance hierarchies and containment, e.g., [Tor15]

The visual exploration techniques are popular in contemporary software engineering, and there are good books and papers about the topic, e.g., [Tel07]. A lot of great data visualization tools exist to accompany the visualization theories, such as Tableau, MS Power BI, QlikSense, and Tibco Spotfire. We encourage all action teams to experiment with the data visualization and use the tools which are the most appropriate for the visualization task at hand.

6.4   Descriptive Statistics

Once we go beyond the simple data visualization, we need to start analyzing the data using statistical techniques. There, we also need to visualize the data, not as individual data points but as groups, trends, or distributions.

In the visualizations and basic statistical explorations, the main descriptive statistics are the most common ones:

- mean and standard deviation—to describe the distribution,
- median and mode—to understand the centrality of the data and the most common value, and
- confidence intervals—to understand what the dispersion of the data is in our data set.

We use these statistics to describe the groups and to show the general tendencies in the data. We compare the impact of our action taking with the baseline before the action taking. In order to be able to reason about the certainty that the observed results are not due to change, we collect many data points. In order to reason about the impact, we need to group the data points using means and medians to check whether there is the difference between these groups.

The charts associated with these descriptive statistics, e.g., the box plots and the histograms, are useful in visual exploration of the data. They aid the action team with the understanding the effect of their action. They also help the action team to communicate the effects to the reference group and the stakeholders.

Visualization of Distributions of Defect Inflow

In the visual exploration of the defect inflow data in Fig. 6.4, the action team understood that there is a difference in the number of defects reported per day. Therefore, the team decided to create the box plot diagram in order to compare the distributions, which is presented in Fig. 6.5.

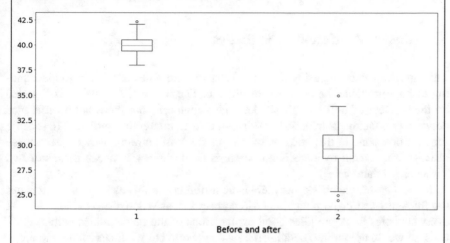

Fig. 6.5 Box plots for the defect distributions

The figure shows that the number of defects changed. The number of defects reported after the action taking is lower than before the action taking. Therefore, the team also decided to visualize the distributions and compare them to the normal distributions with the same parameters, shown in Fig. 6.6.

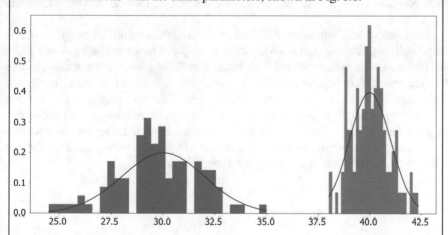

Fig. 6.6 Histogram with the defect distributions. The red line shows the normal distribution with the same parameters as the defect inflow distribution (mean, standard deviation)

The histogram provided the action team with the similar picture—the two data series, before and after the action taking, were different.

The descriptive statistics provide the understanding on the underlying data but do not provide the significance levels, i.e., do not provide any probability that the observed difference in two data sets is caused by chance. For that, we need to use inferential statistics, and we need to get back to the basic principle of the action taking—comparing to a baseline before the action was taken.

6.5   Basics of Inferential Statistics

The significance testing using inferential statistics provides us with the understanding of how probable the observed results are. The inferential statistics is founded on the concept of null hypothesis, i.e., the hypothesis that there is no difference between two factors or treatment levels. All tests in inferential statistics are specific for a purpose, and in this book, we focus on the most common way of using these tests—testing a null hypothesis that there is no difference between means of two variables (or data series).

In most cases, the check that there is no difference in means is done using either the Student t-test or its nonparametric correspondent Wilcoxon [DS+11]. Almost every statistics book provides good explanations of the mathematics behind these tests, so we do not go into details on how they work, but we focus on how to apply them.

In order to know whether we should use t-test or Wilcoxon, we need to check whether the data is normally distributed. This can be done using another test—the Shapiro-Wilk. The Shapiro-Wilk checks what is the probability that the given data series does not come from a normal distribution. If the test determines that the data is most probably coming from the normal distribution, then we can use the parametric t-test.

The t-test checks whether the difference between the means of two data sets is statistically significant. Figure 6.6 shows an example of two distributions—we could see that the peaks were separated from each other. In Fig. 6.4, we could also observe that the series were separate. Visually, we got the indication that the difference in the means is significant. The t-test provides us with the probability of the fact that this difference is due to chance or that any given point can come from either one of the series. The *p-value* of the statistics provides us with the answer to that. The *p*-value is the probability of approving the null hypothesis when the data showed otherwise, i.e., the so-called making the Type II error.

Checking the Normality Assumption and Using t-Test

Once the action team observed the difference in means for the defect inflow per day before and after the action taking, they needed to understand how strong the effect is. Therefore, they decided to run the statistical tests. First, they needed to execute the test for normality, the Shapiro-Wilk test, to find if they can use parametric or nonparametric statistics.

The results from the Shapiro-Wilk test were:

Data	Shapiro-Wilk statistics	p-value
Before	0.986	0.389
After	0.990	0.694

Visually, the Q-Q plots for both data series show that the deviations from the normal distribution are small.

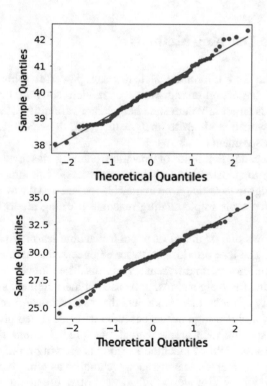

The results show that both before and after, the defect inflow series were distributed normally. Therefore, the team decided to use the t-test to assess the significance of the observed difference in the means of the defect inflow per day before and after the action taking. Together with the t-test, we also run Levene's test for the equality of variances, to make sure that the data for both series can be compared using t-test.

Statistics	Value	p-value
Levene's	34.829	$p < 0.001$
t-test	47.211	$p < 0.001$

Inferential statistics provide us with the ability to reason about our data in the context where we compare the data from the baseline and after the action taking. However, we often need more insight into the data, i.e., grouping similar cases, exploring correlations, or characterizing the data.

6.6   Machine Learning Methods

Data visualization and inferential statistics are powerful tools to analyze the data collected during action taking. However, modern software development tools provide data that is larger in volume and has a larger variability. Therefore, we often can use more powerful methods to analyze this data, draw conclusions, and make predictions and assessments.

In the last decade, the field of machine learning has evolved from being accessible mostly to statistical experts to being accessible to almost everyone with the basic knowledge in statistics. One major role for that was the availability of easy-to-use open source tools implementing machine learning algorithms, e.g., Weka or R.

Figure 6.7 shows one of the most popular machine learning platforms used in research—Weka. The tool provides software engineers, and action teams, with the possibility to experiment with different algorithms. The tool can also generate Java code, implementing these algorithms, to be used in measurement systems.

The availability of tools, like Weka, lets the researchers and action teams work with algorithms for clustering entities based on their measured properties, classify entities given a specific measurement goal, and predict trends in data based on measurements. As the field of machine learning is growing rapidly, we only focus on these three in this chapter, leaving such techniques as reinforced learning, deep learning, and knowledge discovery, to dedicated literature about machine learning [Qui14], [Lan13], [Har12].

For the action team, machine learning algorithms are useful when making sense of the measurement results—providing interpretation to the measurement data.

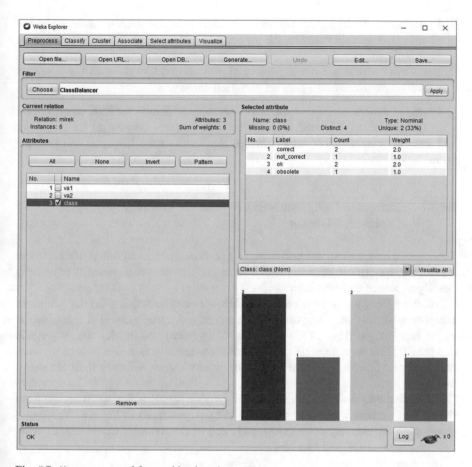

Fig. 6.7 Open source tool for machine learning—Weka

6.6.1   Clustering

One of the applications areas for machine learning is clustering. In action research, the action teams are often faced with the problem of grouping elements based on a given characteristics or finding how many groups of entities are measured by a given data set. The action team can use a number of algorithms to address this challenge of how many clusters of entities exist in the data set, e.g.:

1. k-nearest neighbor (kNN), which is a centroid-based algorithm dividing the data set into clusters based on finding centroids and the distance between data points and centroids.
2. Hierarchical clustering, which is a connectivity-based algorithm dividing the data set into clusters based on the similarity between individual data points and groups of data points

3. Expectation-maximization algorithm, which is a distribution-based algorithm dividing the data set based on the probability that data points belong to the same distribution
4. DBSCAN, which is a density-based algorithm dividing the data set based on identifying regions in the data set of varied density.

From our experience, one of the most useful algorithms is the kNN algorithm for identifying clusters. We used it in our previous studies because of its simplicity and intuitive visualization, which makes the results easy to explain in practice [ASM+14].

6.6.1.1   Example of Using Clustering to Find the Complexity of Software Modules

To illustrate how we can use clustering in practice, when interpreting measurement results, we can explore an example of how to find a perceived complexity of a newly developed source code module.

To make this kind of prediction possible, we need to define what the perceived complexity means. In our example, the perceived complexity is a combination of the size (measured in LOC) and complexity (measured in McCabe cyclomatic complexity). We do not define the thresholds for these values, and instead we want the clustering (kNN) algorithm to find the right clusters. We only limit the set of clusters to three.

To teach the kNN algorithm, we need to provide the algorithm with the data from the current system. In our example, this data is presented in Fig. 6.8. The figure shows nine different modules (1–9), and each of the modules characterized using two measures—LOC and McCabe.

Fig. 6.8 A set of current modules

◢	A	B	C
1	Module	LOC	McCabe
2	1	1	2
3	2	1	1
4	3	2	2
5	4	10	11
6	5	10	12
7	6	11	11
8	7	20	21
9	8	20	20
10	9	21	21
11			

To make the example straightforward, we prepared the modules in such a way that we can clearly see that there are three clusters, low complexity, medium complexity, and high complexity, which we can visualize in the scatter plot in Fig. 6.9.

In Fig. 6.9, we can see that these modules are grouped into three clusters. The newly developed modules are characterized as presented in Fig. 6.10, where we have three modules, also characterized by LOC and McCabe. When we look at the data about the newly developed modules, we can intuitively see that these three modules belong to three different clusters. Now, we can also use the kNN algorithm to classify them.

The script, which we use to make the clustering and find where the newly developed modules belong to, is presented in Fig. 6.11.

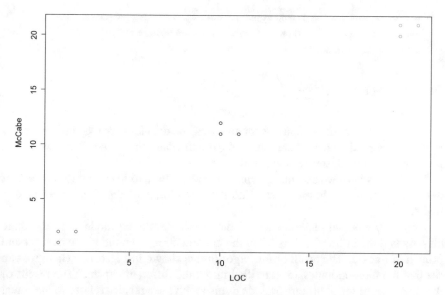

Fig. 6.9 A set of current modules visualized as a scatter plot; colors indicate clusters

◢	A	B	C
1	Module	LOC	McCabe
2	1	2	2
3	2	10	10
4	3	22	22

Fig. 6.10 A set of newly added modules

```
1   # read the data
2   modulesData <- read.csv("clustering_example_data_train.csv", sep=",")
3   newModulesData <- read.csv("clustering_example_data_test.csv", sep=",")
4
5   # removing the names of the modules
6   # as they are not needed in the analyses
7   modulesData[,1] <- NULL
8   newModulesData[,1] <- NULL
9
10  set.seed(1)
11
12  # Finding the clusters
13  fit <-kmeans(modulesData, 3)
14
15  # changing the names of clusters to the text
16  complexityLabels <- factor(fit$cluster, levels= c(1,2,3), labels=c("low", "high", "moderate"))
17
18  # binding the name of the cluster to the data row
19  clusteredModules <- cbind(modulesData,complexityLabels)
20
21  #visualizing the clusters with different colors
22  plot(LOC,McCabe, col=clusteredModules[,3])
23
24  # using the names of the clusters as complexity classes
25  complexityClasses <- clusteredModules[,3]
26
27  # finding the cluster where the new modules are classified
28  newModulesComplexityClass <- knn(modulesData, newModulesData, complexityClasses, k = 3)
29
30  newModulesComplexity <- cbind(newModulesData, newModulesComplexityClass)
31
32  print(newModulesComplexity)
33
```

Fig. 6.11 R script for clustering

Lines 1–10 prepare the data sets for analyses, the data files are read into the arrays in R, and the module names are removed from the data (lines 7 and 8), as we do not need them for the clustering algorithm.

Line 13 is where we execute the clustering algorithm, to find the three clusters of in the data and name these clusters (line 16). The plot, from Fig. 6.9, is presented in line 22.

Finally, the actual classification of the newly developed modules to the three clusters is done in line 28. It is when the classification is bound to the data set and printed in line 32. The result of this algorithm is shown in Fig. 6.12, where we can see that the three modules are classified into three different clusters. The results of the execution of the algorithm provide us also with the statistics related to the actual clustering such as means of squares or distances to centroid. However, these are not needed in practice as they describe the quality of the clustering process.

This simple example illustrates how we can use machine learning clustering to provide interpretation for the measurement results. When we use this machine learning algorithm over time, the predictions get better, and the burden on the stakeholders decreases. The stakeholder need not make manual assessments of the data, but the algorithm can use the previous assessments to derive the new ones. From our experience, this can be very useful when constructing analogy-based prediction models and analysis models.

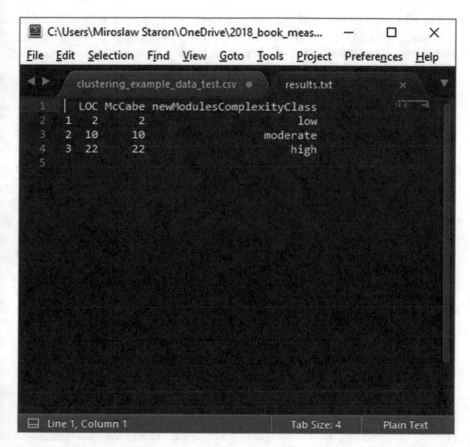

Fig. 6.12 Classification results

6.6.2 Classification

Generally, the problem of classification is similar to the problem of clustering with one significant difference. The classification problem is focused on which class a given new observation belongs. The classes are derived from a training set. In the example of clustering in Sect. 6.6.1, the last step, when we classified the newly developed module, is already touching upon the classification area in machine learning. However, the classification problems can be within a number of areas, e.g.:

1. binary or multiclass—depending on whether the classification results in assigning one of two classes (e.g., defect is easy or difficult to fix) or multiple ones (e.g., defect is very easy, moderately easy, or difficult to fix), and
2. black-box or white-box—depending on whether we know the rules how the classification is done (white-box) or not (black-box)

The current trend in machine learning is the focus on deep learning algorithms with multiple layers of classification, clustering, prediction, etc. This focus has also driven the popularization of simpler techniques such as decision trees for classification.

Decision trees are useful in data analysis, in similar areas to the usage of clustering algorithms, to automatically provide interpretations of the measurement data. The difference between the clustering algorithms and the classification algorithms is that the clustering algorithms are unsupervised, while the classification algorithms are supervised. For the unsupervised algorithms, there are no right-wrong answers, and therefore for the clustering algorithms, there is no such thing as a wrong cluster. For the supervised algorithms, there is a right and a wrong answer, and therefore for the decision trees, there are right classifications and wrong classifications.

The most common and simple decision tree algorithms are:

1. classification tree, which predicts the class which the entity belongs to, and
2. regression tree, which predicts a number like the number of defects next week or the cost of a project.

The decision trees are useful for analysis when we need to check how the classification was done. However, they are not useful when the quantities of data are too large to be used in a simple training pass (e.g., when it comes in batches). For that purpose, we need to use other techniques, e.g., neural networks.

6.6.2.1   Example of Classifying Defects Using Decision Trees in Weka

For this section, we can focus on the classification trees and their usage for solving a problem of classifying defects. Imagine we would like to find if we should prioritize a specific defect or not. Figure 6.13 shows this conceptually.

To exemplify how the classification works, we use a set of defects to train the decision tree on. We use the data set presented in Table 6.1.

In Weka, we use the J48 decision tree algorithm, which produces the classification tree as shown in Fig. 6.14. The classification tree shows that if the submitter is "john," then the majority of defects is "difficult," regardless of which phase they are found. If the submitter is "mary," then the majority of defects is "easy." However, if the submitter is "tom," then the classification depends also on the phase where the defect was found.

Now, as we mentioned before, classification trees are a type of supervised learning, which means that we can test whether the classifications are good in practice. For this, we use the data set specified in Table 6.2.

If we examine the test set, we can see that there are defects which do not fall under the classification easily (i.e., we could expect some deviations between the classification and the test data). For example, defect with ID of 3 is such an example. After applying the classification tree to the test set, Weka produces the output visible in Fig. 6.15.

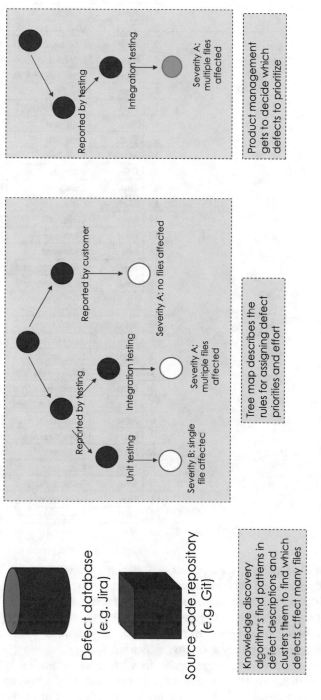

Fig. 6.13 A conceptual view on classifying defects using machine learning

Table 6.1 Existing defect
data—training set

ID	Submitter	Phase	Difficulty
d1	John	Unit_test	Easy
2	Mary	Unit_test	Moderate
3	John	Component_test	Moderate
4	John	Integration_test	Difficult
5	Mary	Component_test	Moderate
6	Tom	Customer	Impossible
7	Tom	Integration_test	Impossible
8	Tom	Unit_test	Difficult
9	Tom	Unit_test	Difficult
10	Mary	Unit_test	Easy
11	John	Integration_test	Difficult
12	Tom	Customer	Impossible
13	Mary	Customer	Easy
14	John	Customer	Easy
15	John	Customer	Difficult
16	Mary	Customer	Easy
17	Tom	Integration_test	Impossible
18	Tom	Integration_test	Impossible

Table 6.2 Existing defect
data—training set

ID	Submitter	Phase	Difficulty
1	John	Integration_test	Difficult
2	Mary	Unit_test	Moderate
3	John	Component_test	Moderate
4	John	Component_test	Difficult
5	Tom	Component_test	Impossible
6	John	Integration_test	Difficult
7	Mary	Component_test	Easy
8	John	Customer	Difficult
9	John	Customer	Difficult
10	John	Integration_test	Impossible
11	Tom	Integration_test	Impossible
12	Tom	Integration_test	Impossible
13	Mary	Customer	Easy

In the output from the classification we can see three parts: (1) summary, (2) accuracy by class, and (3) confusion matrix. The summary part summarizes the parameters of the classification such as the number of accurately classified instances, Kappa statistics, or mean absolute error. The first two lines, the number of classified instances, give us a good overview of how good the algorithm is—in our case, ten defects were classified correctly and three were not.

The detailed accuracy section provides us with more details on which class was the most difficult to classify correctly. In our case, this was the class with the moderate defects as we did not have any moderate defect in the test set. The

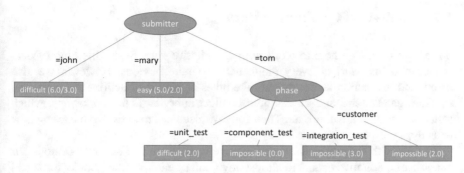

Fig. 6.14 Decision tree build by Weka's J48 algorithm

```
=== Evaluation on test set ===

Time taken to test model on supplied test set: 0 seconds

=== Summary ===

Correctly Classified Instances          10               76.9231 %
Incorrectly Classified Instances         3               23.0769 %
Kappa statistic                          0.6638
Mean absolute error                      0.2315
Root mean squared error                  0.3372
Relative absolute error                 62.4618 %
Root relative squared error             78.4626 %
Total Number of Instances               13

=== Detailed Accuracy By Class ===

             TP Rate  FP Rate  Precision  Recall  F-Measure  MCC    ROC Area  PRC Area  Class
             1,000    0,091    0,667      1,000   0,800      0,778  0,955     0,667     easy
             0,000    0,000    0,000      0,000   0,000      0,000  0,727     0,267     moderate
             1,000    0,250    0,714      1,000   0,833      0,732  0,875     0,714     difficult
             0,750    0,000    1,000      0,750   0,857      0,822  0,875     0,827     impossible
Weighted Avg. 0,769   0,110    0,685      0,769   0,707      0,654  0,865     0,673

=== Confusion Matrix ===

 a b c d   <-- classified as
 2 0 0 0 | a = easy
 1 0 1 0 | b = moderate
 0 0 5 0 | c = difficult
 0 0 1 3 | d = impossible
```

Fig. 6.15 Results from applying the classification algorithm on the test data

class that was classified best was the class of impossible defects. To find out more
about how many cases were classified incorrectly and to which classes, we need to
example the last section—the confusion matrix. The matrix shows how many cases
were classified to which class and where they should be classified.

6.7   Analysis of Qualitative Data

So far, we discussed how to work with quantitative data. Since this kind of data is closer to the heart of every engineer, it is quite obvious. However, we also mentioned that action teams should take notes of how their actions are perceived by the organizations, and they should conduct interviews and workshops, which result in tons of qualitative data. Therefore, we also need to know the basics on how to analyze the qualitative data.

Just as with the analysis of quantitative data, there are several methods for analysis of qualitative data, and almost any good research method books for social sciences provides good references for it. I personally use the book by Robson [RM16], and in this book, we focus on one technique—*thematic analysis*. According to Braun and Clarke [BC06], thematic analysis is "a method for identifying, analyzing, and reporting patterns (themes) within data."

Thematic analysis is organized into five phases followed by reporting:

1. Becoming familiar with the data.
2. Generating initial codes.
3. Searching for themes.
4. Reviewing themes.
5. Defining and naming themes.

The phases progress from the understanding and analyzing the data to synthesizing a coherent set of themes. *A theme* captures a concept which is important in relation to the research question and represents some level of patterned response or meaning within the text [BC06].

6.7.1   Becoming Familiar with the Data

To begin with, we need to read the documents several times. We need to read the text with understanding, and we need to make notes about ideas and meanings that can be extracted from the text. Since we have our original research question in mind, we need to focus on finding the meanings related to it.

For the action team, it is important that we use the assessment framework defined before the action taking as the guide here. If we use the GQM framework here, we identified the questions which need qualitative analysis, and these questions should guide our thematic analysis.

Getting Familiar with the Data

The action team needed to understand the impact of their introduction of the new testing process on the organization. They have collected the data from the interviews and transcribed it. Figure 6.16 shows the results from the first reading of the transcript.

Transcription	Ideas, meanings
... Q: Which challenges did you experience when executing the new testing process for the first time?	
R: At first, I <u>understood that the method was supposed to select the</u> test cases for me. I <u>expected the method to take the code as input and execute the tests</u>. However, it turned out that the method is only suggesting the selection and that I have to do the actual work. I needed to change the test suites in my jUnit set-up. I thought that was a bit on <u>a downside for the method, kind of missed expectations.</u>	Understanding Expected way of working Missed expectation
....	

Fig. 6.16 Transcribed text with the extracted meaning

The extracted meaning was important as it allowed the action team to understand how to improve the method for the next step in the action research cycle. However, they also needed to make the initial codes so that they could link the results to the specific part of the assessment framework.

The outcome of this first phase of the thematic analysis is a text with the annotated meanings on the margins. Once we have these, we can start with the generation of initial codes.

6.7.2 Generating Initial Codes

We can bootstrap the generation of the initial codes by starting with our understanding of the research problem and the intentions behind the action. The initial codes which are extracted from the assessment framework can help us, but they should definitely not be the final set of codes.

In the initial coding, we need to understand and interpret pieces of text and assign codes to them. These codes should reflect the interpretation and meaning of the text and not the intention to capture a specific keyword. Therefore, it is important that we try to interpret each piece of text from different perspectives and also that we reuse some of the codes if needed.

If needed, the initial coding can be repeated several times, and each piece of text can be coded using different codes or even using orthogonal coding schemes. For example, we can code the same text with the codes related to the process (how the action was) and the content/product (what action was taken).

Initial Set of Codes

The team analyzed the transcript and extracted initial codes from the text. Each piece of text has a number of codes associated with them. An example is presented in Fig. 6.17. Each code is linked to the text by using the color.

Transcription	Codes
... Q: Which challenges did you experience when executing the new testing process for the first time?	
R: At first, I understood that the method was supposed to select the test cases for me. I expected the method to take the code as input and execute the tests. However, it turned out that the method is only suggesting the selection and that I have to do the actual work. I needed to change the test suites in my Unit set-up. I thought that was a bit on a downside for the method, kind of missed expectations.	Goal of the method Expected way of working Actual way of working Tooling
....	

Fig. 6.17 Transcribed text with the extracted meaning

In this piece of text, the identified codes are related to how the new methods were used and the context of its use (tooling). The codes identified in the first analysis need to be grouped into themes in the next step.

When creating the initial codes, it is important to identify the links between the codes and the actions taken by the team. It is also important to identify the codes that indicate confounding factors, i.e., factors that contribute to the positive or negative impact of the action but are not caused by the action itself.

For example, a confounding factor related to the introduction of the new testing process is the simultaneous introduction of a new defect management process (not done by the action team). The introduction of the new defect management process can change the way in which engineers report faults, skipping the reporting of unit test-related faults. This affects the defect inflow, so it should be explored further in order to separate the effects of the introduction of the new testing process from the introduction of the new defect management process.

6.7.3 Searching for Themes

Searching for theme starts as an activity of grouping codes and identifying themes. Since themes can form hierarchies, the activity of finding themes can be iterative and can start from grouping individual codes to themes.

A good tool for the thematic analysis is a thematic map, which resembles a mind map but can contain many starting nodes. An example of a thematic map is presented in Fig. 6.18. Codes are linked to subthemes which are linked to themes. The same code (or a subtheme) can be linked to several themes.

A thematic map can be quite large initially, and therefore it is good to use tools for mind mapping and diagramming to draw them, especially as we may need to reorganize the map several times in the course of the analysis. Since the first set of themes is not always (or almost never) good enough, we need to be prepare for such reorganization. It is normal as the initial thematic map is the first visualization of our codes, and it reveals under- and overinterpretations.

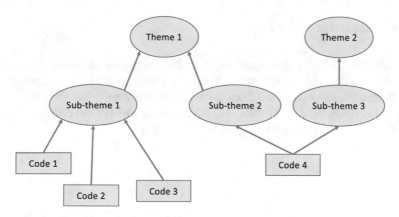

Fig. 6.18 Construction of a thematic map

Identifying the Themes

The action team analyzed the entire transcript and identified the initial codes. The activity of finding themes provided the team with the insight into the potential problems and challenges to address when introducing the new testing method. The initial set of themes is presented in Fig. 6.19 as a thematic map.

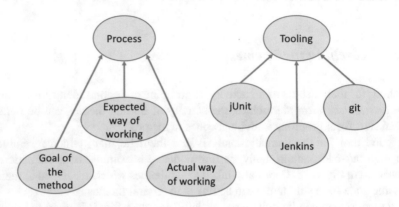

Fig. 6.19 Initial thematic map

The thematic map contained two sets of themes which seemed to be unrelated and where the revision of the thematic map started.

6.7.4   Reviewing Themes

Reviewing and refining the themes are aimed at linking the themes to the research goal. In the case of action research, this linking is done by connecting the hypotheses, questions, or goals from the assessment framework to the initial codes.

When revising themes, we should also investigate whether the codes and themes indicate positive or negative impact of the action taken.

Identifying the Themes

Once the action team started to review the initial themes, they discovered that some of the themes did not reflect the initial goal. The action team revisited the original text behind the codes and themes, renaming the codes and reworking the themes. They also color-coded the codes to reflect positive and negative impact of the action on the organization. The revised map is presented in Fig. 6.20.

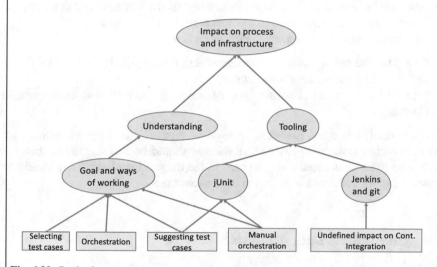

Fig. 6.20 Revised

The map revealed that the impact of the action on the organization was larger than initially expected. It stretched over both process and tooling. It also revealed a few negative effects that the action team did not anticipate at the beginning of the study.

The redefinition of themes is an iterative process. We can revise the codes over and over again; thus, we need to remember about a very important aspect—overinterpretation. When working with revisions, we can be tempted to rename the code slightly to reflect the theme better. However, if we do it several times, we risk losing the original meaning of the code. Therefore, we need to check the underlying text/data for the code before renaming it. We need to assure that the link between the codes and the data is valid at all times.

6.7.5   Defining and Naming Themes

The final defining and naming themes aims at making the themes into a coherent "story" told by the data. We iterate over the themes and put together into a coherent description of the data. In action research, in particular, the coherent description is linked to the description of the effects of the action taking. We describe how the organization experienced the action and describe the positive and negative effects. We also need to note the confounding factors and the further actions that we need to consider in the diagnosing phase in the next action research cycle.

The easiest way to create such a description is to:

- Group the themes according to the assessment framework defined previously.
- List the codes and themes in each group.
- Provide a description of positive and negative aspects related to each theme in the group.

Once the list is done, it should be used as input in the diagnosing phase for the next action research cycle. Not all themes should be investigated further, but they need to be considered and discussed in the diagnosing phase. They should be presented to the reference team and to the stakeholders.

6.8   Continuous Data Analysis

In action research projects which involve continuous changes or continuous experimentation, we need to work a bit differently with the analysis. Naturally, we should keep the principles of experimentation intact, but instead of executing t-tests and continuously collecting/analyzing quantitative data, we need to set up key performance indicators (KPIs, [SNB18], [SMNA16]).

KPIs are used to monitor processes and products over a period of time, and therefore they are well suitable for the monitoring of continuous improvements or action taking over time.

Defining a KPI

In one of the projects, the action team introduced a new way of reviewing source code. This new process impacted the time required to integrate software components into subsystems and to the entire system. Since this process required time to settle and impacted a larger part of the organization, the team set up a dashboard to monitor the evolution. The action team defined a KPI: weekly average of time to integrate code. The KPI was calculated weekly and was presented on a dashboard, together with the raw data, as presented in Fig. 6.21.

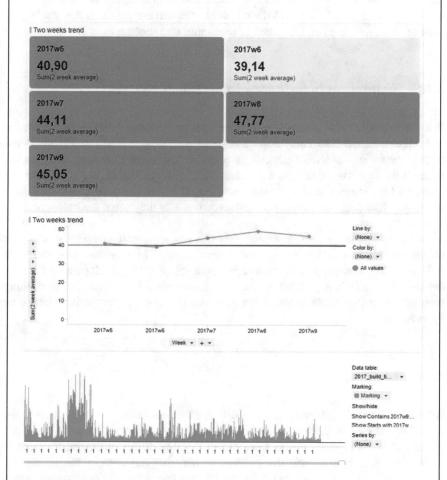

Fig. 6.21 Dashboard with a KPI and raw data

The dashboard provided the team with the possibility to observe the effects of action taking on a longer period of time.

6.9   Evaluation in the Second and Subsequent Action Research Cycles

The data analysis in the second, third, and more cycles is very similar to the first cycle. The main difference is that the assessment framework may have evolved over the cycles. It is quite common as the action research methodology is flexible and aligned with the needs of the collaborating organization.

From the perspective of a researcher, we need to keep track of the evolution of the assessment framework in order to assure the comparability of the results. We need to report the evolution, and if we cannot compare the results across cycles, we need to clearly state when this chain of reasoning was broken.

6.10   Evaluation in Software Experiment Systems

In software experiment systems, we can use exactly the same methods for evaluation as for quantitative data analysis—descriptive statistics, inferential statistics, and machine learning. Machine learning is probably the most common today, as the experiment systems often result in large data sets (so called big data) and the traditional techniques are too time-consuming. It is possible to use them, but new techniques like deep learning ease the data analysis as they often are more robust to noise in the data.

Some companies combine online experiments with real customers, with the offline experiments on the historical data, as described by Gomez-Uribe and Hunt [GUH16]. The company collects, and stores, a lot of data, which provides it with the ability to design experiments that test hypotheses offline. The cost of running such offline experiments is lower but provides the first insight on the alternative hypotheses.

6.11   Summary

After the action taking phase, we have collected data about the effects of our actions. In the evaluation phase, we analyze this data and draw conclusions about the action's effects. This evaluation, which, needless to say, has to be objective, is required as we can have bias toward the positive or negative outcome of the action. As humans, we have some attitude toward the change which we wanted to introduce—sometimes we need the change to fix a problem, but sometimes we make the change to check if something is better than something else. This means that we are biased toward a specific outcome—if we like the change, we look at its effects through this perspective and vice versa.

The role of the evaluation phase is to reduce the biases by objectively analyzing the data. In most cases, the data is a mixture of quantitative and qualitative data. We often collect data from source systems like the Git source code management, and we complement the data with the qualitative one. We may conduct interviews to understand how others perceived the change.

In this chapter, we explored the most common ways of analyzing data in action research. The description is, by no means, exhaustive, and there are many great books devoted to data analysis. The description, nevertheless, gets us quite far as we can use these techniques to analyze a lot of action research results.

However, what we, deliberately, do not discuss in this chapter is how to interpret the data. This is the task for the next phase—to answer the question of what do these results really mean.

References

[ASM+14] Vard Antinyan, Miroslaw Staron, Wilhelm Meding, Per Österström, Erik Wikstrom, Johan Wranker, Anders Henriksson, and Jörgen Hansson. Identifying risky areas of software code in agile/lean software development: An industrial experience report. In *Software Maintenance, Reengineering and Reverse Engineering (CSMR-WCRE), 2014 Software Evolution Week-IEEE Conference on*, pages 154–163. IEEE, 2014.

[BC06] Virginia Braun and Victoria Clarke. Using thematic analysis in psychology. *Qualitative research in psychology*, 3(2):77–101, 2006.

[BFM11] Guido Buzzi-Ferraris and Flavio Manenti. Outlier detection in large data sets. *Computers & chemical engineering*, 35(2):388–390, 2011.

[BPM04] Gustavo EAPA Batista, Ronaldo C Prati, and Maria Carolina Monard. A study of the behavior of several methods for balancing machine learning training data. *ACM SIGKDD explorations newsletter*, 6(1):20–29, 2004.

[BRE13] Tanja Blascheck, Michael Raschke, and Thomas Ertl. Circular heat map transition diagram. In *Proceedings of the 2013 Conference on Eye Tracking South Africa*, pages 58–61. ACM, 2013.

[ÇSM18] Gül Çalikli, Miroslaw Staron, and Wilhelm Meding. Measure early and decide fast: transforming quality management and measurement to continuous deployment. In *Proceedings of the 2018 International Conference on Software and System Process*, pages 51–60. ACM, 2018.

[DS+11] David P Doane, Lori Welte Seward, et al. *Applied statistics in business and economics.* New York, NY: McGraw-Hill/Irwin,, 2011.

[GUH16] Carlos A Gomez-Uribe and Neil Hunt. The Netflix recommender system: Algorithms, business value, and innovation. *ACM Transactions on Management Information Systems (TMIS)*, 6(4):13, 2016.

[Har12] Peter Harrington. *Machine learning in action*, volume 5. Manning Greenwich, CT, 2012.

[Lan13] Brett Lantz. *Machine learning with R*. Packt Publishing Ltd, 2013.

[Qui14] J Ross Quinlan. *C4. 5: programs for machine learning.* Elsevier, 2014.

[RM16] Colin Robson and Kieran McCartan. *Real world research*. John Wiley & Sons, 2016.

[SHF+13] Miroslaw Staron, Jorgen Hansson, Robert Feldt, Anders Henriksson, Wilhelm Meding, Sven Nilsson, and Christoffer Hoglund. Measuring and visualizing code stability—a case study at three companies. In *Software Measurement and the 2013 Eighth International Conference on Software Process and Product Measurement (IWSM-MENSURA), 2013 Joint Conference of the 23rd International Workshop on*, pages 191–200. IEEE, 2013.

[SMNA16] Miroslaw Staron, Wilhelm Meding, Kent Niesel, and Alain Abran. A key performance indicator quality model and its industrial evaluation. In *Software Measurement and the International Conference on Software Process and Product Measurement (IWSM-MENSURA), 2016 Joint Conference of the International Workshop on*, pages 170–179. IEEE, 2016.

[SNB18] Miroslaw Staron, Kent Niesel, and Niclas Bauman. Milestone-oriented usage of key performance indicators–an industrial case study. *e-Informatica Software Engineering Journal*, 12(1), 2018.

[Tel07] Alexandru C Telea. *Data visualization: principles and practice*. AK Peters/CRC Press, 2007.

[Tor15] Adam Tornhill. *Your code as a crime scene*. Pragmatic Bookshelf, 2015.

Chapter 7
Specifying Learning

> *Tell me and I forget. Teach me and I remember. Involve me and I learn.*
>
> —Benjamin Franklin

Abstract In this chapter, we describe methods used to increase the learning in the organization. We focus on the role of the researchers in this process and the need to reduce the bias introduced by them. We base this chapter on the theories and practices from the software process improvement field. However, we focus on identifying learning outcomes from studies, organizing them in categories, and packaging for the next action research cycle.

7.1 Introduction

In action research projects, specifying learning plays an important role. It provides the opportunity for the practitioners to communicate the results in an appealing way which leads to wider spread of the knowledge. The researchers, on the other hand, have the possibility to describe how their actions contributed to theory building and to the state of the art in their research area.

Figure 7.1 shows the action research cycle focused on learning. The figure shows that this phase of the action research cycle is important for two other parts—the evaluation and the diagnosing for the next cycle. The link to the evaluation part is important because all learning needs to be well anchored in the evidence collected and evaluated in the current cycle. The link to the diagnosing is also very important as the learning phase can direct the decisions related to the next cycle's research focus. The diagnosing phase of the subsequent cycle uses the learning and evaluation results to find which important research problems should be addressed in the next phase.

© Springer Nature Switzerland AG 2020
M. Staron, *Action Research in Software Engineering*,
https://doi.org/10.1007/978-3-030-32610-4_7

When specifying learning, we deliver two types of artifacts—industrial, targeted toward practitioners, and academic, targeted at the scientific community. We also need to understand that there are two sides of each of these—how things are and how they should be (e.g., how the organization should learn from the cycle and how it actually did learn) [Tsa97].

For the practitioners, each action research cycle should result in the development and evaluation of a product, process, new organization, ways of working, and/or methods. It is important, therefore, that the action team specifies learning along these lines.

For the academia, each action research cycle should result in the development of new knowledge, learning, and/or theory. This means that each action research cycle could, in principle, result in a short paper about the development and evaluation of a specific industrial deliverable (e.g., new product) in the light of an existing or a new scientific theory. Therefore, specifying learning needs to have the same scientific rigor as any type of publication.

Finally, when specifying learning, we must document the experiences from the research itself. For example, we should note down the observations of how the organization receives the action team, the research type, and the way of presenting the results to them. We use the research logbook as the starting point for the documentation. These experiences help the research team and the organization in the subsequent action research cycles or projects.

7.2 Specifying Learning for Companies and Teams

When discussing the learning of the organizations, we need to look back at some of the older theories dating back some 30 years. These theories were developed in the time when research into organizations started to be popular and researchers started to develop theories which described how the organizations are structured, how they function, and how they learn. One of such theories is the organizational change theory by Goodman [Goo82].

Goodman's model for understanding the degree to which an organization change is institutionalized consists of five facets of the change:

- behavior—the extent to which an individual has knowledge of a specific behavior,
- performance—the extent to which the behavior is performed in the organization,
- preference for the behavior—whether a participant likes or dislikes the behavior,
- normative consensus—to which extent there is a consensus about the appropriateness of the method,
- values—social consensus about the values relevant to a specific behavior and consensus about how things "ought or ought not to be" [Goo82].

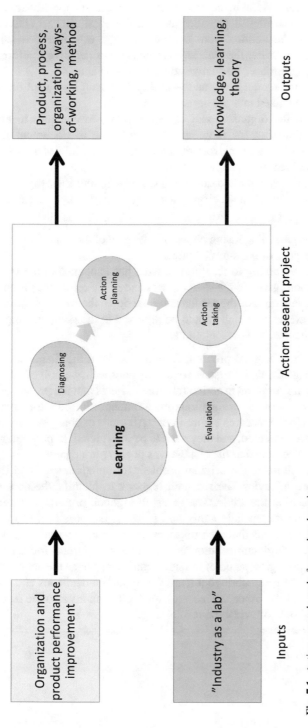

Fig. 7.1 Action research cycle focused on learning

The model is very useful in the context of action research in software engineering when specifying learning. It provides us with the possibility to reason about the degree to which the actions were accepted by the organization (behavior and performance) and whether the reactions are positive or negative (preference for the behavior) and appropriate (normative consensus and values).

In particular, the model gives us the ability to reason how well the learning is actually institutionalized into the organization.

In addition to the organizational change theory, we can turn to ethnography in software engineering for more guidance on how to document and specify learning [SDDS16], where the role of the research log and notes of the behavior of individuals and teams are documented.

Although we can specify and document learning in multiple ways, I recommend a structured approach when specifying learning. In particular, we can follow these steps:

1. Revisit the original diagnosing phase and the goal of the study to recapitulate the goals and purpose of the current sprint.
2. Revisit the research log to recapitulate what has happened in the study. Review the presentations given to the stakeholders and to the reference group.
3. Review the evaluation of the results and note down the most important findings.
4. Identify the elements which should be archived at the company, e.g., data sets, scripts, documents, and presentations.

By revisiting the original problem formulation from the diagnosing phase, we recapitulate the goals, and we start reflecting how well we solved the diagnosed problem. It is quite common in action research projects that the project evolves a bit from the original problem formulation, due to changes in the setup, availability of data, or changes in the research environment. All kinds of changes from the original plan need to be documented, and they need to be interpreted. In particular, the action team needs to reflect whether the change was positive or negative.

Once we recapitulated the original problem formulation, specified the learning from it, we need to review the research logbook to identify the new knowledge that we found during the study. The research logbook provides the record of all our actions during the specific study and gives us the possibility to reflect upon our actions. All decisions that are important for the research study are documented in the logbook. This documentation is particularly important for action research projects, since the original setup of the study can change once the action starts. What we extract from the research logbook are the important decisions and the rationale behind these decisions. Since the research logbook contains also the results, we use the research logbook to review the results (Fig. 7.2).

Revisiting the Logbook

When conducting a number of simulation trials with neural networks, the team
kept a research logbook where they documented each trial, its parameters,
and the confusion matrix (the result). The goal was to get the best possible
classification result given the available data set.

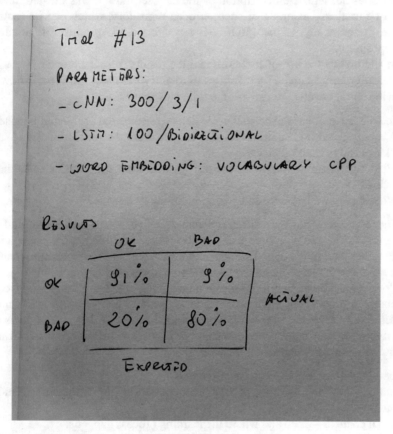

Fig. 7.2   An example page from the research logbook

The logbook for this particular trial did not provide any satisfactory results, and
therefore the team decided to change the setup. The change was documented on
the next page of the logbook, and it was used together with these results to justify
the change in the setup.

When specifying learning, it is important to share the data within the company, to the extent possible. In the open source community, and increasingly in the scientific community, there is a trend to share data sets used in research. Openly sharing proprietary or commercial data from companies is not equally popular. When it comes to sharing the data within the company, this is much easier. We can strive to share the data within the same organization in a similar way in which open repositories do, with the description of the data set, how it was created, and how it can be used. An example of such an open repository, which can be replicated within the company, is the PROMISE repository http://promise.site.uottawa.ca/SERepository/.

In addition to the use of logbooks and the results from each cycle, we use the reference group to conduct workshops to identify the most important knowledge from the current cycle. We can ask the following questions:

- To which extent has the current cycle helped to solve the problem diagnosed?
- What are the most important lessons learned from the problem-solving (action taking) and evaluation phase?
- What are the most important lessons learned from the process of taking the action?
- What should we take into consideration for the next cycle?

The reference group has a different, more objective, perspective on the study than the action team. The reference group is also more embedded in the context of the study rather than in the actual actions and interventions. Therefore, we should use their experiences to document the learning from the action research cycle.

However, useful and high-quality documentation of the new knowledge requires a structured process for eliciting the knowledge. For that purpose, we can use a model, Syllk (Systemic Lessons Learned Knowledge, [DW16]), to guide us when specifying the learning for the organization. The model prescribes considering the following elements when specifying learning:

- learning—how people learn as individuals,
- culture—how the learning process is supported by the management and colleagues,
- social context—when and where the learning process happens,
- technology—the tools used to support the learning process, e.g., dashboards,
- process—how the learning is used to change the operations of the company, e.g., best practices and guidelines, and
- infrastructure—how the company's infrastructure facilitates learning, e.g., colocation of teams vs. remote teleconferencing equipment.

Organizational learning is a process of institutionalization of knowledge in the organizations. The process of learning can be individual when the action team comprises only one researcher working at the software development company. However, even the team of two persons, like one researchers and one practitioner, requires discussion and dissemination. The culture differences between academia and industry can be either an obstacle or an opportunity. If the researchers and practitioners are open to new ways or working and accept the other's differences, the learning becomes richer and deeper—the mutual understanding helps to increase the rigor of reporting and the ability to use the results in another organization.

The model identifies a number of facilitators that help in learning in the organization, such as the facilitators for the learning, [DW15]:

- Mentoring (and one-on-one coaching).
- Small workshops (in-house) with the persons of the same skill level to learn from one another.
- Willingness to share and learn from each other and others willing to listen and accept new ideas; for us, we have a large and growing multidisciplinary that compliment and respect each other.

In order to learn, the organizations use such practices as stories and storytelling, communities of practice, and mentoring/coaching.

Storytelling has become one of the modern ways of specifying learning. Instead of focusing on facts and numbers, we focus on events, people, and stories related to action taking and evaluation. We describe when and where the stories happen, but we often replace the real names of the people with the fictional ones in order to avoid ethical issues and to keep the integrity of the personal data of our partners intact (Fig. 7.3).

Describing Metrics Research as a Storytelling

In one of the projects, the action team had the opportunity to create a film that showcased the research. The team has created a film that showed how to choose a dashboard. This film was used in training and in disseminating the information in a form that was accessible from mobile phones and computers.

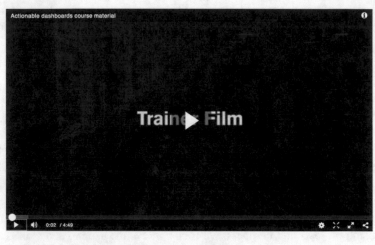

Fig. 7.3 Screenshot of a trainer video demonstrating the use of dashboards. The full video is available at https://play.gu.se/media/Actionable+dashboards+course+material/0_srzxnwv0

The screenshot above illustrates the movie, which is similar to modern YouTube videos but stored at the university server, thus retaining the copyright. The action team used this video to showcase the method and to provide the audience with the first glimpse of it. The interested people were referred to websites and tutorials about the method.

Communities of practice are based on the idea that learning is a social activity and that we learn by examples and "word of mouth." The communities of practice are seminars and meetings that are based on specific topics. An example community of practice can be a community of configuration managers discussing the challenges in introducing continuous integration into their company. The communities of practice usually create a website or a wiki page where they describe their experience with a specific topic [PL14] (Fig. 7.4).

Packaging Method for Company Internal Reuse

In the project, the action team decided to describe the learnings from the project as a website. The website shows how the method is to be used and starts up the communities of practice around the method.

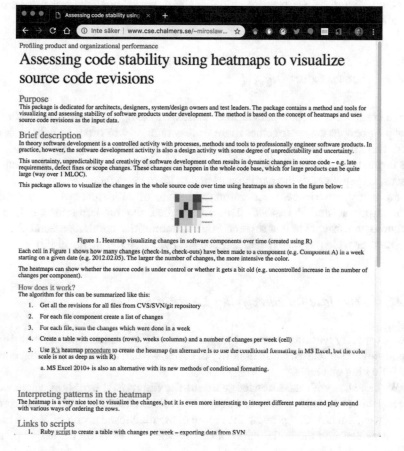

Fig. 7.4 Screenshot of a simple website showing how to use a method for visualizing code stability [SHF+13]

The webpage is used as an instruction, and it includes the links to all the scripts and papers describing the method. The action team used it to collect all information about the method to disseminate it.

Specifying learning can also be done by disseminating the information through such technological tools as dashboards, portals, and wiki pages. They are particularly useful for the communities of practice, but they can also be used when extracting information from a research log and describing it for the purpose of dissemination.

Mentoring and coaching are important in dissemination of knowledge. In action research, therefore, we prepare guidelines and workshops where we teach others about the methods and tools developed in the project.

7.2.1 Active Learning

Some companies adopt a paradigm of *action learning*, which is a process when a group of people gather together more or less regularly in order to help each other learn from their experience, according to Dick [Dic97]. In many cases, these groups are formed around communities of practice or seminar series, where the focus is to discuss experiences of the participants and to learn from them.

From my experience, these communities are often virtual, where participants come from around the globe. This means that the modern videoconferencing technology is crucial in that respect. Some communities combine a number of local sites and provide physical meeting space with videoconferencing abilities.

7.2.2 Template for Specifying Learning

We can specify learning in several ways, starting from bulleted points to full-fledge reports and dashboards, but in majority of cases, we can create a report that contains the following elements.

We can start with the **knowledge about the diagnosed problem** where we can specify what new we have learned about the problem itself. In every action research cycle, we learn new things about the nature of the diagnosed problem. We go beyond the interviews and the initial data collection when we work on the action planning and on action taking.

Once we specified the new knowledge about the nature of the problem, we can specify the new knowledge about the **organizational context**, where we describe the new knowledge about the organization where we conduct our action research. This new knowledge is important as we need to be aware about the social aspects of the action taking and specifying the lessons learned for the company. We need to consider who was affected about the action taking, whether the action taking went beyond the behavior of the team and was accepted as organizational practice (aka normative reference in Goodman and Dean's model [Goo82]).

We also need to specify the **learning from the action taking**, where we describe the results from the evaluation of the action. We provide the collected data from the action taking, and we present the evaluation of it. We also need to consider the interpretation of the evaluated data in relation to the baseline, the reference data, from before action taking.

Finally, we need to specify the **guidelines for the company** regarding how to scale up the results, practices, and actions beyond a research project so that they can be adopted by a wider audience in the company. For that, we need to compile a compendium about how the method should be used and when. These guidelines can have a form of a webpage where we create a step-by-step instruction of how to use a method. However, modern companies work with short instructor films and movies where the learnings are specified in terms of instructional videos. These videos provide a good way of engaging younger generations of software engineers who are more used to that way of learning about new methods and tools.

Finally, when we specify the learning, we need to reflect upon the **infrastructure** in the project. We can reflect upon the available tools and data sources as well as the ability to scale up our results based on this infrastructure. For example, we can reflect upon the fact that the introduction of new method requires investments, and we can list what needs to be changed to make the new method work. Such reflections provide the company's management with the ability to make better decisions upon the adoption of the methods used in the company. This reflection is also one factor that distinguishes action research from other types of research methods. As the action team is embedded in the company, they can provide such a calculation.

7.3   Contributing to Theory Building

Specifying learning for the scientific community sounds familiar to every researcher as it is similar to preparing a full-fledge publication. However, as every research methodology is based on specific premises, the focus of documenting action research is on the process, the context, and the learning from it. The development of the product for the industrial partner is a bit secondary in this context. It is described as a learning for the particular host organization where the action research takes place.

For the contribution to theory building, we need to address the question—*What new have we learned from this study?* We need to revisit the diagnosing phase where we explored which theories we can apply in the cycle. In an article discussing how to write for the IEEE Software magazine, McConnel [McC02] poses the question slightly different, although with the same meaning—*Does [the article] make a contribution to the software engineering literature?*. According to McConnel, all authors of IEEE Software should ask themselves this question. In my view, this guidance applies for specifying learning in action research projects.

Runeson et al. [RHRR12] provide good guidance on reporting of case studies for the academic audience, which we can adopt for specifying learning for the academic audience. These guidelines provide the starting point for considering what we have contributed with.

One important aspect of specifying learning is to ensure that the study can be replicated, so we need to prepare a protocol that can be useful for researchers who want to replicate the study in their own organization. The replication should allow to compare the results and the learnings. In order to ensure replicability, we need to think about the following when specifying learning:

1. The importance of the finding: why is it worth disseminating?
2. The significance of the finding: why should other researchers care about our finding?
3. The implications for the theory: do we create a new theory or confirm/reject an existing one?

A rule of thumb in identifying the implications is to understand how our findings relate to the state of the art, which can be as follows:

1. Confirm the existing findings (e.g., through replication): when our study confirms the results of the previous research, in a different context, a different organization, or by changing an element of the original study.
2. Contrast the existing findings (e.g., by refuting an established hypothesis): when our study finds that the existing theories and research results do not apply for the specific context under investigation.
3. Refine the existing findings (e.g., by studying one specific aspect more deeply): when our study explores one specific aspect of the original research and goes in more depth.

When we cannot specify whether our results fall into one of the above three categories, we can say that we do not contribute to that particular field of science. This does not mean that we do not have a contribution; it simply indicates that we should look for new theories or that we establish a completely new theoretical model.

7.3.1 Examples of Types of Contributions

Petre and Rugg [PR10] identify a number of ways in which one can make contributions.[1] We can adapt and discuss these types in the context of action research studies.

Applying a technique in a new context, testing an existing theory in a new setting, or showing the applicability of a model to a new situation is the type of contribution where the action research study uses existing tools and methods to solve a problem at a specific company. This type of contribution can be seen quite often when the action team got inspired by a research study conducted at another company or a theoretical new techniques which they want to validate.

---

[1]This book is an example of many which provide advice on how to identify contributions in research studies.

Applying Research from Open Source in Industrial Context

In this project, the action team's diagnosed problem was the fact that the company had a lot of cloned code, but not all clones were significant. Therefore, they decided to look for existing theories in code cloning to understand these phenomena in the industrial context.

The action team found the theories about code clones in the open source community and applied them to their context. Figure 7.5 shows the clones between different components in the same system.

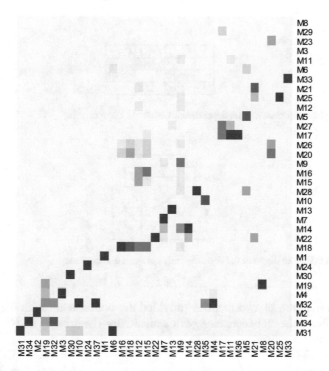

Fig. 7.5 Heatmap showing the cloned code between components (M1–M34) [SME$^+$15]

The theories from the open source were extended by introducing a new classification scheme for clones. It was the access to the architects and designers that provided the necessary insight to design and evaluate the scheme.

Quite often, the contribution of a particular action research cycle is a combination of two or more ideas, showing that the combination leading to new results is another example of the contribution. We often can find relevant theories that need adjustment to the current context. When looking for this adjustment, we often use another theory. For instance, we can combine the analysis of source code with a visualization used in city plannings and thus create this kind of contribution [PBG03].

Combining Statistical Analysis of Codependencies with Architectural Design Visualization

In this project, the action team's diagnosed problem was the need to predict whether a specific source code change can cause changes in different modules.

The action team combined the visualization of code changes using heatmaps [SHF+13] (Fig. 7.6) with the visualization using architectural design [KS05] (Fig. 7.7).

	X	Y	Z
X		99%	100%
Y	80%		100%
Z	50%	50%	

Fig. 7.6 Heatmap showing the dependencies between components

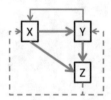

Fig. 7.7 UML-like diagram for dependencies between components

The combination of two theories provided the action team with the ability to reason about the dependencies both statistically (heatmaps) and design wise (architecture diagram).

It is also quite common that in the first action research cycles, we demonstrate a concept. We provide evidence that something can be done in the context of our collaborating organization. Alternatively, we can show that something cannot be done or it is inefficient to do something. For example, we can design a prototype program that demonstrates feasibility of a specific technique or approach (Fig. 7.8).

Demonstrating a Concept of Metrics Cloud

In this project, the action team has developed a prototype of a program that distributed measurement systems using cloud approach.

The action team developed a prototype system which demonstrated the feasibility of this approach.

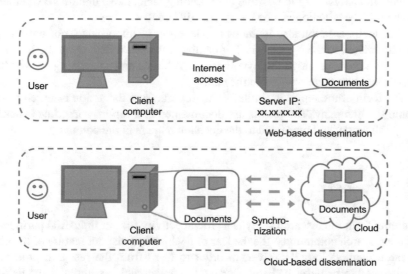

Fig. 7.8 Conceptual model of a metrics cloud (bottom) compared to the traditional one (top) [SM18]

The demonstrator provided the action team with the ability to reason about the feasibility of this way of distributing measurement systems in terms of performance, robustness, and scalability.

Creating the prototypes can show that it is feasible to implement a theory in practice. It provides us with the possibility to understand the limitations of the theories in the industrial contexts.

We can, finally, provide a new solution to a known problem where there are solutions available. Providing a new solution to a known problem entails demonstrating the solution's efficacy. We can show that the new solution is faster, more accurate, or better with respect to some parameter, compared to the existing solutions.

7.4 Specifying Learning from Experiment Systems

In the experiment systems, where the customers are involved in the research, the specification of the learning is related directly to the hypothesis. We analyze the metrics collected during the experiment, and we show whether the null hypothesis can be rejected in favor of the alternative one. In the description, we also need to include an analysis of the possible confounding factors. We document whether the results of the evaluation can be interpreted differently.

The documentation also includes any learning of importance, not only the one directly related to the hypothesis. For example, we can reflect upon the hypothesis itself—whether we judge the hypothesis as valuable and interesting or whether it turned out to be quite obvious in the end.

The form of the report is similar as the reports from the action research projects within the company. The results are documented in a report, sometimes packaged as a publication, and presented to the decision makers in the company.

7.5 Summary

Learning from the research study is a crucial activity for our industrial partners and for the research community. It's the learning which is a distinct feature of the action research methodology. However, in order to learn from the research project, the results need to be described and packaged in a way which stimulates the learning. We need to conduct workshops to identify learnings and good practices, and we need to document these practices.

In this chapter, we described a number of methods that can be used to elicit lessons learned from a research study, and we show how to document these learnings. In addition to organizational learning, we also described how to make a contribution to theories in software engineering.

In order to deepen our knowledge on how to identify organizational practices that emerged during the study, we can turn to ethnographical methods in software engineering. Ethnography is a research methodology which contains the component of learning and is often focused on activities, just like the action research [SDDS16]. The major difference is that action researchers intervene with the daily work of software engineers, while the ethnographers do not.

In the next chapter, we dive into the challenges of documenting research studies and writing up our results in form of research reports.

References

[Dic97] Bob Dick. Action learning and action research. 1997.

[DW15] Stephen Duffield and S Jonathan Whitty. Developing a systemic lessons learned knowledge model for organisational learning through projects. *International journal of project management*, 33(2):311–324, 2015.

[DW16] Stephen M Duffield and S Jonathan Whitty. Application of the systemic lessons learned knowledge model for organisational learning through projects. *International journal of project management*, 34(7):1280–1293, 2016.

[Goo82] Paul S Goodman. Creating long-term organizational change. Technical report, CARNEGIE-MELLON UNIV PITTSBURGH PA GRADUATE SCHOOL OF INDUSTRIAL ADMINISTRATION, 1982.

[KS05] Ludwik Kuzniarz and Miroslaw Staron. Best practices for teaching UML based software development. In *International Conference on Model Driven Engineering Languages and Systems*, pages 320–332. Springer, 2005.

[McC02] Steve McConnell. From the editor: How to write a good technical article. *IEEE Software*, (5):5–7, 2002.

[PBG03] Thomas Panas, Rebecca Berrigan, and John Grundy. A 3d metaphor for software production visualization. In *Proceedings on Seventh International Conference on Information Visualization, 2003. IV 2003.*, pages 314–319. IEEE, 2003.

[PL14] Maria Paasivaara and Casper Lassenius. Communities of practice in a large distributed agile software development organization–case Ericsson. *Information and Software Technology*, 56(12):1556–1577, 2014.

[PR10] Marian Petre and Gordon Rugg. The unwritten rules of PhD research (open up study skills), 2010.

[RHRR12] Per Runeson, Martin Host, Austen Rainer, and Bjorn Regnell. *Case study research in software engineering: Guidelines and examples*. John Wiley & Sons, 2012.

[SDDS16] Helen Sharp, Yvonne Dittrich, and Cleidson RB De Souza. The role of ethnographic studies in empirical software engineering. *IEEE Transactions on Software Engineering*, 42(8):786–804, 2016.

[SHF+13] Miroslaw Staron, Jörgen Hansson, Robert Feldt, Anders Henriksson, Wilhelm Meding, Sven Nilsson, and Christoffer Höglund. Measuring and visualizing code stability–a case study at three companies. In *2013 Joint Conference of the 23rd International Workshop on Software Measurement and the 8th International Conference on Software Process and Product Measurement*, pages 191–200. IEEE, 2013.

[SM18] Miroslaw Staron and Wilhelm Meding. *Software Development Measurement Programs: Development, Management and Evolution*. Springer, 2018.

[SME+15] Miroslaw Staron, Wilhelm Meding, Peter Eriksson, Jimmy Nilsson, Nils Lövgren, and Per Österström. Classifying obstructive and nonobstructive code clones of type I using simplified classification scheme: a case study. *Advances in Software Engineering*, 2015:5, 2015.

[Tsa97] Eric WK Tsang. Organizational learning and the learning organization: a dichotomy between descriptive and prescriptive research. *Human relations*, 50(1):73–89, 1997.

Chapter 8
Action Research vs. Design Research

> *Every discourse, even a poetic or oracular sentence, carries with it a system of rules for producing analogous things and thus an outline of methodology.*
>
> —Jacques Derrida

Abstract Action research is one of many research methodologies used in contemporary empirical software engineering. Its practical orientation and embedding in the context of a company are its main appeal. However, the embedding can be challenging as it requires active participation from industrial partners. Therefore, we can sometimes change the course of our studies and use a methodology that is closely related—design science research. In this chapter, we explore the basic principles of design science research and make the comparison between these two methodologies.

8.1 Introduction

We choose our research methodology based on the goal of the research at hand. Some research projects require studying software development methodologies [CR08] and developing new tools [CH11] or methods [SKT05], while others focus on the social aspects of software engineering, like team composition [LFW15]. Given a specific goal of each research study, the researchers focus on different aspects. When focusing on the studies where social aspects are in focus, we use research methodologies which are close to social sciences like experiments, case studies, or ethnographical studies. When the focus of a research study is on the technological aspects, we use engineering research methods like simulations, prototyping, and technology adoption.

The combination of both social and engineering research in the field of software engineering makes it a broad discipline, with many flavors. Software engineering's body of knowledge (SWEBOK, [BF+14]) lists over a dozen of different areas and

© Springer Nature Switzerland AG 2020
M. Staron, *Action Research in Software Engineering*,
https://doi.org/10.1007/978-3-030-32610-4_8

subareas of software engineering. These areas range from computer science to social science.

Design science research is a methodology which we can place close to the engineering, technical areas of software engineering. Design science is the design and investigation of artifacts in context [Wie14]. A design science research project, therefore, seeks to solve an empirical or industrial problem, with the help of an artifact. It recognizes two contributions—the construction and evaluation of the artifact and the development of new knowledge.

Design science research projects are similar to action research projects in many ways. They seek to work in close collaboration with the context of the study. This context can be the organization or company where the research is done. However, it does not require the project to be done by practitioners or having practitioners as part of the research team. Although the practitioners can be part of the team, the methodology of design research does not require it.

My students and industrial collaborators often ask when they should use one or the other. In this chapter, we learn what design science research is and when to use it over action research, or when to use action research over design science research.

8.2   Design Research

Design science research is used in different ways, and here, we use the definitions by Wieringa [Wie10] and [Wie14]. Wieringa's way of defining, describing, and practicing design science research is the most suitable for software engineering. It links strongly to the principles of empiricism in software engineering.

Figure 8.1 presents the basic principle of design science research—interaction between an artifact and its context.

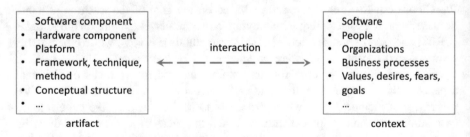

Fig. 8.1 Basic principle of design science research—interaction between an artifact and its context. Adapted from Wieringa [Wie10]

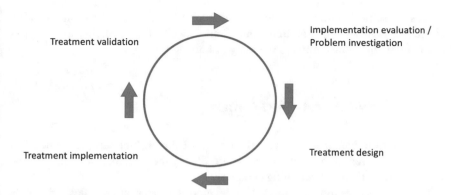

Fig. 8.2 Design science research cycle, adapted from Wieringa [Wie10]

In essence, this interaction between the artifact and the context is similar to the principles of action research. However, the focus of design science research is different from the focus of action research. The context is also different.

The design science research is used to evaluate the artifacts in their context. The most commonly used research questions oscillate around the topics of how well the artifacts work in a given context or what the effects of using a specific artifact in the contexts are.

The context of the design research is used when discussing the evaluation part of the design research. The design science researchers often use the context, and the companies, in a model where "industry as a lab" is dominating the needs of improvement of the companies. This means that the design science researchers seek contexts, or companies, which fit the need of their evaluations. This means that the design science research teams seek to find the conditions where their artifacts can be applied and where they can find how well their laboratory-designed artifacts can be tested and validated in industrial contexts.

Wieringa [Wie10] presents design science research as a cyclic activity, as shown in Fig. 8.2.

Although it is presented as a cyclic graph, design science research often entails only one or two cycles. In the first cycle, the design science research teams make the first evaluation, and in the second cycle, they improve their artifact and evaluate the improvement.

8.2.1 Awareness of the Problem or Problem Investigation

The first phase of the design science research aims at the development of the requirements for the artifacts. The design research team uses the same techniques as requirement engineers to understand the needs of the stakeholders and to design the new method, tool, software, or other artifacts, so that these needs are fulfilled.

This phase is also important for the understanding of the details of the scientific problem to address. The research team should specify this explicitly as they need this to define the contribution to the body of knowledge.

8.2.2 Treatment or Artifact Design

Once the requirements are elicited, the design of the artifact can commence. The design science research team can work off-site on the design, although they can work on-site of their collaborating company.

The treatment design is intended to develop the external specification for the artifact to be developed and implemented in the next phase. It is similar to the design and implementation phase of software engineering projects.

In this phase, the development of the treatment or artifact takes place. The development means that at the end of the phase, there is a tool, method, or measure that can be used in the company.

8.2.3 Treatment or Artifact Implementation

In the implementation phase, the research team applies the artifact to the original context. This means that the concept of implementation is similar to business research where we apply a method to a problem. The implementation is hence different from the concept of implementation in software engineering.

8.2.4 Treatment or Artifact Evaluation

The last phase of the design science research cycle is the evaluation of the treatment. This phase is an assessment of how well the artifact solves the problem identified in the problem investigation phase. It is similar to the evaluation of the action research cycle, where we analyze whether the artifact solved the problem or whether we need to change the artifact or evolve it.

8.3 Similarities and Differences

Design science research and action research come from two different origins— the engineering science and the social science. However, they have evolved and adapted to different settings, and nowadays, they have both similarities and differ-

Table 8.1 Similarities and differences between action research and design science research

	Action research	Design science research
Focus	Intervention and action	Artifact and treatment
Location	On-site	Off-site
Researchers	Industry or industry + academia	Academia or academia + industry
Contribution	Practice and theory	Practice and theory
Include learning	Yes, explicit	Yes, implicit in the evaluation
Evaluated entity	Action and its impact	Artifact and its design
Impact of research is primarily on	Client organization	Developed artifact
Intervention	In the problem setting of the client organization	In the local organization where the artifact is to be used

ences [Jär07]. Iivani and Venable [IV09] examined these two methodologies and concluded that there can be varying degree of overlap but no total overlap.

In Table 8.1, we grouped the main differences and similarities between these two methodologies.

However, the main difference between these two methodologies is that the design science research often perceives the industry as a lab. In this perception, the role of the industry is to help to design a software tool or a method that can help software engineers in their work. This means that the design science researchers often design tools that are more generic than the tools designed by the action researchers. Since the model of "industry as a lab" means that the researchers often seek the right context for their work, the alignment of the designed artifact is better than when the researchers are designing an artifact to solve a particular organizational problem in action research.

In the examples in the boxes below, we see how two similar studies are organized according to design science research and as action research (Figs. 8.3, 8.4, 8.5, and 8.6).

Defect Prediction as a Design Science Research Project

In this project, a researcher designed a study to evaluate a number of defect prediction models based on industrial data. The goal was to evaluate how well the models can predict the defect inflow from a number of industrial projects.

The models were constructed before contacting the company, based on data from other projects, e.g., from research projects conducted at NASA. Since the models were constructed in the 1970s and 1980s, there was a need to evaluate whether they were still applicable in the 2010s [RSM+13]. The following models were evaluated:

1. Goel-Okumoto, [GO79],
2. Musa, [MO84],
3. Delayed S-shaped model [YOO83],
4. Rayleigh model,
5. Inflection S-shaped model [Pha03],
6. Yamada exponential imperfect debugging model (Y- ExpI) [YTO92],
7. Yamada linear imperfect debugging model (Y-LinI) [YTO92], and
8. Gompertz model [OOD09].

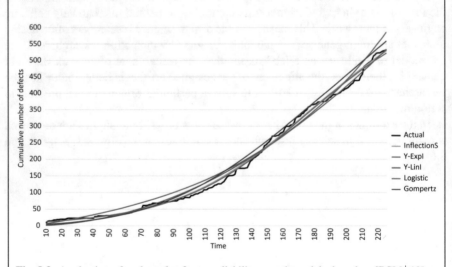

Fig. 8.3 A selection of evaluated software reliability growth models, based on [RSM+13]

The researcher found that the software reliability growth models can still be used with the modern software development. Based on the evaluation using mean squared error, the researcher could provide guidelines on which models to use.

Fig. 8.4 Mean squared error for the evaluated models

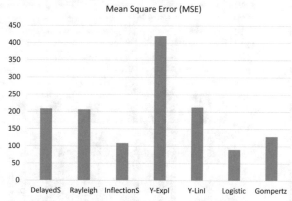

Defect Prediction as an Action Research Project

In this project, the action research team set off to understand the dynamics of the defect inflow profiles in industry. The goal of this project, therefore, was to design and evaluate a method for predicting the number of defects reported per week.

During the course of the project, in the diagnosing phase, the action research team discovered that the industrial partner expected to know the number of defects with a 3 week's prediction horizon.

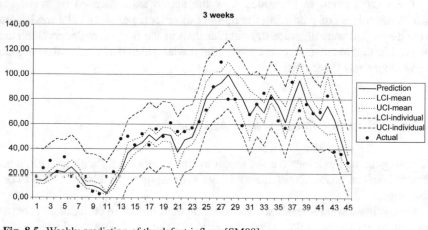

Fig. 8.5 Weekly prediction of the defect inflow, [SM08]

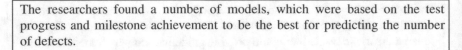

The researchers found a number of models, which were based on the test progress and milestone achievement to be the best for predicting the number of defects.

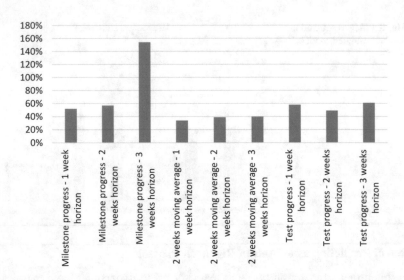

Fig. 8.6 Weekly prediction of the defect inflow, mean magnitude of relative error [SM08]

The two examples above illustrate a difference between the two research methods. In the first example, the focus was on the prediction models. The goal of the researcher was to assess whether old models are still applicable in practice. The researcher was not focused on the impact of the models in practice but on the quality of the models.

The second example illustrated how the action team focused on solving an industrial problem of predicting the number of defects per week. The models that were developed were significantly simpler than in the first example, and the study evolved further to create a robust prediction model which was used in the company a few more years [SMS10].

8.3.1   When to Choose Which Methodology

Choosing the methodology for the research study can be a difficult process, but to choose between action research and design science research does not have to be a challenge.

Firstly, if we want to evaluate a specific method or tool in an industrial context, we should not focus on the action research. We should choose the design science research methodology and rigorously follow it. Instead of diagnosing the problem, we can focus on developing the tool and the method and finding the right context to evaluate it and, finally, to assess the tool or the method.

However, if we want to develop our understanding of the problem, and focus on the impact of our work on the industrial practices, we should choose action research. We spend the time on understanding the problem, on making an intervention, and on specifying learning. Using action research allows us to explore both the technical and social aspects of making the intervention.

Secondly, when our research problem is related to the technical aspects of software engineering, e.g., developing new tools, we should choose the design science research. Choosing that method helps us to understand the technology rather than the context.

However, if our goal is to understand the context of the technology a bit more than the tooling, then we should definitely choose the action research methodology. It provides us with the right mind-set from the beginning and helps us to document both the theory development and the practice development.

Thirdly, when our research team consists of academic researchers and is done primarily in an academic lab using the industrial context as validation, then we should choose the design research. Even the best researchers can only be observers if they do not partner up with practitioners in the research team.

In contrast, having practitioners in the research team makes the dynamics completely different. The practitioners provide a very practical perspective on the study and, in most cases, direct the research project in the direction of making an impact in the industrial practice. This kind of setup makes the action research more natural that the design science research.

Fourthly, if our research project is time-limited and the amount of time is less than 6 months, then we should choose the design science research over action research. Entering the company, creating the understanding of its inner workings, and building the trust take time. We cannot build trust in a short time, and establishing a good access to the company's infrastructure can be jeopardized by the short time frame.

Therefore, my master or bachelor students seldom use action research as the methodology. They follow the design research unless they have a prior relation to the company, e.g., because they did an internship there. My students often appreciate the ability to work with a company but not "putting the faith of their grades" in the company's ability to adopt or disregard the results from their thesis project.

Finally, if we do not have a long-term relationship with the industrial partner, if we do not have the full access to their infrastructure, we should choose the design science research. The lack of full access makes the research team becoming observers and therefore not action takers.

Nevertheless, if we have a long-term relationship, then using action research helps to strengthen that relationship even further, beyond the research project. It provides the benefits that are beyond research results and create an impact for real [SC17].

8.4   Summary

Design science research and action research are similar, yet different. In this chapter, we reviewed the principles behind design science research and contrasted them with the principles of action research. We also examined how a study can be designed using one or the other methodology.

The intention of this chapter was to compare these two methodologies, not to pick up a winner. Both methodologies have their strong and weak characteristics, but both are equally used in industry in general. In software engineering, the design science research is a bit more popular as we, as a field, are still more oriented towards technology development rather than in human and social aspects of our profession (although this is changing since the beginning of the 2000s) [ST09].

There exist other kinds of methodologies that are popular in software engineering, although they are less rigorous because they focus on technology transfer. One example of such methodology is the one presented by Gorschek et al. [GGLW06]. These kinds of methodologies are important for research projects where the researchers work off-line and off-context in the design and development of methods. However, in action research, and in design research, the research teams work on-site and in-context and therefore do not need a specific methodology for transferring their results to industrial practice.

References

[BF+14] Pierre Bourque, Richard E Fairley, et al. *Guide to the software engineering body of knowledge (SWEBOK (R)): Version 3.0.* IEEE Computer Society Press, 2014.

[CH11] Koen Claessen and John Hughes. Quickcheck: A lightweight tool for random testing of Haskell programs. *SIGPLAN Not.*, 46(4):53–64, May 2011.

[CR08] Lan Cao and Balasubramaniam Ramesh. Agile requirements engineering practices: An empirical study. *IEEE software*, 25(1):60–67, 2008.

[GGLW06] Tony Gorschek, Per Garre, Stig Larsson, and Claes Wohlin. A model for technology transfer in practice. *IEEE software*, 23(6):88–95, 2006.

[GO79] Amrit L Goel and Kazu Okumoto. Time-dependent error-detection rate model for software reliability and other performance measures. *IEEE transactions on Reliability*, 28(3):206–211, 1979.

[IV09] Juhani Iivari and John Venable. Action research and design science research-seemingly similar but decisively dissimilar. In *ECIS*, pages 1642–1653, 2009.

[Jär07] Pertti Järvinen. Action research is similar to design science. *Quality & Quantity*, 41(1):37–54, 2007.

[LFW15] Per Lenberg, Robert Feldt, and Lars Göran Wallgren. Human factors related challenges in software engineering: an industrial perspective. In *Proceedings of the Eighth International Workshop on Cooperative and Human Aspects of Software Engineering*, pages 43–49. IEEE Press, 2015.

[MO84] John D Musa and Kazuhira Okumoto. A logarithmic poisson execution time model for software reliability measurement. In *Proceedings of the 7th international conference on Software engineering*, pages 230–238. Citeseer, 1984.

[OOD09] Koji Ohishi, Hiroyuki Okamura, and Tadashi Dohi. Gompertz software reliability model: Estimation algorithm and empirical validation. *Journal of Systems and Software*, 82(3):535–543, 2009.

[Pha03] Hoang Pham. Software reliability and cost models: Perspectives, comparison, and practice. *European Journal of Operational Research*, 149(3):475–489, 2003.

[RSM+13] Rakesh Rana, Miroslaw Staron, Niklas Mellegård, Christian Berger, Jörgen Hansson, Martin Nilsson, and Fredrik Törner. Evaluation of standard reliability growth models in the context of automotive software systems. In *International Conference on Product Focused Software Process Improvement*, pages 324–329. Springer, 2013.

[SC17] Anna Börjesson Sandberg and Ivica Crnkovic. Meeting industry: academia research collaboration challenges with agile methodologies. In *Proceedings of the 39th International Conference on Software Engineering: Software Engineering in Practice Track*, pages 73–82. IEEE Press, 2017.

[SKT05] Miroslaw Staron, Ludwik Kuzniarz, and Christian Thurn. An empirical assessment of using stereotypes to improve reading techniques in software inspections. *ACM SIGSOFT Software Engineering Notes*, 30(4):1–7, 2005.

[SM08] Miroslaw Staron and Wilhelm Meding. Predicting weekly defect inflow in large software projects based on project planning and test status. *Information and Software Technology*, 50(7–8):782–796, 2008.

[SMS10] Miroslaw Staron, Wilhelm Meding, and Bo Söderqvist. A method for forecasting defect backlog in large streamline software development projects and its industrial evaluation. *Information and Software Technology*, 52(10):1069–1079, 2010.

[ST09] Paulo Sergio Medeiros dos Santos and Guilherme Horta Travassos. Action research use in software engineering: An initial survey. In *Proceedings of the 2009 3rd International Symposium on Empirical Software Engineering and Measurement*, pages 414–417. IEEE Computer Society, 2009.

[Wie10] Roel Wieringa. Design science methodology: principles and practice. In *2010 ACM/IEEE 32nd International Conference on Software Engineering*, volume 2, pages 493–494. IEEE, 2010.

[Wie14] Roel J Wieringa. *Design science methodology for information systems and software engineering*. Springer, 2014.

[YOO83] Shigeru Yamada, Mitsuru Ohba, and Shunji Osaki. S-shaped reliability growth modeling for software error detection. *IEEE Transactions on reliability*, 32(5):475–484, 1983.

[YTO92] Shigeru Yamada, Koichi Tokuno, and Shunji Osaki. Imperfect debugging models with fault introduction rate for software reliability assessment. *International Journal of Systems Science*, 23(12):2241–2252, 1992.

Chapter 9
Ensuring Sustainability of Knowledge

Wilhelm Meding and Miroslaw Staron

Better Safe than Sorry.

—unknown

Abstract Contemporary companies and organizations have understood since long the value of close cooperation between them and academia. Technology today takes huge leaps forward for every year that passes by, and ways of working evolve dramatically in order to cope with technology. Companies are no longer able to keep up with this "insane" speed of technology and ways of working; they know more possibility to learn and adapt by themselves. The solution to this challenge is called "action research," an effective and efficient way for companies to keep up with what's new and necessary for them to succeed in today's hard competition. This book presents prerequisites needed for both parties to succeed in this type of collaboration, while this chapter focuses on a checklist to be used once such a relationship has been established.

9.1 Introduction

Action research can be seen as one of several ways of introducing new knowledge into companies, as we discussed in Chap. 8. However, not all knowledge "sticks" in the company. If the research project addresses short-term problems, the solutions tend to be short-term as well. There is nothing wrong with that, and this kind of research projects are perfect for short-term collaborations, for example, for master theses [Par98].

On the other hand, many software engineering environments are built with long-term collaboration in mind. Collaborations with large software development companies are often focused on the long-term value for both researchers and the companies, e.g., Microsoft Research in Seattle [DASH10] or Software Center in Gothenburg, our home university [SC17], [SPA11]. In this chapter, we focus on the latter—long-term collaborations with the focus on long-term results.

© Springer Nature Switzerland AG 2020
M. Staron, *Action Research in Software Engineering*,
https://doi.org/10.1007/978-3-030-32610-4_9

Action research is one of the collaboration models that can be the fastest and most effective way for companies to keep up with new technological leaps and never-ending introduction of increasingly effective and efficient ways of working.

There has been since long a mistrust between software industry and academia or more formally between practitioners (as academics call all nonacademic) and academics. This is not that strange given that (often) practitioners are seen as "research objects" by academics, and academics are seen as too theoretical, that they lack understanding of the "real" world. Practitioners are not always able to specify exactly what they need is, and academics have been "afraid" to be seen and used as consultants.

Significant improvements have happened the last years to close the gap between practitioners and academics, with good results we may add. As this book makes evident, there are a lot of things that need to be in place for a successful cooperation between the two parties. There are mainly two types of action research projects, those that are initiated by software industry and those initiated by academia. The focus of this chapter is on the first one. The checklists have thus this focus and put heavier emphasis on the stakeholder of the research project at the software company, though some tips are given also for the researcher.

In order to get the right perspective for this chapter, it's been written as a collaboration between academia and practice, in the spirit of action research. Together with my coauthor, Wilhelm Meding, we have understood that we need to provide action teams, stakeholders, and the reference team with the support how to structure the action research projects, not only to conduct the projects but mostly in order to ensure that the results of the projects overlive the projects and become used practices.

Action research's benefits and setup are presented extensively in this book, while this chapter focuses on the listing a checklist that can be used when companies and academia run action research projects. Please note that in the checklists the word "company" is used. The correct way is to use "company/organization," but for simplistic reasons, we mention only companies. The checklists presented here follow the structure of the book and refer to Chaps. 3 through 7.

9.2   Researcher's Perspective on the Sustainability of Knowledge

The researchers' perspective on the sustainability of knowledge is about how to assure that our research results are valid for more than one company. It is important for the scientific community and for the researcher's career—being able to work with multiple companies and developing the scientific theory beyond the one action research project.

Developing a Research Program Over Multiple Cycles with Several Companies

The action team set off to investigate how to provide software architects with the support in analyzing the stability of their products over time.

The work has been conducted in a number of cycles where several companies were involved. The goal has evolved over time, and the involved companies have also changed. However, both the action team and the reference team were the same.

The action team consisted of one researcher and three practitioners, and the reference team consisted of seven company representatives from different companies. The results from this project evolved in the following way:

1. heatmaps for monitoring code stability [SHF+13],
2. code change waves to predict the changes in code and improve testing [SMH+13], and
3. portfolio of architecture measures to support architecture evolution [SM17], [SM18],

The knowledge generated in each of these research cycles was packaged in instructions and research papers. The packages contained scripts and theory and therefore were easily applicable to other contexts. They became practices in several of the collaborating companies.

As researchers, we also need to make sure that our work is protected from two events:

1. premature termination of the project and
2. prohibited publication of the results.

The first event can occur when the collaborating company changes the direction and terminates the collaboration. Although this happens quite seldom, it can happen. Companies restructure, reorganize, and change their focus. Some companies do not understand the nature of research and require results too quickly, neglecting the research protocols. Sometimes, the so-called chemistry between the company and the researchers does not work, and therefore, the company terminates the contract.

In these cases, it is important that we keep the action research cycles short, to ensure that we both deliver results quickly and limit the risk that a lot of results is lost because of the lost collaboration.

We also need to be proactive and regulate what happens when the collaboration contract is terminated. For example, we can ensure that we can finalize the collaboration with results packaged for further reuse.

Packaging Intermediate Results for Further Work in Another Context

The research project was terminated in the middle, and the researchers, together with the company, agreed to finalize it with a survey. There were no plans for publication.

A few years later, the researcher could replicate the same survey at another company and therefore could provide a great complement to the results from the first company.

The knowledge generated by the study provided very useful contribution to the community, even though one of the companies did not adopt the results from the project.

This example illustrates a mature termination of the project without the loss of valuable knowledge.

It is important for the researchers and for the practitioners to have a good dialogue in a research project and align their goals. Otherwise, we risk the premature termination or that we produce research results that are not adopted by companies.

9.3   Practitioner's Perspective on the Sustainability of Knowledge

Practitioners have a different view on the sustainability of knowledge. On the contrary to the common stereotypes, most of my collaborators were not interested in short-term results. They wanted to observe the project progress, but they wanted to see results that could make improvements in the long run.

In our research projects, we learned that the most important factor that determines the success of the collaboration is mutual understanding. The researchers need to understand that the results from the project need to be applied in industry. The practitioners need to understand that high-quality research takes time.

To ensure that the research projects are approved in industry, the action team needs to ensure that the goals of the research projects are aligned with the company's goals and that these goals provide value to the organization.

The goals also need to provide value to the researchers as, otherwise, the research will not be sustainable and short-lived.

9.4   Diagnosing

The diagnosing phase of each action research cycle is needed to understand the nature of the problem to be solved. It helps us to plan which problem needs to be addressed without going into the detail how.

Table 9.1 Checklist for the diagnosing phase

Question	Comment for stakeholder	Comment for researcher
Research projects cost time and claim resources. So, the very first question to ask is: Why do we need to have this research project?	• What motivates a research project? • Have alternative approaches been evaluated? • Have there been previous attempts to address this research question? • If yes, what was the outcome?	Is it motivated to have a research project? The researcher need to be cautious not to be used as a resource/consultant!
Since research projects usually require the active participation of members of the company, it is important to get their support. So, what is the perception of the company about the research project?	Which activities do you plan to execute to get the understanding and support of your company?	• What is the perception of the company about research in general? • Will you get support from the company during the research project?
In general terms, what need is the research project addressing?	What is the overall question to be answered by the research project? Which organizational need is addressed?	What is your competence and experience in the area that the research project will address?

As the researcher, in the beginning of the project, you can establish if you are suitable to conduct the research project given the needs of the company. It is important to understand the needs and value for the community, see the checklist in Table 9.1. If we find that one of our colleagues is more suitable for the project at hand, we should be able to involve them rather than trying to, quickly, get the expertise on our own.

In addition to the understanding of the problem, we need to examine our possibilities at the host company. We need to make sure that we have the right prerequisites for the project, the right support, and the right resources.

9.5 Action Planning

Our experience shows that research projects fail because they were ill-defined, the scope was too big, and/or the time planning was poor. These three "areas" need to be addressed extensively and thoroughly. Table 9.2 presents a number of checks that help to assure that these are addressed.

Table 9.2 Checklist for action planning—part I

Question	Comment for stakeholder	Comment for researcher
Is the scope of the project's cycle well defined?	A well-defined cycle requires a project specification, including (but not limited to) what we wrote in Chaps. 3–6. Start by addressing the research question and the outcome of the project and then identify actions needed and plan them over time	Put extra effort into specifying the objective of the cycle, which actions need to be taken, and start defining the measurement framework to assess the effects of the actions
Is the scope of the research project well delimited?	Define intermediate and final deliveries. At each such delivery, plan how to evaluate their outcome. If there are (even small) signs of problems, stop and reevaluate the scope and time plan of the project	The scope of the research project (regardless of size) must address the research question. You must thus verify that by the end of the research project you have enough material to, e.g., write and submit a paper. Also, it is in this phase that you must decide where you will submit your paper(s): journal, conference, workshop, or others. The reason being that this will decide that structure, shape, and size of the paper
Is the cycle well delimited in time?	We recommend that research projects should run for a maximum of 4–5 months. For a 4–5 months cycle, there should be at least two intermediate deliveries	You need to balance solving the entire research problem and provide intermediate deliveries. You may need to plan for more than one cycle to prepare the full publication of high quality. For intermediate results, consider presentations at workshops to get feedback from the research community
What is/are the deliverable(s) of the research project?	The more focus you put on this question, the easier it will be to get relevance from the deliverables in this cycle!	Consider preparing publications in progression. Start with workshop papers and build the material to gradually develop the publication for high-quality venues

Our experience has taught us that on several occasions, the absence of a stakeholder leads to defective evaluation of the results which in turn leads to unsuccessful implementation in the company.

Another problem we have seen also is that many times persons perceive themselves to be stakeholders, without being that. One typical outcome that we have observed is that there will be disagreements/conflicts when the results from the research project are to be evaluated and/or implemented in the company. Therefore, the checklist in Table 9.3 groups the checks that help to secure the presence of the stakeholders. They also help to secure that there are no surprises in terms of access to infrastructure or people.

Table 9.3 Checklist for action planning—part II

Question	Comment for stakeholder	Comment for researcher
Is there a stakeholder appointed? Does the stakeholder have the mandate to drive and implement the results of the research project?	Make sure that (a) you are indeed the stakeholder of the research project and that (b) you have the mandate to implement the results of the research project in the company	As a researcher, you must a have a counterpart in industry—a stakeholder. You may be able to write and submit a paper, but if the company does not have a "recipient" and/or does not gain anything from your research results, there will be able to perform more research projects again
	You must anchor these two questions with your company	Verify that the person you are working with has the mandate to drive and implement the results in the research project. Verify also that this is how the company understands it to be the case
Have security issues been addressed prior to the start of the research project?	You have the responsibility to go through security issues prior to the start of the research project. For example, • Has the researcher signed the NDA (nondisclosure agreement)? • What is the security access of the researcher? • Is the researcher allowed to take material outside the company? • What can and cannot be written in the academic report?	Examples of security-related questions: • Have you signed the company's NDA? • Can you take research-related material outside the company? • Can you access the intranet of the company from the outside? • What can be and not be part of your publication?
Are employees identified that are going to support the research project?	Many times, research projects require the involvement of your colleagues. For instance, they need to act as the reference team during the research project and/or when evaluating the results of it. Another example can be that they need to take active part in the research project since the subject of the research project is their ways of working	If other employees, except of the stakeholder, are going to be part of the research project, take contact with them from the very beginning of the project. It is important that they feel "being seen and heard" and not be treated as research "objects." Minor as some researchers find this, good social relationship with the employees of the company is of utmost importance for the success of the research project

(continued)

Table 9.3 (continued)

Question	Comment for stakeholder	Comment for researcher
If additional colleagues are participating, how are they going to be kept informed of the progress and results of the research project?	Plan from the very beginning how your colleagues are going to be kept informed during the execution of the research project, as well as when the project is done and concluded	Remember to include the information activities in the action planning

For the researchers, it is important that special attention must be paid on respecting and complying to the security rules of the company. Failure (for whatever reason) to follow security rules can lead to that you are banned from the company or worse.

The checks in these checklists provide both the stakeholders and the action team with help to ensure that the planning is done in a good way.

9.6   Action Taking

When taking the action, the most important part is the ability to measure the effects of the action and to work closely together. A collaboration where the researchers leave the premises and use the practitioners as a sounding board should change into a collaboration where both researchers and practitioners are involved.

The stakeholder and the researcher must keep close cooperation during the research project. They need to meet regularly; the frequency of these meetings depends on different things, e.g., the size of the project and how often the researcher is on site. The checklist in Table 9.4 helps to ensure that the collaboration is well aligned with both practitioners and researchers.

The checklist contains elements that are important for the setup of the action taking. They help to establish trust and set a collaboration that is effective. For example, the access to resources is crucial but always comes with certain security constraints. The action team needs to respect these.

Although we recommend that the researchers from the action team have the same access as the employees, it is sometimes not profitable to make it this way. If one of the team members has the access to the right data and the data can be exported for the purpose of the research project, not all members of the action team need to have the access. The action team will know what is best in which situation.

Table 9.4 Checklist for action taking

Question	Comment for stakeholder	Comment for researcher
Are there regular meetings taking place between the stakeholder and the researcher?	As a stakeholder, you must keep frequent meetings with the action team, to ensure that you are informed about the progress and/or challenges encountered. Failure to do so will result in non-applicable/non-useful results	Keep frequent contact with the stakeholder. This is the most important activity that will guarantee the success of the research project! Bear in mind that many times, such meetings do not have to be formal and (administrative) heavy but may as well take place over a cup of coffee
During these regular meetings, is the time plan discussed/followed up on?	Check that the time plan is kept. Small deviations are signs of (potential) problems and should be discussed. Address deviations regardless of how small they may be, immediately and without hesitation. Prompt discussions lead to trust and better collaboration	See the time plan as the "contract" between you and the stakeholder and treat it accordingly. At the earliest sign of deviations, inform the stakeholder so that the two of you can work them out immediately and take actions needed to either change the plan or get back on track
During these regular meetings, is the scope discussed/followed up on?	Check that the action team keeps his/her activities within the scope of the project. We have seen that, sometimes, action teams expand or limit the scope of the project. A reason for this can be that they may stumble across something that they perceive to be (more) interesting. Or that the action team perceives the research project to be too big, or too complicated, thus limiting the scope of it. And again, address deviations regardless of how small they are immediately and decisively	Avoid changing the scope of the research project mid-cycle. If this is needed, terminate the cycle, evaluate the action, and specify learning and then use the learning as input to diagnosing. As action research projects are collaborative, do not be afraid to ask for help. Companies value honesty and will help you!
During these regular meetings, are the deliveries discussed/followed up on?	Check that the planned deliveries have the expected quality. For example, check that preliminary results are thoroughly documented, that planned milestones have been reached and action taken, and that underlying material is sufficient to motivate the written conclusions	Make sure that your deliveries keep high quality—it is these that will judge how you are perceived as a research team! Ascertain that your chain of reasoning has the appropriate quality and quantity to support your findings/conclusions

(continued)

Table 9.4 (continued)

Question	Comment for stakeholder	Comment for researcher
During these regular meetings, are the work-related issues discussed/followed up on?	During the stay of the researchers from the action team, you have the responsibility for him/her, including his/her working environment. For example, that the researcher has a good working place (desk and computer access), access to related data, and sitting close to you and/or by the employees he/she will work with	Though you are guest at the company, you should have the same working environment standard as its employees. Do not accept anything less! When it comes to working in the company, respect that the employees (most often) have much to do and may not always be available for you. It is better to have more shortly meetings that a few lengthy ones. A tip is to sit close to those you are working with!
During these regular meetings, is the security discussed/followed up on?	Security is and should be priority number one! You must verify and follow up that • The researchers from the action team has signed the NDA • The researcher knows and understands the security rules of the company • The researcher complies to all security regulations • The data cannot be taken outside the company, unless this is explicitly written and approved by your manager Any action of the researcher that is not in line with the above can result in the revoking of his/her access to the company, including legal consequences	Since you are a guest, it is of the highest importance that you respect and fully comply to the security rules of the company. Failure to do so may have severe consequences, e.g., termination of the research project and legal actions if the violations lead to loss of business. Be aware that it may also have strong negative impact for the company, e.g., loss of technological advantages to competitors. For your university, it may give bad will/reputation and revoke of collaboration with the company

9.7 Evaluating

The evaluation phase is about understanding the effects of the taken action, interpreting the collected data, and drawing the conclusions. The action team should focus on storing the data properly and assuring that the analysis procedures are conducted correctly. They also need to ensure that the conclusions are relevant for both the practitioners and researchers.

During the action taking phase, data is collected and stored. The action team must emphasize frequent collection and storage of the data, which needs to be done systematically and orderly. Failure to do so will result in having to redo the whole action taking phase. Therefore, we need to carefully consider the checks from Table 9.5.

Table 9.5 Checklist for the evaluation phase

Question	Comment for stakeholder	Comment for researcher
Is data collected and stored orderly?	During the action taking phase, data needs to be collected and stored in dedicated areas at the company's site. It can be in folders or data tables in databases. Whatever means used, define this before the action taking phase and follow until the evaluation of the data	It is your responsibility as a researcher to see to it that data is collected and stored orderly. See to it that the structure is detailed, including dates, sources, purpose, action taking iteration, and others. The more metadata you have, the easier it will be when you start evaluating the data and writing on your academic report. Experience shows that you will come back to the data stored more than once, to cross-reference results, e.g., between different iterations and/or with other studies, or to redo the evaluation to be certain about the results
Having the mechanisms for data storage defined and in place is only the first step. Other aspects that must be fulfilled are access of data and security handling. So, does the storage of the data guarantee easy access and, at the same time, fulfillment of security rules?	Stored data should be easy to access, both for you and the action team. Also, it should be easy for the action team to create substructures, if needed. That said, it is imperative that all security regulations of your company are met when it comes to the handling of collected and stored data. This is your responsibility! If you are uncertain, contact your security function in your company. Remember, failure to address this can have severe impact on your company and may result in you losing your job	Once data is stored, it is important that access to it is easy, both manually and by automated means. Do not forget to understand and comply to the security rules that refer to handling of data. Failure to do so may result in negative impact for the company, and you may face legal consequences

Evaluation of data can be split into two phases: intermediate and final. Intermediate analyses and evaluations take place during the execution of the research project, whereas final evaluation is done at the very end of the project, when the action taking phase has been concluded. Therefore, checklist from Table 9.6 helps us to assure that we evaluation is done properly.

In order to make the outcome of the evaluation phase more long-term, we need to make sure that we prepare replication packages for other scientists and for practitioners. We need to make sure that we guide the organization in interpreting our results, both as diagrams and as statistical analyses.

Table 9.6 Checklist for the evaluating phase—part II

Question	Comment for stakeholder	Comment for researcher
First, the data is refined, analyses are performed, results are presented, and preliminary conclusions are drawn. So, how are the preliminary analyses and results handled?	This phase is usually most intense for the action team than you. The reason for this is, e.g., that the use of advance tools, mathematics, and algorithms may occur. If that is the case, then you must see to it that the preliminary results (e.g., tables and diagrams) are presented in such a way that you can understand them. The action team may (mostly unintentionally) present results that are difficult for practitioners to grasp. It is your responsibility that the results that are used to draw conclusions can be understood by you (and related colleagues). Never accept an "it is not possible" answer from the action team. It is his/her responsibility to break down the results in such a way that they can be understood by you and your colleagues	This is usually the most intensive phase of the research project. Structured and systematic approach data analyses are the very key for success. Results and conclusions must be supported by rigorous analyses. You must always be ready to back trace your findings, from the table/diagram to the data source. When you present the results to the stakeholder, the action team, and the reference team, put extra effort to use (as far as possible) their "language." If they do not understand (whole or parts of what you present and say), the outcome of the research project will not be used. During those presentations, pay attention on the comments and reactions of the practitioners. They may not always express their thoughts or concerns. A common reason for this is that they either see you as an expert and are "afraid" to argue with you or they may not understand what you say. Remember, it is the feedback you get from these meetings that will strengthen your research results and your academic report!
During the second phase, results are put together to support findings and conclusions. So, are results from the evaluation rigorous enough to support the outcome of the research project?	The final evaluation sums up the results of the research project and reasons about the conclusions. It presents evidence to support the success or failure of the research project. It is important that you inform your company about the final results. It is also important that you store the results in an orderly fashion and that they are made easily accessible	For the action team, the outcome of a research project is always positive. This is because even if the outcome of the research project did not give the expected results, you still generated new knowledge. You need to keep in mind that for a practitioner this is not always the case. An unsuccessful research project may result in monetary loses and may hinder further research activities in the company. This is one of the reasons why it is so important to verify that intermediate results (will) lead to the successful conclusion of the project. If this is not the case, the research project should be terminated as soon as possible

9.8 Specifying Learning

A common misunderstanding is that when a research project is concluded, nothing else needs to be done. However, a lot of work remains. The purpose of running research projects at companies is:

- to solve the problem at hand
- that they are informed about the outcome and findings of the current research project, and
- that they learn, implement, and utilize the knowledge from research projects.

The checklist presented in Table 9.7 helps to understand how to ensure that the learnings from the project are documented in the way which is relevant for both practitioners and researchers.

In this checklist, we also added additional actors—the company. From our experience, it is important that the company is involved in the research and that there are people willing to adopt the results afterward. It is the responsibility of the stakeholders to involve the relevant persons in the organization, both in the research project and in the handover of the research results.

It is often the case that the results from one cycle are used both in the diagnosing phase and as part of practices at the company.

Lack of Involvement of the Organization Leads to Lack of Adoption

The action team set off to design new methods for assessing quality of test cases. They have worked with testers and developed a new method, which required changes in requirement specifications.

The stakeholders and the action team did not involve the requirement management team in their work.

The results were that the action team was not able to hand over the results to the company. When the action research project was close to conclusion, the stakeholders were not able to show the results to the requirements team. There was a threat that the requirements team would see these results as a threat to their work.

This example illustrates that it is important to involve all kinds of stakeholders to ensure that no one in the organization is "offended" by the research project.

9.9 Summary

Companies and researchers can collaborate in different ways and with different goals. Depending on the goal, the collaboration stresses different aspects. In action research projects, the focus is on working together, on-site, using the company's

Table 9.7 Checklist for specifying learning

Question	Comment for stakeholder	Comment for the company	Comment for researcher
How do you specify the results and knowledge to maximize the impact?	It is your responsibility that the results of the research are spread in the company. The action team can present their results, but you need to make sure that the results are presented to others	Companies must have mechanisms in place that ensure that they learn and implement (whenever applicable) findings from them. Those mechanisms (ways of working) guarantee that results from research projects become common knowledge and that they benefit the whole company!	In order to assure continuity of the project, you need to make sure that you take the learnings from one phase to the diagnosing in another phase
How should the company be informed about the outcome and findings of research project?	After the conclusion of the research project, you should inform the company about the results and findings of the research project. Since the understanding of the research topic varies among your colleagues, emphasis must be put on giving two different types of presentations: one on a high level to increase awareness and one on a detailed level to teach others how your results "work." The first type of presentation should be on such a level that (almost) everyone understands. See also next table cell	Companies must have established and well-known routines that guarantee that results and findings from research projects are always presented to the company. The purpose of "high level" presentations is to make the results of research projects known and available to the whole company. Companies appreciate these types of presentations as they allow their employees to keep up both with the latest research results and findings and also with the direction/focus of their company about research in general. In addition, we have seen that such presentations inspire the start-up of new research projects. The detailed level presentations aim at the stakeholders and the involved parties to spread the details, teach others, and to reason about the next steps. They can, e.g., draw conclusions about continuing/discontinuing with research projects within the same topic	Participating is in this phase is optional (unless stated otherwise in the formal agreement). We strongly recommend that the researchers participate since it provides so many benefits for all parties involved. For example, it is not certain that the stakeholder can answer all questions he/she receives during the presentations. You can make in-depth analyses and explanations, related to theory, and draw parallels from research project at other companies. Participation in these meetings expands your network and (not seldom) results in the start-up of new research projects

(continued)

Table 9.7 (continued)

Question	Comment for stakeholder	Comment for the company	Comment for researcher
How can the company learn, implement, and utilize the knowledge gained from research projects performed?	Your responsibility is to summarize the results and findings to the research-responsible parties of the company, in such a format that it can be stored by them	There must be a team that is responsible for collecting and storing data from research projects and making it available to the company. The team should also be the driver in informing and seeing to it that new methods and tools are understood, implemented, and used by the company. We have seen, unfortunately, many times how good/useful research results were lost/forgotten, because no one took care of them. This is not the task of stakeholders of research projects; it is the responsibility of the companies	N/A

premises, and taking actions that make direct changes in the company's ways of working.

In this chapter, we worked together to identify what makes an action research project leave long-lasting positive impact on the company. We prepared our finding in form of checklists that different roles can use in different phases.

The next chapter is about identifying threats to validity of our results, which is important in understanding the scope and limitations of the impact of our project.

References

[DASH10] Prasun Dewan, Puneet Agarwal, Gautam Shroff, and Rajesh Hegde. Mixed-focus collaboration without compromising individual or group work. In *Proceedings of the 2nd ACM SIGCHI symposium on Engineering interactive computing systems*, pages 225–234. ACM, 2010.

[Par98] David Lorge Parnas. Successful software engineering research. *ACM SIGSOFT Software Engineering Notes*, 23(3):64–68, 1998.

[SC17] Anna Börjesson Sandberg and Ivica Crnkovic. Meeting industry: academia research collaboration challenges with agile methodologies. In *Proceedings of the 39th International Conference on Software Engineering: Software Engineering in Practice Track*, pages 73–82. IEEE Press, 2017.

[SHF⁺13] Miroslaw Staron, Jörgen Hansson, Robert Feldt, Anders Henriksson, Wilhelm Meding, Sven Nilsson, and Christoffer Höglund. Measuring and visualizing code stability–a case study at three companies. In *2013 Joint Conference of the 23rd International Workshop on Software Measurement and the 8th International Conference on Software Process and Product Measurement*, pages 191–200. IEEE, 2013.

[SM17] Miroslaw Staron and Wilhelm Meding. A portfolio of internal quality metrics for software architects. In *International Conference on Software Quality*, pages 57–69. Springer, 2017.

[SM18] Miroslaw Staron and Wilhelm Meding. *Software Development Measurement Programs: Development, Management and Evolution*. Springer, 2018.

[SMH⁺13] Miroslaw Staron, Wilhelm Meding, Christoffer Höglund, Peter Eriksson, Jimmy Nilsson, and Jörgen Hansson. Identifying implicit architectural dependencies using measures of source code change waves. In *2013 39th Euromicro Conference on Software Engineering and Advanced Applications*, pages 325–332. IEEE, 2013.

[SPA11] Anna Sandberg, Lars Pareto, and Thomas Arts. Agile collaborative research: Action principles for industry-academia collaboration. *IEEE software*, 28(4):74–83, 2011.

Chapter 10
Validity Evaluation

> Science is a way of thinking much more than it is a body of
> knowledge.
>
> —Carl Sagan

Abstract Conducting a research study is always linked to questions about whether
we can trust the results or not. Since the goal of each action research project is to
make software engineering practices and tools better, we need to be able to assess
the validity of our research finding very critically. Therefore, we need to be able
to combine the impact of the research results with the limitations of it. We need to
be able to provide the stakeholders of the action research projects with a solid and
as-objective-as-possible account of the research validity.

10.1 Introduction

When planning and conducting research, as well as when analyzing it and drawing
conclusions, there is a lot to think about, and a lot can go wrong. We can plan for
the perfect study, but then the reality can turn out to be quite different. For example,
we can have a perfect design of our intervention, and then a reorganization at a
company side can confound our measurements, and thus we cannot say whether the
improvement is caused by our intervention or by the reorganization. Therefore, we
often talk about the validity of our research.

As researchers, we need to be critical to the effects which we observe and whether
these effects can be traced back to the interventions we made in our research.

We also discuss the potential problems that can render our research invalid;
we call them *threats to validity*. The concept of research validity, in particular, in
the empirical research, has been discussed widely since the work of Campbell and
Stanley [CS63] and Cook and Campbell [CC79]. In software engineering, probably
the most commonly used reference is the book about experimentation by Wohlin et
al. [WRH+12], which provides an interpretation of the common validity threats in
the context of experimentation in software engineering.

© Springer Nature Switzerland AG 2020   169
M. Staron, *Action Research in Software Engineering*,
https://doi.org/10.1007/978-3-030-32610-4_10

Action research is prone to problems with validity as any other research. Since action research often combine both potential threats to validity from social research and constructive research, we need to evaluate the validity from both perspectives.

When we design the study, we need to list which potential problems of the design of our study we need to avoid. In other words, we need to decide which threats to construct validity we have and how to minimize them.

Once we design the study and are in the process of its execution, we need to discuss which threats to internal validity we have and how to address them.

Finally, after we have executed the study, we need to understand the limitations of our data analysis by listing out which conclusion validity threats are relevant and how we can minimize them. Thus, we need to understand how generalizable our findings are, by understanding the external validity threats.

10.2   Construct Validity

The first category of research validity is the construct validity. It is related to our research design and how we create the measurement instruments that measure the effects in our study.

Action research requires the research team to be embedded in the research context, and therefore, the validity of the constructs in the study is extremely sensitive to bias. For example, we may seem to know the organization well enough to skip initial interviews about the context of the study. In this way, we reduce our ability to find all confounding factors in the design of the study.

In the first place, we need to consider the following categories of threats to the validity of our research design, from https://socialresearchmethods.net/kb/consthre. php. These are presented in Tables 10.1 and 10.2 with examples of threats from action research projects.

The set of construct validity threats in Tables 10.1 and 10.2 provides a few examples of which threats of validity we can have in each category. However, there are many more instances.

As the construct validity threats are related to the design of the study, they relate mostly to a subset of the elements of an action research, as shown in Fig. 10.1.

Therefore, in order to understand which threats we have in an action research study, we need to analyze our design from the following perspectives:

- the research problem diagnosed in the diagnosing phase,
- formulation of the research question,
- planned activities and interventions in the planning phase, and
- designed measurement framework.

Table 10.1 Threats to construct validity, their explanations, and examples

Threat	Explanation	Example
Inadequate preoperational explication of constructs	This means that our constructs and measures are not related to the concepts which we want to evaluate. We plan to study one thing, but we measure something else	We plan to study development's quality, but we measure size of the software
Mono-operation bias	This means that we study only one specific instance of the setting. This is quite common for action research projects as we often are embedded in the context	We study only one software development team in a short period of time; instead we should study more teams and thus validate out finding there
Mono-method bias	This means that we measure the effect with only one variable, thus do not capture the breadth of the entire effects	We measure the impact of our actions only on the productivity of the team, forgetting to observe the effects of the action on the quality of the product
Interaction of different treatments	This means that the observed results of the study can be caused by other treatments, not the one intended. In action research, this happens if our actions are taken in parallel with other improvement activities, which we do not control	We introduced a new complexity measure and observed lower number of defects; at the same time, the organization adopted a different testing method, which could influence the number of defects discovered
Interaction of testing and treatment	This means that just taking the action in the context makes the change; our preparations and diagnosing of the action may change the context of bias the subjects	We ask about the perception of *low* quality, and therefore we indicate that the quality needs to be improved
Restricted generalizability across constructs	This means that our action caused unintended consequences that we did not observe	Our intervention of introducing a prediction model changed the test organization but also caused increased effort and extra resources. In consequence, we cannot distinguish whether the improvement was caused by the predictions or the allocation of extra resources
Confounding constructs and levels of constructs	This threat occurs when we can parameterize our actions and interventions and we select too few parameters to generalize	We use a threshold of 50% when categorizing defects as severe vs. non-severe and found too many false-positives (i.e., non-severe defects which were classified as severe). We concluded that the method is not accurate enough. If we used a level of 90%, then the number of false-positives would be lower, and we would accept the method

Table 10.2 Threats to construct validity, their explanations, and examples (continued)

Threat	Explanation	Example
Hypothesis guessing	This means that our collaborating practitioners and their organization can anticipate the goal of the study and adjust their behavior accordingly. This biases the observed results	We describe that we expect the new software development method to be "faster" than the previous one, instead of describing the study of the impact of a new development method on the company's performance
Evaluation apprehension	This threat is about the subjects behaving differently when observed; they can get stressed during an interview, or they want to "look good" when being observed	When we analyze the code of a designer, he/she may write the code differently because of being observed; for example, the designer adds more comments than usual. This leads to bias in the observations about internal quality of the code
Experimenter expectancies	This threat comes when the researcher designs the study where he/she knows what to expect and biases the design so that the results can be expected	We know that increased number of tests executed will increase quality but slow down the development. Therefore, we design the study so that we focus only on the speed disregarding other factors

Once we diagnosed the problem, we need to evaluate whether we have understood the problem correctly and whether we can develop an intervention to actually address it. If we have doubts, then we need to list them as threats in the category of *inadequate preoperational explication of constructs*. Examples of such threats can be:

- we want to check if we observe "an improvement" without actually defining what we mean by that; since the concept of improvement is broad, we risk that we do not measure the right aspect of the improvement
- we intervene in one area, but we measure another area like we make a change in defect reporting and observe speed of software integration; we do not establish the correct links between the intervention and the measurement of the effect.

When we formulate the research question, we can also be "vague" and therefore cannot design the study that addresses this question. We can also end up in designing

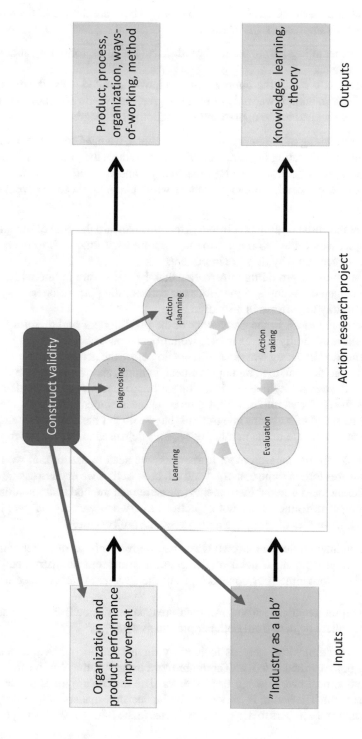

Fig. 10.1 Phases relevant for scrutiny when finding threats to construct validity

the study that addresses the question only partially. These are threats to the *mono-operation bias*. Examples of such threats are:

- we study the team just before the intervention and just after, forgetting about the long-term impact.
- we define a study where the intervention can have multiple levels like different degrees of automation; if we study only one degree, then we do not know whether the results are related to the operation (automation) or its degree.

During the planning of the interventions and actions, we need to remember how we prepare the collaborating organization in order to reduce the potential problems with *hypothesis guessing*, *experimenter expectancies*, and *evaluation apprehension*. Examples of threats, which we can encounter while planning these interventions, are:

- we prepare the collaborating practitioners too much toward the goal of our study; for example, we devote too much time to describe what kind of improvements we expect to see and why they are important,
- we bias the study by providing information that the actions are in line with some sort of management order, and therefore our collaborating practitioners may see this as their duty to perform in a specific way,
- we intervene too much in the daily work of the practitioners, and therefore they do not behave naturally; for example, we introduce observations of their daily work during action taking which we did not do before the action taking, or
- we have a specific goal, e.g., an improvement, in mind, and we design the action evaluation in such a way that we look for the improvement, but we neglect the negative effects; for example, we introduce the measurement of speed, and we measure the speed of software integrations, but we do not measure the quality of the integrated software or the number of features delivered to the customer.

When we design the measurement framework, we need to assure that we have multiple measures for the same construct and effect as well as we need to assure that we have different measurement instruments (measurement method triangulation), if our measurement instruments are not objective (e.g., when we rely on people to report things). Examples of threats in action research projects are:

- we make an intervention in our own work, and we rely only on our own opinion about the improvement, instead of designing a measurement instrument that collects data from either our context or from the systems which we use in our work,
- we make an intervention, and we ask measure data only once from one system, instead of collecting data from both people and systems

The above examples can help us to identify threats for our particular design, but they are not an exhaustive list. There are more examples that can be found in literature, and almost every design has its flaws. The important part is to identify them and list them. The listing is important for the decision-makers in industry and for our colleague researchers to design more studies in the future. It is also important for us as input to new action research cycles when diagnosing the problems; sometimes we need to replicate a cycle with some modifications to avoid biases (e.g., the mono-method bias).

10.3   Internal Validity

Once the design of the study is done, we need to explore the potential threats to the validity of the operation of the study. In action research projects, this means that we need to make an in-depth analysis of our action taking.

The internal validity evaluation of the action research study means that we scrutinize the operation of the action taking. We also need to evaluate whether there are any threats that relate to the evaluation (data collection) and planning (measurement framework). Once again, there are a number of characteristics of action research projects that make it more prone to certain threats than to others. For example, since in action research projects we advocate long-term relations to build trust, we need to be more aware about the history effects, i.e., changes in the environment that are related to time rather than to actions and interventions that we do in the action research project.

There are a number of categories of threats to internal validity of the studies. In the first place, we review the ones presented by Yu [YO10], which we list in Table 10.3.

The examples provided in Table 10.3 provide a number of examples, but the list is not exhaustive. Figure 10.2 shows that the threats to internal validity apply mostly to the action taking phase but also are relevant for action planning (e.g., subject selection) and evaluation (e.g., regression to mean).

Action research projects are more prone to the effects of the long-term collaboration, and therefore we need to be more cautious about the following threat categories:

- History effects—as we conduct cycle after cycle, the organization learns, and we, as researchers, learn, which means that the history affects us a lot. When we work with a single company, we may forget that this is a specific case, not representative for the entire software industry.
- Maturity—across the cycles, the company learns and matures, not because of our actions but because of the continuous competence development in general. The longer our study, the higher potential of the maturity threats.
- Biased selection of subjects—since we work with practitioners in the action team, we may be tempted to work with them as subjects, and we also may be tempted to work with the same people in the company because we have good collaboration experiences. However, this may introduce biases in subject selection.

Table 10.3 Threats to internal validity, their explanations, and examples

Threat	Explanation	Example
History	Some specific events occur between the first and second measurement, and these events can influence the outcome of the second measurement	We evaluate the code quality before and after our action of changing a test strategy, yet at the same time, the software has matured by itself (defects were fixed)
Maturation	The passage of time makes things better or worse and not our intervention. This is very important for long-term action research projects and longitudinal studies	We ask the same questions about code quality about the same code fragment. The respondent learns more about the code every time he/she reads it, and therefore the last response is more informed than the first one. Hence, the response is affected by the learning effect equally as the actual quality improvement
Testing	The measurement of the performance before the action taking can influence the results of the action taking	When we ask a software development team before the study about their perception of the quality of the tests, and the questions are about the problems with testing. This can affect their perception that there is a problem with their testing strategy
Instrumentation	The instruments can change over time, and thus the measurement results can change and affect the results	When we change from ClearCase to Git source code management, we need to use a different measurement instruments that counts the number of changes; there can be a difference in how the tools count the change. The observed difference, therefore, can be caused by either the new tool or the new measurement instrument
Statistical regression (regression to mean)	When we remove subjects based on their extreme statistical properties (so-called statistical outliers), instead at examining their empirical properties	We observed one designer to cause twice as many errors in continuous integration; without examining the causes of that, we removed the designer's data as outlier
Biased selection of subjects	We can select subjects of different characteristics for our measurement before and after the action taking	We chose to interview junior designers when diagnosing the problem, but we interviewed the senior designers after the action taking to assess the effect
Experiment/study mortality	We lose the subjects during the study, which biases the comparison before and after the action taking	The company decides to move the development of the most important features off-shore, and we can only study the features which are not off-shored

(continued)

Table 10.3 (continued)

Threat	Explanation	Example
Selection-maturation interaction	When we select the comparison groups, we do not take into consideration the maturation effect	For the diagnosing problem we chose one team that consists of mostly junior designers; for the post-action taking assessment, we chose a group that was with the company at least 4 years
John Henry effect	John Henry was a worker who outperformed a machine under an experimental setting because he was aware that his performance was compared with that of a machine	We provide an explicit comparison baseline, and our subjects know about this and "compete" with the baseline. We do not know if the results are better because of the intervention or just because of the "competition" with the baseline

- John Henry effect—similar to the point above, we may tend to work with individuals who are generally interested in improvements and competition. So the actions taken do not necessarily cause the effect but merely contributed to the effect that would happen anyway.
- Experiment/study subject mortality—since action research projects take a longer period of time, we observe changes in the subject which we work with. Participants change roles in the company, companies reorganize, and people join or quit teams. This means that the set of persons that we start with in action research cycle 1 is not the same as in action research cycle n.

Many of the aforementioned threats to validity can be observed over a number of cycles, not just within one cycle. An example of such threats is the history effect. For a collaboration which takes place over months or over years even, the industrial participants learn about the topics, and therefore their assessments are not as objective as they were in the beginning of the action research project.

Therefore, we need to make sure that we work closely with the reference team and the stakeholder of the project. Since they are not as involved in the study as the action team is, they can provide us with more objective view on the potential biases in our study. We also need to embrace the fact that the history can plan a role in action research and seek to compare the results with other contexts. An example of that kind of remedy is to involve other companies in the evaluation of the research study.

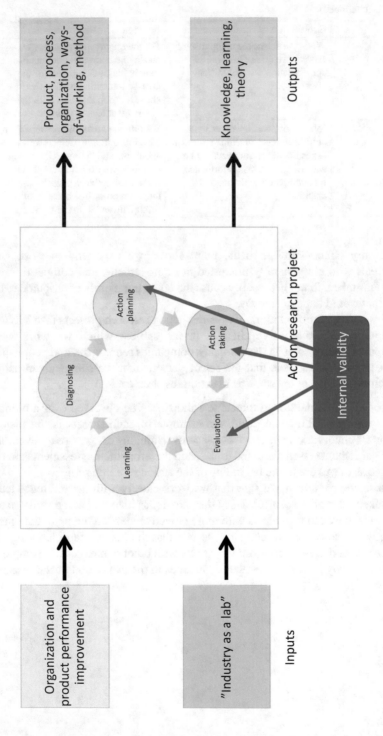

Fig. 10.2 Phases relevant for scrutiny when finding threats to internal validity

Involving Multiple Companies in One Action Research Project
In this project, the action research team set off to investigate the impact of code
changes in large code bases. They studied one company and developed a method
for creating a visualization of changes in their code base. They used the concept
of code churns developed by Microsoft Research [NB05], [NB07]. The team
combined that with the visualization of test case progress [FSHL13].

An example of the visualization of the code churns is presented in Fig. 10.3.

Fig. 10.3 Visualization of the code churns using heatmaps. The figure shows a subset of the
code of open source project Notepad++

In order to validate the results, the action team studied involved more
companies in the study. The involvement of additional companies confirmed the
observations in the original company [SHF+13].

We also need to be careful when we evaluate the results of the action taking. For
example, the John Henry effect can be identified when we evaluate the data. We can
ask the reference team about the potential signs on of this effect and ask them to
independently assess the presence of this effect.

When we plan, conduct, and evaluate the action, we must establish a good
baseline for the measurement instruments. We need to know our measurement
instruments in order to avoid the *instrumentation bias*. In action research, it is quite
common that we change the measurement instruments during the action taking.
Since we want to observe the effects of the action taking, it is often impossible
to keep the same instrument, as we often need to recalibrate the instrument or
change them because it is requires by the action. Imagine a large organization which
changes a process from a V-model to Agile software development and measures the
number of delivered customer features. The measurement instrument needs to be
adjusted as the V-model is plan driven and delivers what is planned in the scope
(so we can just count the number of features in the project scope), whereas Agile
software development advocates ability to adjust to customer needs and delivery of
one feature per sprint (so if we count number of features per project/sprint in this
case, then the numbers cannot be compared). To avoid this kind of "trap," we need

to measure the number of features delivered in the Agile project over the same time as the V-model project; this will allow us to compare the measurements.

Another aspect important in the instrumentation is the measurement error of the instrument, both the random error and the systematic error. If we keep the same measurement instrument, like a script, we have the same systematic error, and it's only the random component that changes. However, if we change the instrument, the systematic error also changes. This fact is important as the systematic error changes the mean value of the distribution of the measurement result, thus potentially biasing the statistical analyses [SDR17].

Long-Term Collaboration and Changing Models

In this project, the team studied the dynamics of defect inflow and constructed defect prediction models.

The models evolved over time:

- The first models worked well for project following a predefined plans, e.g., waterfall development, and used such predictors like test cases and work packages [SM08].
- The second models used moving averages and basic statistics to predict defect backlog (number of open defects) [SMS10].
- The third method used test progress and defect backlog as the predictors or release readiness instead [SMP12].

10.4   Conclusion Validity

After we have diagnosed the problem, planned the action, and taken it, it's time to evaluate the results. This activity is also potentially threatened by a number of factors—*conclusion validity threats*. Even for the studies that are designed flawlessly and executed flawlessly, we can make mistakes when drawing conclusions. We could be so much into the study, and we want to see the effect so much that we see it when it is not there (or vice versa, we are blind for an effect that is there).

Many young researchers mistake the conclusion validity with the statistical validity, as it is often the case in software engineering that we conduct quantitative research. However, conclusion validity is much more than that—it's our ability to draw correct conclusions from our observations. Since action research combines both the quantitative and qualitative research elements, we need to consider both.

Action research projects are prone to such specific biases when drawing conclusions, simply because the action team is involved in taking the action. We are simply less objective when it comes to judging the effects of our own actions than we are when judging the effects of the actions of others. We need to be aware of that, and we need to assure that we both understand the categories of conclusion validity threats and that we take precautions to reduce them.

In Table 10.4, we present the most common conclusion validity threats, adopted from https://socialresearchmethods.net/kb/concthre.php to action research projects.

Conclusion validity relates to the process of analyzing data, finding patterns in it, and drawing conclusions. It relates to the subset of phases in the cycle, as presented in Fig. 10.4.

When we take the action and make the interventions, we can prevent certain threats to validity from occurring. For example, we can maximize the data collection by including as many products, subjects, and organizations as possible in order to minimize the threats related to *low statistical power*. We can also maximize the number of persons who we interview in order to minimize the problems related to *random heterogeneity of subjects*. At the same time, we need to ensure that the data collection in one action research cycle does not last too long. From the experience, the best action research cycles last ca. 1–3 months, and therefore we need to adjust the data collection periods to that. If this is not enough, it's much better to plan the next cycle as more "evaluation heavy" rather than prolong the data collection period.

When we take the action and collect the data, we need to be on the lookout for the effects of *low reliability of measures*. If we observe that our measurements do not show any difference, but we still observe effects of our actions, we need to adjust the measurement framework. The best approach to this is to note the required change and to plan to make this change in the measurement framework for the next cycle.

On the other hand, if we observe that we may have problems with the *low reliability of treatment implementation*, we need to change our activities so that we can increase the reliability. For instance, if we conduct interviews in a group and we realize that one of the group members dominates the discussion, then we should adjust our plan and conduct a series of individual interviews. We need to adapt the data analysis methods accordingly, but it is better to make the change in the course of our action taking rather than waiting for another cycle, mainly because we only have one change to get the initial reactions on the action taking. In the subsequent cycles, we can take other actions and therefore collect data for another setup.

One of the threats, however, is very difficult to predict and to address beforehand. It is the threat of experiencing *random irrelevancies in the setting*. When conducting action research, we are embedded in the organization, and we need to adjust to the environment around us. This means that reorganizations, people changing roles, new managers, or products affect the study. Therefore, the shorter the action research cycle, the lower probability that we will experience this kind of disturbances.

Table 10.4 Threats to conclusion validity, their explanations, and examples

Threat	Explanation	Example
Finding no relationship when there is one (or "missing the needle in the haystack")	This means that our analysis methods can miss an important observation, and thus we can draw conclusions that there is no effect of our actions, when there are	When we analyzed data about reported defects, we missed the defects which were reported by designers in a new system
Finding a relationship when there is not one (or "seeing things that aren't there")	This means that our analysis methods can provide us with observations that are not related to our intervention	When analyzing the defects, we included defects from more than one project, which resulted in additional defects, unrelated to the action taken
Low reliability of measures	Our measurement instruments can be unreliable, or open to interpretation, thus resulting in low quality of collected data	We asked questions that were ambiguous, and therefore we do not know if the subjects interpreted them in a consistent way
Low reliability of treatment implementation	This means that we cannot trust the procedures which we applied during the study. We did not conducted our intervention carefully enough	We collected the data from different defect reporting systems, but we did it during different points of time (one project in the beginning of the week, in another project at the end of the week). The consequence was that we could not compare the number of defects reported per week, because there could be up to 1 week difference between projects
Random irrelevancies in the setting	This means that we were exposed to random events that confounded the study	When taking the action of exporting defects, the database server was crashing frequently, resulting in low quality of the data. The low quality of the data discouraged the stakeholders from using the measures created by the action team. This meant that we do not know whether the failure of the action taking was caused by the database outage or the measure
Random heterogeneity of respondents	Individuals vary in their responses and actions regardless of treatments, and therefore there is always certain degree of randomness in observations	When the action team provided the same measurement system to two different stakeholders, one of them adopted it, and the other one did not. There was no consensus in the action team whether that was because of the measurement system or because of the random variability between these two stakeholders
Low statistical power	When using statistical tests, low number of data points or high variability in data can result in low p-values or low beta-values	When the action team used statistics for ten data points (t-test), the number of data points was too low to use inferential statistics

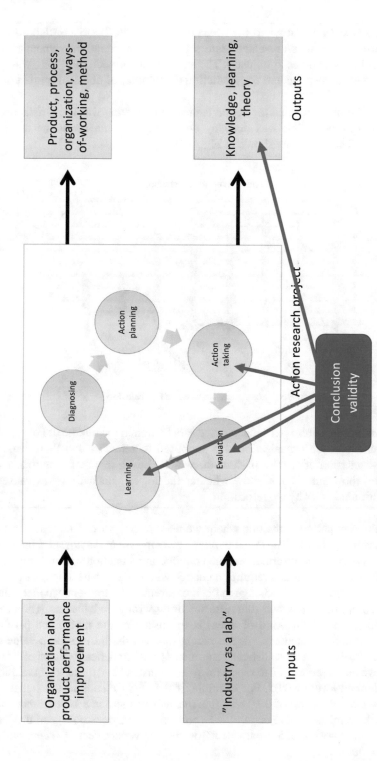

Fig. 10.4 Phases relevant for scrutiny when finding threats to conclusion validity

Changing Location Disturbed the Measurement of the Team's Satisfaction
In this project, the action research team set off to understand the dynamics of the defect inflow profiles in industry. The goal of this project, therefore, was to design and evaluate a method for predicting the number of defects reported per week.

One of the measures that the action team was observing was the satisfaction of the organization. This was done by collecting the data about the team's satisfaction. The results are shown in Fig. 10.5.

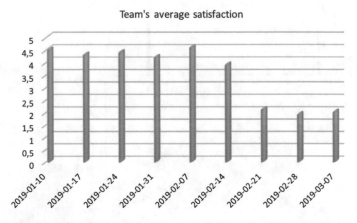

Fig. 10.5 Chart showing team's satisfaction, an average on scale 1–5

The researchers observed the decreased satisfaction in the middle of February. They found that the organization was supposed to relocate, and there was a general discussion about the placement, which caused a lot of disturbances. Therefore, the team did not know whether the lower satisfaction was caused by the action taken or by the relocation.

The evaluation period is the one where we need to pay special attention to the conclusion validity threats. The threat of *missing the needle in the haystack* happens when we miss important information when conducting an action research study. It happens often when our action requires a change where we also need to change the measurement instrument. The change in the measurement instrument can mean that we miss an important fact, and therefore we draw wrong conclusions. The most prominent example of this kind of threat is the usage of the predefined p-value in statistical tests. As scientists, we are taught that we should use the p-value of 0.05 as the cutoff between statistically significant and statistically nonsignificant results. However, I recommend to report the p-value instead and discuss it in relation to the predefined level of 0.05. For example, if the study results in the statistical significance from the t-test of 0.1 level, this means that there is a 10% chance that we may make a mistake of rejecting the hypothesis, but it does not mean that our study is suddenly not valid. Similar is true for the vice versa effect of *seeing things that are not there*.

10.5   External Validity

Once the study has been conducted, data were collected and analyzed, and conclusions were drawn, we need to reflect on the impact of our results. We need to understand whether our conclusions apply only to the action team, their company, or whether they are representative for the entire industry or even universally valid.

Although the goal of all kinds of research projects is to have as large impact as possible, action research is conducted in a specific context and does not control the external environment. This means that we cannot claim the generalizability of our results to all kinds of context and all kind of projects and companies.

However, since action research projects are done outside of the lab and therefore are externally validated, they are definitely applicable to industrial context directly, and, if we make certain preparations, they are even applicable to other companies.

Table 10.5 presents the most common categories of threats to external validity of our results, from [YO10].

Table 10.5 Threats to external validity, their explanations, and examples

Threat	Explanation	Example
Reactive or interaction effect of testing	In the preparation for action taking, we can ask the subjects about pre-action taking preferences, and this may increase or decrease a subject's sensitivity or responsiveness to the experimental variable	In the diagnosing phase, the action team were actively asking for participation of software development teams, asking for teams experiencing problems with continuous integration. This biased the results as the teams themselves thought that they "could" have problems there
Interaction effects of selection biases and the experimental variable	We can choose a context which is particularly suited for the action taking, and therefore the results are not representative for any other context	
Reactive effects of experimental arrangements	If we control the context too much, it gets difficult to generalize to nonexperimental settings if the effect was attributable to the experimental arrangement of the research	To study the effects of introducing continuous integration on speed, the team prepared a dedicated server where the continuous integration was the only task This was not a typical setup and biased the results as the arrangement (setup of the server) speeded up the integration by itself
Multiple treatment interference	If we take two or more actions at the same time, it is difficult to control for the effects of prior treatments	The action team introduced new testing tool and new continuous integration tool. The effect of these two tools on the speed and quality was difficult or impossible to separate

Table 10.6 Threats to external validity, their explanations, and examples, cont

Threat	Explanation	Example
Selection biases	When we select the context that is not representative for the population	Out of 20 software development teams, we select the ones that volunteer. However, the volunteers are the teams that are not busy, which is not representative for the company
Constructs, methods, and confounding	Our measurements and methods do not allow us to generalize outside of the studied context	We studied the effect of pair programming on software quality. However, we want to generalize to pair-modeling as well; since these are two different constructs, we cannot make this generalization
The real-world setting vs. experimental setting	Our experimental setup is too distant from the normal company operations	We set up an experiment as part of one action research cycle; however, the experiment is offline and does not use any of the company code, which makes it difficult to generalize to the context of the company

Furthermore, we can examine a number of external validity threats which come from the guidelines for writing PhD theses from http://dissertation.laerd.com/external-validity-p3.php#threat1 in Table 10.6.

External validity is about how much we can generalize our results, and therefore they are related to three parts of the action research model, as presented in Fig. 10.6.

When it comes to the external validity in relation to theory building, we need to be transparent about our context. In action research, the action team is embedded in the organization and is part of the action taking. This means that there is often the danger that the study and its results are dependent on the action team itself. The action team has a stake in getting positive results, otherwise they would not conduct it, and therefore they are intrinsically biased. This means that the action team needs to be very careful when claiming generalizability outside of their original context. They also need to be transparent about the study being conducted with the participation of the researchers as part of the action team.

However, for the improvement of the practices in the company, the action team can be much more transparent compared to the theory building. The team can provide almost all details about the projects, products, and teams involved, since it is often part of the company's internal reporting. The action team can also provide demonstrations and show how the action was taken in their product without the need of obfuscation of the data or theoretical presentations.

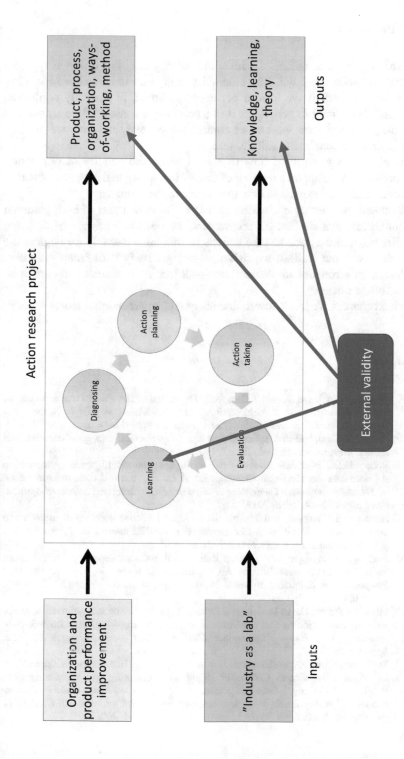

Fig. 10.6 Phases relevant for scrutiny when finding threats to external validity

10.6   Summary

Every research project is burdened with some validity issues as different types of validity balance each other out. The external validity and the conclusion validity require some trade-off. If we have a perfect experiment, in perfectly controlled environment, it's difficult to generalize it to a company's context. If we embed our study in the company, then we cannot control the context, and thus we need to carefully review the conclusion validity threats.

In this chapter, we explored how to reason about the validity of our action research projects. We mapped a number of threats to validity to the phases of action research cycles, and we explained how they relate to these phases.

We discussed the validity evaluation as it is an important part of both planning and executing research studies. As researchers, we need to be aware of different validity threads, and we need to take actions to minimize them. If we neglect the validity analysis of our studies, we risk conducting a study with faulty premises, flawed design, or erroneous implementation—all leading to results that cannot be trusted and effort wasted.

In the next chapter, we learn how to document and report action research studies.

References

[CC79] Thomas D Cook and Donald T Campbell. The design and conduct of true experiments and quasi-experiments in field settings. In *Reproduced in part in Research in Organizations: Issues and Controversies*. Goodyear Publishing Company, 1979.

[CS63] Donald T Campbell and Julian C Stanley. *Experimental and quasi-experimental designs for research*. Ravenio Books, 1963.

[FSHL13] Robert Feldt, Miroslaw Staron, Erika Hult, and Thomas Liljegren. Supporting software decision meetings: Heatmaps for visualising test and code measurements. In *2013 39th Euromicro Conference on Software Engineering and Advanced Applications*, pages 62–69. IEEE, 2013.

[NB05] Nachiappan Nagappan and Thomas Ball. Use of relative code churn measures to predict system defect density. In *Proceedings of the 27th international conference on Software engineering*, pages 284–292. ACM, 2005.

[NB07] Nachiappan Nagappan and Thomas Ball. Using software dependencies and churn metrics to predict field failures: An empirical case study. In *First International Symposium on Empirical Software Engineering and Measurement (ESEM 2007)*, pages 364–373. IEEE, 2007.

[SDR17] Miroslaw Staron, Darko Durisic, and Rakesh Rana. Improving measurement certainty by using calibration to find systematic measurement error—a case of lines-of-code measure. In *Software Engineering: Challenges and Solutions*, pages 119–132. Springer, 2017.

[SHF+13] Miroslaw Staron, Jörgen Hansson, Robert Feldt, Anders Henriksson, Wilhelm Meding, Sven Nilsson, and Christoffer Höglund. Measuring and visualizing code stability–a case study at three companies. In *2013 Joint Conference of the 23rd International Workshop on Software Measurement and the 8th International Conference on Software Process and Product Measurement*, pages 191–200. IEEE, 2013.

[SM08] Miroslaw Staron and Wilhelm Meding. Predicting weekly defect inflow in large software projects based on project planning and test status. *Information and Software Technology*, 50(7–8):782–796, 2008.

[SMP12] Miroslaw Staron, Wilhelm Meding, and Klas Palm. Release readiness indicator for mature agile and lean software development projects. In *International Conference on Agile Software Development*, pages 93–107. Springer, 2012.

[SMS10] Miroslaw Staron, Wilhelm Meding, and Bo Söderqvist. A method for forecasting defect backlog in large streamline software development projects and its industrial evaluation. *Information and Software Technology*, 52(10):1069–1079, 2010.

[WRH+12] Claes Wohlin, Per Runeson, Martin Höst, Magnus C Ohlsson, Björn Regnell, and Anders Wesslén. *Experimentation in software engineering*. Springer, 2012.

[YO10] Chong-ho Yu and Barbara Ohlund. Threats to validity of research design. *Retrieved March*, 24:2019, 2010.

Chapter 11
Reporting Action Research Studies

Writing, to me, is simply thinking through my fingers.
—Isaac Asimov

Abstract Conducting an action research study improves practices at our industrial partners. The improvement can range from elevating the competence of the action team to changing the way in which the partner company or organization develops software. The ideal outcome, however, is the change in the way of working or in the product. While improving the industrial practice, action research also contributes to developing and evaluating theories in software engineering. Therefore, it is important that we report our action research studies in a rigorous way, so that others can learn from our experiences. In this chapter, we describe how to report studies, both in the standard format of research papers to focus on the impact of the actions and as a storytelling to focus on the actions taken alongside of the impact.

11.1 Introduction

The goal of action research is to directly improve industrial practices and to contribute to the body of knowledge. The first is achieved by conducting the action research project in industry, together with or by practitioners, and thus changing the way in which industry works. However, the challenge with the action research projects is that they often stay within the walls of the company—either because the practitioners lack time to prepare a full publication or because the results are too sensitive to be published.

We need to remember that the goal of many software development companies is to develop, maintain, and sell their products and services, thus maintaining their businesses. In small businesses, these activities are distributed among very few

M. Staron, *Action Research in Software Engineering*,
https://doi.org/10.1007/978-3-030-32610-4_11

individuals who often need to struggle to get enough revenue from the customers to survive. In larger companies, the employees have an easier task to find time between assignments to prepare the publication. However, this needs the approval of management.

An important obstacle in publishing results of action research is often the sensitive nature of the results. Since the research is done as part of the operations of the company, on real products, with real people (in comparison to lab environment and toy problems), the results contain direct links and references to products, problems, or improvements. Not all companies are willing to let such sensitive results be published. In this chapter, we discuss how to handle this in a good way.

Before we start writing up our results, we need to carefully plan the publication. We start from studying the typical structure of the journal where we want to submit our study. We need to prepare the paper based on their recommended structure; at the same time, we need to align the structure with the structure of action research— cycles and phases. Smith et al. [SRS10] present a number of best practices, which start with just that—preparing the right structure and planning the actual paper.

From my experience, writing up the results in a report is where most researchers struggle the most, especially in the field of engineering. We are engineers, so we like structures, programs, algorithms, and diagrams. Discussions and elaborations are our strong sides as long as they do not require writing. However, I've also observed that the threshold of the first paper can be overcome if we work systematically and focus on the reader's perspective of the report at hand. Therefore, let us go through the elements of reporting and see how we can take the results collected in an action research project into a coherent report, interesting for the scientific and professional community.

11.2   Basics of Reporting Action Research Studies

A report of a scientific study has a number of purposes to fill. It communicates the results to practitioners who were not part of our study and to the scientific communities. Since the action research methodology requires us to be placed at the company and work with the stakeholders in the study, we do not need a special report for them. They are usually informed through our presentations in the study. They are included in the knowledge creation and therefore seldom require a separate report from the study.

The other practitioners' goal with reading about action research is to extract new practices and ways of working, which they can adopt in their context. Therefore, the reports targeted toward them should include details of how the results can be applied. For example, if our research project resulted in a new method, the method should be described in detail. The description can be included in the report or included as additional material if the format of the report does not allow it. The main goal, however, is still the same—to provide others with the possibility of applying this method in their context without anyone from the action team present.

The scientific community's goal in reading about action research is, often, to extract the practices which are used in industry and to learn about how the technology transfers from academia to industry or how the technology is cocreated by academia and industry. If the action research projects involve only practitioners, then the reports often include experiences from industry, which are extremely important for researchers, teachers, and students in academia. Therefore, reports targeted toward the scientific community should focus on the results, research design, and operation, so that other scientists and researchers can learn from the project. We need to remember that sometimes the journey to the results is more interesting than the results themselves!

Ip [Ip17] after Feldmann and Weiss [FW05] advocates to focus on a number of elements in the report. These elements do not need to form the structure of the paper, but they need to be part of it:

1. Describe the context where the action research takes place.
2. Contain a statement of your research focus.
3. Detail the method(s) used.
4. Highlight the research findings.
5. Suggest implications.

The description of the context of the study is the description of the main characteristics of the organization, product, and team which takes part of the action research project. The context of the study helps the readers to understand whether these results are applicable in their own context. When describing the context, we should focus on the characteristics of the context rather than the details of a particular company. For example, instead of writing that we conducted a study at Company XYZ, it's more beneficial to describe that it is a company of 100 developers, projects are usually for one customer (solicited), and the project teams use Java to integrate components for a web system. Although it is tempting to write the name of the company as the readers can check the company's website to find details, it is not the case. Companies change over time, and we have no control over when the readers pick up our publication and whether the company still exists or whether it is in the same business—simply, we cannot control what we do not write in the publication. Table 11.1 explains the typical characteristics of the context that we should include in our publications.

Table 11.1 Typical characteristics of the research context to include in publications

Characteristics	Explanation
Domain	The domain of the company is important as it is often linked to development styles, types of products, and quality assurance. Examples of domains are embedded software, web systems, safety-critical software, cloud systems, enterprise systems, and healthcare systems
Type of collaboration	We should describe how the collaboration is organized—whether it was initiated by the company to solve a specific problem or whether this it was initiated by the university to test a theory. We should also state the kind of financing that the project obtain, e.g., that it was financed directly by the company. This helps the readers to understand how the collaboration is organized and understand from which perspective the study was done
Size	The size of the company can be included for information, but the most important is the size of the organization where we conducted the project. For the readers, there is a difference between one team in a 100,000 developers company and a team in an SME
Development process	We should report the type of development process employed by the company. We should also provide as many details about the development as possible. The details include the length of sprints, the number of software developers in a typical team, and the characteristics of the customers. The readers need to understand whether the software is developed using principles of XP (extreme programming) or the traditional V-model for safety-critical systems
Characteristics of the product	We need to describe the product in terms of its properties. We should describe whether this is an embedded software, web software, or a safety-critical microcontroller software. We should include, if possible, approximated size of the software, but the details are not so important. The readers need to know whether the software is a 10,000,000 LOC Linux Kernel type of software or 1000 LOC microcontroller code
Characteristics of the architecture	We can include a short characteristics of the architectural style used. For example, we can describe the product as a monolith or a component-based software. This helps the readers to understand what kind of product we have studied
Theories used	We should describe which theories were applied in the study or considered but rejected. The readers need to understand the context in terms of theoretical framing of the problem

---

Characterizing the Company

In this project, the action research team set off to improve the speed of software development. Since the topic is, by nature, sensitive, the companies were characterized and not mentioned by name [SMSB18].

Company A: The company is a large infrastructure provider from Sweden. The studied organization within this company has over 100 developers who work in a combination of Agile and Lean principles. They develop an embedded software product which has been on the market for over 10 years and has a stable, mature code base. It is based on the proprietary operating system. The product is sold to the infrastructure operators, who in turn provide the services to their customers. The organization has adopted practices of continuous integration for over 5 years.

Company B: The company is a medium-size consumer product provider from Sweden. The studied organization within this company has over 100 developers who work according to Agile principles. They develop an embedded software product, based on Linux, and they adopted continuous integration for over 5 years. Compared to Company A, Company B's product is much smaller (at least an order of magnitude) and has much larger variability as it is sold to consumers.

Similarities: Both companies use a similar setup of modern software development tools, including Jenkins for continuous integration and Gerrit for code reviews. The process of code reviews, code integration, and testing is the same for both companies. The size of the teams is similar too.

Differences: Testing tools and equipment are different, as the products are different. The roles in the companies, which are involved in the processes, are also different. At Company A, the reviews are done within the same team, whereas at Company B, the reviews are often done by external roles to the team. The setup of the code repositories is also different, which we describe in the Results section.

The statement of the research is a description of what the goals of the research are and how the study is designed. Examples of what the description can contain are a short description of which action research phases we have, the goal of each phase, and the summary of the learnings. When describing the focus, it is also important to state whether the focus is on the improvement of the operations of the company, improvement of its products, or improvement of its organization.

The description of the methods used is the description of the details of our action research. To describe the action research, we should describe each cycle and its phase of these cycles. The description should be detailed and contain all the information that we deem as relevant for the readers, both to understand the study and to assess its quality and validity. Furthermore, we should describe how

Table 11.2 Typical elements of the description of methods

Element	Explanation
Hypotheses or research questions	We need to describe which research questions and hypotheses we pursued in the study. The readers need to understand the goal of the study
Data sources	We need to describe which sources of data we used. If we used interviews, we need to describe the subjects, the population, and the sampling methods used. If we use quantitative methods, we need to describe where the data was taken from, e.g., which databases. The readers need to understand where the data comes from and if they can collect the same data
Data collection	We should describe which data collection methods we used, for example, how we conducted the interviews and how we collected the data
Measurement instruments	We need to describe in detail how the data collection was done. For example, for interviews we need to provide the questions. For the quantitative data collection, we should provide the code of the scripts used to collect the data (or links to where the code is available). The readers who want to replicate the study will be helped by the materials shared in the study
Data analysis	We should describe how we analyzed the data and how we drew our conclusions. The analysis methods and links to their descriptions are very important for the replication. The readers can get a good understanding of how the conclusions are drawn if we are transparent about how we analyzed the data

we collected the data (e.g., measurement instruments), how we analyzed it, and how we drew our conclusions. The typical elements which need to be included are presented in Table 11.2.

The description of the research findings is the main part of the research publication. The findings contribute to the body of knowledge and therefore is appreciated the most by the readers. For the action research studies, we should focus on two parts of the findings—research findings and the recommendations for other companies. The first part is about the relation of our findings to the existing theories, our hypotheses, and our research questions. The second is about actionable recommendations for other companies for how to apply the results and how to conduct similar studies in the future.

Recommendations for the Companies

In this project, the action research team set off to improve the maintenance of measurement systems. Alongside the contributions, the team prepared a set of recommendations for companies willing to adopt the self-healing approach [SMT+18].

1. To start with the implementation of self-healing, the organization should start with defining the most common failures, i.e., a simple taxonomy, to understand how much impact these failures have on the organization and develop means to identify them in an automated analysis based on data that can be obtained by monitoring.
2. The repair strategies covering the most common failures can be derived from the daily practice of the operators as experiences by the studied company. In the considered system, it was important that they are triggered both by the execution problems and the information quality problems. This allows to assure the high quality of the information and reduce the risk of making decisions based on erroneous data.
3. Self-healing can be realized in an effective way using simple repair strategies like re-execute or restore. Even such simple strategies save significant effort for the organization, as shown in both studied companies.
4. When deploying the infrastructure, include the mechanisms for (simple) self-healing. Once the initial learning threshold has been overcome, the organization should focus on introducing the automated mechanisms for handling the most common failures of the infrastructure and, in this way, move toward a self-healing infrastructure with higher degree of automation.

The recommendations helped other companies to adopt the same approach. Instead of copying the entire technology stack, the companies can choose which part of the approach they can adopt.

To describe the implications of the findings, we focus on which possibilities the findings open up. We can think about this part of the publications as the ending to the following sentence: *Now that we have found the following in our study, we can . . ..* This part of the publication is intended to show the readers what can be done thanks to the results of our study. When discussing the implications, we can think about the potential next steps of our findings. This also helps us to design new studies, find new industrial partners, and open up new research directions.

11.3 Working with Results That Are Sensitive to Our Industrial Partners

When we report the studies, we often need to deal with confidentiality of the results. Most companies do not want to reveal their business secrets in form of the publications, and they have full right to do that. It's also not really necessary for reporting of studies. The scientific community is not interested in whether it was company X or Y that produced the results. It's more important to describe the characteristics (see Table 11.1).

Although this seems to be against the principles of academic freedom and transparency of research, in reality, it is not at all in conflict with them. From my experience, we can use a number of different techniques to make the results nonsensitive while keeping the academic freedom of publishing all results.

The first rule of thumb is to always work together with our industrial partners on the publication. We need to keep them "in the loop" from the very beginning, discussing the drafts of the publication and discussing how to present the results. The industrial partners help us with the understanding of what is and what is not a sensitive aspect of the publication. We, on the other hand, help them to understand why we want to publish these results. This mutual understanding always leads to being able to publish relevant results without jeopardizing our partner's business, organization, or products.

When discussing how to hide the real data from the competitors, it's our, researchers, responsibility to make sure that we preserve the privacy of the data. At the same time, it is our obligation to be transparent and true to the readers [Ber18].

When publishing results that can be sensitive to the company, we can use techniques to obfuscate the data, which are presented in Table 11.3.

In addition to the obfuscated data that preserves the privacy of the data, we need to ensure that we do not jeopardize the business of our industrial partners by choosing wrong terms and concepts when writing.

Table 11.3 Techniques which help us to obfuscate the results

Technique	Explanation
Data transformation	Instead of providing real values, we can transform the data to hide the real values but do not violate important properties of the data. For example, instead of reporting number of defects, we scale it to 100, so that the highest number is 100. This helps to replicate the results but does not reveal the real numbers from the company. A good resource for the techniques of data obfuscation is the work of Bakker et al. [BRB+04]
Subject privacy protection	Instead of providing names or positions of the collaborators, we describe their roles and experience. For example, instead of writing that we interviewed the chief executive officer, we describe his experience and characterize his position (high line management). This helps the readers to understand the perspective of the collaborators but does not reveal the collaborator's identity
Data sanitization	Instead of providing the real data when conducting analysis of information from Internet sources (e.g., social media), we can replace the sensitive information with proxies. For example, instead of writing the name of the person who provided the information, we change it to Mrs. X. In this way, the readers can trace the information throughout the study but cannot find the identity of Mrs. X. It is also important that we manually assure that searching the Internet does not lead to revealing the identity of Mrs. X [CHGL18]

We should avoid writing about which company problems we solve and focus on solving universal problems. For example, instead of writing that Company X has problems with large number of defects, we should phrase it in more neutral terms: We study the defect management practices at Company X in order to identify improvements. Once again, we should include our industrial partners in these discussions so that they can help us with the formulations in our publications.

If, against all odds, we cannot obfuscate the data or change the privacy, we should ensure that we do not fabricate results or jeopardize our research integrity. This is "rule number one" of the research ethics.

Obfuscated Defect Inflow

In this project, the action research team set off to improve the predictions of defects in large software products. In the course of the study, the company was keen on not revealing the real number of defects, in order to prevent the business of the company.

In Fig. 11.1, the action team presents the inflow of defects which is scaled to 100, which does not prevent replications and preserves the privacy of the company. The figure also hides the real length of the project by removing a number of data points (months) from the figure.

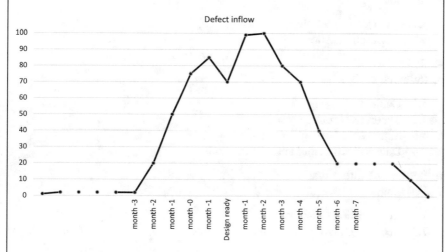

Fig. 11.1 Rescaled defect inflow

The protection of the privacy provided the action team with the possibility to publish the results and thus disseminate important knowledge in the community.

11.4   Reporting Studies Focused on Results

In many cases, we can report action research studies in the same format as any other empirical study—case study or observation. These type of reporting is often focused on the results, and the research methodology is of secondary importance. Therefore, we can summarize the action cycles instead of describing them fully cycle by cycle and describe the learnings before we describe diagnosing of new cycles.

The format for reporting which is focused on the results of action research, included in this section, is based on the guidelines presented by Runeson and Höst [RH09] and Runeson et al. [RHRR12]. They propose the format of reporting of case studies, after conducting a review of existing ways of reporting empirical studies. We can adapt their guidelines to the purpose of reporting of action research—adding summary of the action research cycles, extended description of the context, and recommendations for other companies.

A research report describing an action research project should be structured around the following headings:

1. Title
2. Abstract
3. Introduction

    3.1. Problem formulation
    3.2. Research questions

4. Related work[1]
5. Research design

    5.1. Context
    5.2. Theoretical framework
    5.3. Summary of research cycles
    5.4. Data collection and analysis methods

6. Results and interpretation
7. Learnings

    7.1. Contribution to theory
    7.2. Recommendations for other companies

8. Validity evaluation
9. Conclusions and further work

---

[1] Some authors prefer to write the related work as the section before the Conclusions. It is perfectly fine and depends on the whatever is comes more naturally.

Each of the sections of the report has a specific goal and contents. One general advice is to use the past tense. It's easier to use the past tense when describing the study because the nature of action research. It is a flexible research design methodology, which means that the design of the study changes as we go along with the study. It is not given how many action cycles we have á priori, and we do not know what each cycle focuses on. Therefore, instead of using the present tense to describe the design of the study and the results, or use the past tense for the results, it's better to use the past tense for the entire paper.

The goal of the **abstract** is to provide an overview of the entire report, and therefore it needs to be as informative as possible, yet very concise. It is nowadays quite often written in the form of structured abstract, where we organize the abstract into the following parts: background, objective, method, results, and conclusions. This way of organizing abstracts helps us to structure them so that the readers can quickly get an overview of the article.

Structured Abstract

In this project, the action research team set off to identify methods for measuring speed of software development. They reported that in a paper and considered the following structured abstract.

Background Continuous integration and continuous software deployment depend on the mix of automated and manual activities. The automated build and test processes are often intertwined with manual reviews and bug-fixing activities.

Objective In this paper, we set off to study how these manual and automated activities influence the speed of reviews and integration.

Method We conduct a case study of two companies developing embedded software, measure the time required for reviewing and integrating software code (alias speed), and conduct a workshop to identify factors which explain the quantitative results.

Results Our results show that the measurement of speed is a good alias for calendar time and triggers improvements better than using measures for velocity. We have also found that the distribution of code repositories, frequent reminders, and team proximity decrease the time needed to deploy the software.

Conclusions We conclude are that there is a difference in the structure of code repositories between the fast and slow integration cases, which contributes to the debate on the pros and cons of different repository structures in modern companies.

Introduction can be structured using the CARS model (e.g., [Swa90], [Swa11]), and its modification to software engineering [Ant99], where we create a research space by shortly reviewing the existing work, creating a niche, and outlining the contribution (https://libguides.usc.edu/writingguide/CARS). For the action research studies, we recommend that the latter two parts—the niche and the solution—are clearly separated as problem formulation, research questions, and outline of the contribution.

The role of the **related work** section is to describe how our research related to the existing body of knowledge. No research is done without building on existing theories and empirical results. Therefore, we need to help the readers with the review of the most relevant literature and results in the field relevant to our action research project. In this section, we need to provide an overview of the field, not overview of individual publications. It is important to identify relevant areas and important trends in research in these areas, summarize the main works in these trends, and then clearly show how our study expands the current results in these areas.

The goal of the **research design** section is to describe the details of how we designed our action research project. It should describe how we designed the cycles, summarize each phase in each cycle, and show how we collected and analyzed the data. We should elaborate on the design choices we made in the research and motivate them. We should also describe the theoretical underpinnings and the context of the study.

In the first part of this section, we describe the **context** of the study. We describe the company and the organization where we conducted the study, describe its characteristics, and describe the setup of the action team. It is important for the readers to understand who conducted the action research project and in which context. It is also important to note who has been sponsoring the study for transparency reasons. The description of the context should include the descriptions of the subjects and objects.

In the **theoretical framework** section, we present the theoretical framework important for the research at hand. This theoretical framework is the theory which we use and the theory that we develop as part of our study. The theory does not need to be called a theory in a strict sense (e.g., like the set theory) but has to be a published evidence and/or published theoretical, analytical, or synthetical knowledge.

Theoretical Framework

In this project, the action research team set off to design a way in which we can assess the quality of a measurement program. In order to design the measure of quality, the action team used a number of different theories and included them in a common model [SM16].

In Fig. 11.2, we can see the part of the model developed based on combining a number of theories—the theoretical framework.

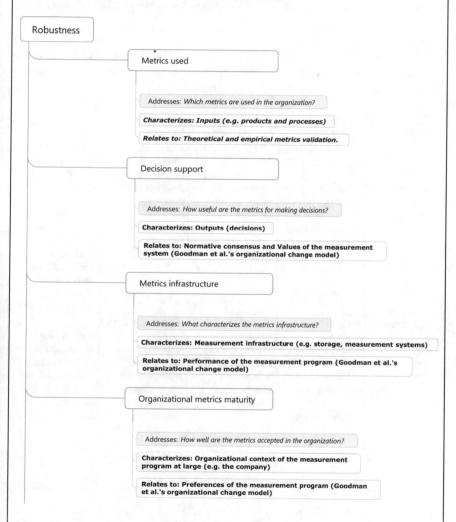

Fig. 11.2 Excerpt of a theoretical model behind a MeSRAM method

Using a mind map to collect the theories into one coherent model helped the action team to understand the relations between these theories.

To describe the **summary of action cycles** we can use a tabular format to summarize the information about the action research cycles. It is important to communicate how the research ideas developed over time, how the learning influenced next cycles, and which problems we investigated in each cycle. For this format of publication, this section should explain how we designed the study. However, since action research is per definition a flexible design methodology (i.e., changes during the course of the study), this section is a bit of a mix of findings with design as the learning of one cycle influences the diagnosing of the subsequent one.

Summary of Research Cycles

In this project, the action research team set off to identify methods for measuring speed of software development. They reported that in a paper, and their action cycles were summarized in the following table.

Diagnosing	Action planning	Action taking	Evaluating	Learning
What are the most common measures of speed in industry?	We planned an analysis of literature and a survey of industry practitioners in the collaborating company	We conducted the semi-systematic review and a survey of 100 software developers	The results showed that velocity and its derivatives were the most common measures	We learned that the measure of velocity can be easily manipulated if one changes the way how story points are counted. Therefore, we need a more objective measure of speed
How can we use duration as a measure of speed of software development?	We planned to study the measure of duration of software reviews and use it as a proxy for the measure of speed	We collected the data from over 50,000 reviews from the Gerrit code review system at one company	We evaluated it with the stakeholders at the company to check whether the measure reflects the stakeholders' perception of the review speed—empirical validation of measures	The outcome was that the duration was a good proxy for the measure of speed and was not prone to the same problems as the measure of velocity

In this summary, the action team provided a description of how the study was conducted, what was done in each cycle, and how the team's understanding changed over the course of the study.

The research design section must also contain the details of **data collection and analysis methods**. The details about what kind of data sources we used and how are important for the readers to both replicate the study and to be able to trace the results back to their sources. In action research projects, these kinds of details are often included in the action planning and action taking phases of the action cycles. In this way of reporting, we do not need to detail which method comes from which cycle, just trace which method resulted in which data.

The description of data collection is usually complemented with the description of data analysis methods used in the study. Here, just like with the description of the action cycles, we mix the description of what we planned with what we did.

After the description of our research design, we move on to the **results and interpretation**. In this part of the report, we show all data collected, usually in form of diagrams, tables, and summaries. Usually we do not show the entire data sets in terms of interview transcripts or data tables, but we show the results of the analysis. The full data is kept either in the company premises or it is provided as open data sets so that other researchers can use it for further studies. If we provide the data as open data sets (e.g., in a form of a data file shared at www.zenodo.org), we need to ask the company for the permission, and we need to obfuscate it. In the interpretation of the results, we should reflect on the research questions and hypotheses posed in the beginning of the report.

Finally, before the end of the paper, we dive into the **learnings**, where we summarize the findings and provide the recommendations. In this section, we should reflect on which **contribution to theory** we made in the study. This means that we take our findings and discuss them in the light of existing theories—the theoretical framework. This discussion is important for other researchers to understand how we developed the theories further.

In addition to the contributions to the theory, we should also provide the separate section with the **recommendations for other companies**, where we group and present our findings in an actionable way. The recommendations are important for the readers as they help them to operationalize the results in their own company.

After presenting the recommendations, and before concluding the paper, we need to critically reflect upon the **threats to validity** of the study. We go through the list of threats to validity, as we described in Chap. 10, and we discuss whether these threats to validity were present in our study. We also account for which actions we took to minimize these threats.

Finally, we provide the **conclusions and further work**, where we summarize the paper, outline the results, and finally provide pointers of what new research directions our findings open up. The summary should include a brief statement of what we set off to achieve, how we conducted our study, and the outline of the findings.

11.5   Reporting Studies Focused on Actions

When reporting action research studies, we can often use a format which is focused on cycles, actions, and learnings. When we have a free choice of the format or no space limitations, we can choose to elaborate more on the learnings and on the theories developed in the action research study. This kind of reporting reads more like a "story" of action research and is more appealing for the readers. The format of this report is different from the format of the report described in the previous section, yet we still should keep the scientific rigor of reporting and provide all facts from the study.

A research report describing an action research project with focus on actions should be structured around the following headings:

1. Title
2. Abstract
3. Introduction

    3.1. Problem formulation
    3.2. Research goals
    3.3. Contributions

4. Related work[2]
5. Theoretical framework
6. Research design

    6.1. Context
    6.2. Summary of research cycles

7. Execution and results

    7.1. Cycle 1

        7.1.1. Diagnosing
        7.1.2. Action planning
        7.1.3. Action taking
        7.1.4. Evaluation
        7.1.6. Learnings

    7.2. Cycle 2

        7.2.1. Diagnosing
        7.2.1. ...

8. Validity evaluation
9. Conclusions and further work

---

[2]Some authors prefer to write the related work as the section before the Conclusions. It is perfectly fine and depends on the whatever is comes more naturally.

There is a lot of similarity of the reporting in the first four sections. The notable differences are in the **introduction**, where we often stress the contributions of the action research study. Since this format can be longer than the previous one and in each subsection of the results we focus on one cycle, there is a risk that the main contributions are hard to spot. Therefore, it makes it easier for the readers to focus on the main topics of the paper. We also do not focus on the research questions but instead introduce the **research goal**. The research questions are included in the description of each action research cycle, where they belong more naturally in the diagnosing section.

The main differences start in section 6, **research design**, where we do not discuss the data collection methods or the research questions. Instead, these elements are described in more detail in the section describing each action research cycle.

Section **execution and results** is the main reason why this format of reporting is more natural for action research studies. Since action research is a flexible research design methodology and is not set á priori before the study, it is easier to describe it as a story of the research. Each cycle can be seen as separate with its own research questions, which are derived from the research findings from the previous cycle.

In the description of the **diagnosing** phase of each cycle, our focus should be on the research problem that we solve in this cycle and how we found that this is the actual problem to solve. We need to provide an account of our activities that led us to diagnosing the particular problem. For example, if we conducted interviews, we need to report on them, include the interview protocol, and report on the analysis of it. If we used quantitative data analysis, we should provide the diagrams and analyses. If we used literature review as part of diagnosing, this should be reported too. This section should include the research questions which we address in this particular action research cycle.

In the description of the **action planning** phase, our focus is to report on how we designed the action taking of the cycle. We can see this description similar to the description of the design of a study. Here, we need to include the data collection and analysis methods, procedures for validating the process of data collection, and description of our design choices.

In this format of reporting, we can easily describe changes in the focus of the study from quantitative to qualitative and vice versa. As each cycle can use a different approach, we can explain the change given the learnings from the previous cycle and the goal of the cycle at hand.

The **action taking** description is an account of how we conducted out study. It shows what we did and how and describes whether the action taking was done according to the plan from the previous section and, if not, what kind of adjustments were made. We should also provide the results of the action taking, in forms of raw data (if it is relevant), diagrams, and summaries. However, we leave the analyses for the next section.

In the description of the **evaluation** phase, we focus on how we analyzed the data and how the analysis addresses the research questions. We need to provide the results of the analysis, and we need to explicitly answer the research questions posted in the diagnosing section.

Finally, in the section describing the **learnings** from the cycle, we should focus on:

- what the results mean and what next steps can/need to be taken in the next cycle,
- findings that contribute to our theory building, and
- recommendations for other companies.

These first element is very important for the "storyline" of the report; it helps us to link two cycles together and helps the reader to understand why we need to investigate new research questions in the next cycle. The last two elements are similar to the findings and recommendations described previously. The difference is that these findings and recommendations are more detailed as they are directly linked to the action research cycle at hand.

Description of One Action Research Cycle: Diagnosing

In this study, the action team set off to investigate how to automate the assessment of coding quality based on proprietary coding guidelines in industry and example-based machine learning tools.

The goal of the cycle was to investigate the coding guidelines of our industrial partners. In particular, we wanted to understand the types of rules that are in the companies' guidebooks.

We investigated rules in the Company A and B guidebooks and categorize them based on the information required to identify their violations. We assessed the quality of the rules and consulted our findings with software engineers from both companies.

Description of One Action Research Cycle: Action Planning

After reviewing the literature, we learned that there is no agreed taxonomy that could be used to categorize coding guidelines (and their violations). For instance, [NKo10] compared four static code analysis tools and showed that each of the tools uses a different set of categories, and even within a single taxonomy, multiple criteria are often used to define these categories. For instance, some categories refer to syntax and programming concepts (e.g., naming conventions, code layout, exceptions handling), while others are defined by referring to quality attributes of software products that could be affected by certain violations (e.g., maintainability, security, or performance problems).

Since we wanted to automatically identify lines of code violating coding guidelines, we proposed a different taxonomy that categorizes violations based on the information that is required to recognize them in the code. The taxonomy is presented in Fig. 11.3. It groups guidelines into three main categories.

Fig. 11.3 Taxonomy of code guidelines violations

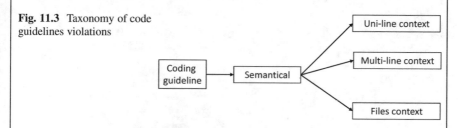

The first root category "semantical" requires understanding the meaning of a text in its context. Depending on the size of the context, we distinguish four subcategories: a uni-line context, we need to understand the meaning of the tokens/words in a single line (e.g., the rule stating that there can be only one statement in a line); multiline context, we need to understand the meaning of words/tokens in a sequence of lines (e.g., braces must be used for all compound statements); and files context, we need to be able to relate the code in different files or understand file properties (e.g., unused functions must be deleted).

Description of One Action Research Cycle: Action Taking
When classifying the rules into the categories, we identified three groups of outlying rules:

- *rules as documentation*: no style-related coding guidelines but rather hints about what libraries or interfaces to use or what protocols to follow when calling an interface,
- *optional rules*: either a whole rule or its part is optional to follow,
- *rules on external information*: rules that require information outside of the studied code, e.g., user requirements.

Rules that serve as documentation and rules on external information might be extremely difficult to identify and certainly have special needs to an static code analysis approach, such as consideration of multiple files at once. On the other hand, optional rules might as well be ignored by any approach. Therefore, we defined these three types of rules to be out of scope for the further investigation (Fig. 11.4).

Fig. 11.4 The number of coding guideline rules found, per category

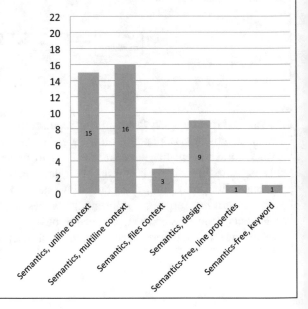

> **Description of One Action Research Cycle: Evaluation**
> The performed analysis resulted in narrowing our study to rules belonging to four categories: semantical uni-/multiline context and semantic-free line properties and keywords. We observed that the rules belonging to the three remaining categories were either not related to code (process rules), violations could not be mapped to particular lines (design semantics, e.g., usage of design patterns), examples were not available in the guidebook and would be very difficult to get (design semantics), or they span through multiple source files (semantical files context, e.g., unused functions should be deleted).

> **Description of One Action Research Cycle: Learning**
> Most of the coding guidelines are different between the companies, which means that the potential tool has to be adapted and tuned on a per-company basis. We also found that several coding guidelines are not related to code but the process of coding. These guidelines cannot be checked by any automated tool and should be removed from further analyses.

Finally, the last two sections of this kind of reporting are similar to the previous way of reporting, described in Sect. 11.4.

11.6 Summary

Conducting a study is an important contribution to science, and reporting the study makes the contribution more complete. In this chapter, we explored how to report action research studies. We discussed which elements are the most important in the reporting and showed different styles of reporting.

As the action research method is close to other methods like collaborative case studies and design science research, some authors prefer to package the results of action research into the format of other studies. Some authors divide the action research into a series of case studies in order to assure that the publications are coherent and self-contained. As long as we can use the same elements as in the case study or design science research in the report, it boils down to how we can best communicate the research results to the readers and how we can inspire other companies to action. We should, however, not jeopardize the research ethics and change the way in interpretation of the results or do not report important elements, methods, and results of the study.

Although the elements presented in this paper are important for the success of the report and the dissemination of knowledge, they often need to be adjusted to the venue where it is reported. Many conferences have their own requirements and formats. They also have limited space, and we are required to make prioritizations of what to include in the conference paper. The same is true for several journals; they have their formats and requirements, and we need to respect it.

Therefore, before the publication, we should look at the style required by the journal and conference where we intend to submit our work. Once again, we need to keep our research integrity and ensure that we can communicate our research results in an appealing way that inspires action of our readers.

There are a number of great style guides on how to write academic articles, both online and in print. Depending on the venue where we want to publish or if the study is included in a dissertation or a master thesis, we need to choose the right format. There, I recommend to choose the guide which is recommended by the venue. When it comes to the academic style, I'm particularly fond of Sword's *Stylish Academic Writing*, [Swo12], which provides a guide on how to make the text appealing to the readers by advising on how to choose headlines, construct sentences, and disposition the text. Sword's text can be easily complemented with Pinker's *The Sense of Style* [Pin15], which is a more modern version of the style guides for academic writings from the 1980s and 1990s.

References

[Ant99] Laurence Anthony. Writing research article introductions in software engineering: How accurate is a standard model? *IEEE transactions on Professional Communication*, 42(1):38–46, 1999.

[Ber18] Jeremy Berg. Obfuscating with transparency. *Science*, page 133, 2018.

[BRB⁺04] David E Bakken, R Rarameswaran, Douglas M Blough, Andy A Franz, and Ty J Palmer. Data obfuscation: Anonymity and desensitization of usable data sets. *IEEE Security & Privacy*, 2(6):34–41, 2004.

[CHGL18] Zhipeng Cai, Zaobo He, Xin Guan, and Yingshu Li. Collective data-sanitization for preventing sensitive information inference attacks in social networks. *IEEE Transactions on Dependable and Secure Computing*, 15(4):577–590, 2018.

[FW05] A Feldman and T Weiss. Suggestions for writing the action research report. In *University of Massachusetts Amherst Conference Paper*, 2005.

[Ip17] Tiffany Ip. Linking research to action: A simple guide to writing an action research report. *The Language Teacher*, 41(1):37–39, 2017.

[NKo10] Jernej Novak, Andrej Krajnc, and RokŽontar. Taxonomy of static code analysis tools. In *MIPRO, 2010 Proceedings of the 33rd International Convention*, pages 418–422. IEEE, 2010.

[Pin15] Steven Pinker. *The sense of style: The thinking person's guide to writing in the 21st century*. Penguin Books, 2015.

[RH09] Per Runeson and Martin Höst. Guidelines for conducting and reporting case study research in software engineering. *Empirical software engineering*, 14(2):131, 2009.

[RHRR12] Per Runeson, Martin Höst, Austen Rainer, and Björn Regnell. Case study research in software engineering. In *Guidelines and examples*. Wiley Online Library, 2012.

[SM16] Miroslaw Staron and Wilhelm Meding. Mesram–a method for assessing robustness of measurement programs in large software development organizations and its industrial evaluation. *Journal of Systems and Software*, 113:76–100, 2016.

[SMSB18] Miroslaw Staron, Wilhelm Meding, Ola Söder, and Magnus Bäck. Measurement and impact factors of speed of reviews and integration in continuous software engineering. *Foundations of Computing and Decision Sciences*, 43(4):281–303, 2018.

[SMT+18] Miroslaw Staron, Wilhelm Meding, Matthias Tichy, Jonas Bjurhede, Holger Giese, and Ola Söder. Industrial experiences from evolving measurement systems into self-healing systems for improved availability. *Software: Practice and Experience*, 48(3):719–739, 2018.

[SRS10] Laura Smith, Lisa Rosenzweig, and Marjorie Schmidt. Best practices in the reporting of participatory action research: embracing both the forest and the trees $1\psi 7$. *The Counseling Psychologist*, 38(8):1115–1138, 2010.

[Swa90] John Swales. *Genre analysis: English in academic and research settings*. Cambridge University Press, 1990.

[Swa11] John M Swales. *Aspects of article introductions*. Number 1. University of Michigan Press, 2011.

[Swo12] Helen Sword. *Stylish academic writing*. Harvard University Press, 2012.

Chapter 12
Conclusions

> *Success is a science; if you have the conditions, you get the result.*
>
> —Oscar Wilde

Abstract This book introduced action research as a research methodology for software engineering research. It is one of many methodologies available today and is best suited for organizations centered around collaboration and knowledge co-creation between academia and industry. In the book, we introduced all phases of action research, compared it to the most similar research methodologies, and discussed how to document and report action research studies. In this final chapter, we focus on providing guidelines on where to go next. We look into the case where action research can be applied in multiple organizations and how to tackle collaborations with multiple organizations, by time-sharing the research time and activities.

12.1 Experiences from Working According to Action Research

As a scientist, I've had the privilege to work with several software development companies, ranging from only a handful of employees to large global companies with market-leading products. I've also had the opportunity to test different research methodologies, and I can say that I've really liked action research, although case studies and experiments were equally appealing at times.

However, there are a few companies where I've kept good relations and thus been able to work according to the principles of action research. I'd like to say that these organizations and projects are the coolest ones I could imagine as a scientist. They challenged my view of the world, they challenged my view on scientific impact, and they, simply put, changed my view on software engineering.

M. Staron, *Action Research in Software Engineering*,
https://doi.org/10.1007/978-3-030-32610-4_12

One of my early experiences from action research is that one needs to be part of the company in order to be able to work according to action research. We need to get the access card and be part of a team and a project. This kind of embedding in the industrial context helped me to understand the difference between theory and practice.

I can provide an anecdote from a discussion with one of my colleagues. During the project meeting, during a discussion about how to solve a problem, I was advocating a simple, quick-and-dirty script that could help us to collect the data. However, my colleague wanted to have a generic model and solution that would work for several companies. After a long discussion, one of my industrial colleagues interrupted and said that in industry no one wants generic solutions; engineers want simple, quick solutions that solve the problem. The generic solutions are for academics.

Now, after a while, I lean toward being in the middle, in-between the quick-and-dirty and fully generic. This experience has taught me that it's necessary to provide quick results to industrial partners, but we also need to spend time to make the solutions more generic. If we do, we can replicate studies, and we can involve many companies.

I've learned that the ability to provide quick solutions is the key to a successful collaboration. As researchers, we need to be able to learn and make mistakes, and for that, we need to show the results. If we do not show the results, the industrial partners can get discouraged and turn to other researchers and teams for solutions.

Yet another thing that I picked up during my years as an action researcher is the fact that we need to work with trust. We need to be able to trust our colleagues, and they need to trust us. From my experience, the only way to build this trust is to work together, make mistakes together, and co-create results. Co-creation and collaboration also mean that the team takes the responsibility together, which builds trust.

12.2   Where Action Research Fits Best

Action research is a great way of collaborating with industry, but it does not fit all contexts. There are a few cases where it is hard to use action research and other methodologies work better. An example of that is a bachelor or a master thesis project. Many of my students try to use action research and then end up with making a case study—either explorative (if they focus on the diagnosing phase for too long) or constructive (if they focus on the action taking and artifact construction for too long). The major reason for the abandonment of action research is the fact that my students have difficulty to get familiar with the context sufficiently in their thesis time, a time that is often limited by their study programs.

However, the action research is a perfect opportunity to build longer-term relationships between senior researchers and their industrial partners. In the context when the senior researcher has a project that is at least 2 years long and involves the industrial partners, the action research methodology is a perfect match. Planning and taking actions on the premises of the company, together with its engineers, as one action team, result in new theories, improvements, and elevated knowledge. It provides the researchers with the satisfaction of achieving a real improvement, something that goes beyond a publication only.

The action research methodology is also suitable for post-doc projects where we want to help young scientists to understand the complexities of working with industry. When post-doctoral researchers engage with industry, they have a better view on their future careers. Some choose to stay in academia and become professors [FJ19], while others choose to go to industry and focus on product development using critical thinking to improve the company's operations. Finally, there is a group of scientists that focus on the place in-between—usually a research institute. A research institute provides the possibility to conduct industrial research but have no requirements on publications or theory development. Many young scientists find this to be very attractive and appealing [RS17].

When we see that using action research would be problematic or would require shoe-horning the methodology to fit the context, it's better to choose another methodology—experimentation when we want to control the context, case study when we do not want to make an intervention, or design science research when we want to focus on the artifact rather than the action. One of my colleagues gave me one advice that I remembered well—it's better to do one thing and do it well than to do many things and do them sloppy. I use this advice when I choose my methodology—instead of planning for many cycles, I sometimes use other methodology and keep my options open for the continuation. By the end of the day, the context around us can change outside of our control, and we need to be flexible to terminate our studies, publish and disseminate our result, and move on to the next study.

12.3   Combining Action Research with Other Methodologies

Once in a while, I get questions from my students and colleagues whether it is possible to combine different methods as part of action research. The short answer is "yes, it is possible" [Min01]. The only requirement is that we need to combine the methods systematically [DG02]. The concept of a methodology means that it requires instantiation to become a research method applied in a particular study. In the action research methodology, we have a number of places where we can combine different research methods. Let me quote a few examples.

The first example is the diagnosing phase where we can combine interviews and mining software repositories as data collection methods. The qualitative interviews are cross-validated by hard data from the software development tools. The hard data from the software development tools also gets a meaning when interpreted during the interviews and, thus, provides a better, more complete, picture of the situation and the research context [KD88].

Another example is when we combine different interventions in the action taking phase. We can mix changing our own ways of working (if we are practitioners) with changing the ways of working for our team. This means that we have a cause-and-effect relationship and can observe the effects of the actions taken on both us and the team.

Finally, we can also combine different methods for specifying learning—we can combine workshops with surveys of the feedback. The workshop provides us with new perspectives on our action cycle, whereas the survey provides the ability to understand the impact of our actions on the entire organization.

12.4   Where to Go Next: Action Research with Multiple Companies

In this book, I focused on action research projects which involved one organization. However, there are collaboration projects which involve multiple companies. In these kinds of collaborations, there are two models of collaboration—one where research (action) teams work in parallel and one where the research (action) teams move from one company to another over time.

The second model is something that my team used in several studies, for example, when we studied stability of source code [SHF+13]. In this collaboration, our major constraint was the research resources. We could not scale by adding more researchers, so we decided to organize the study sequentially in steps.[1]

Figure 12.1 shows how action cycles at multiple companies can be linked to each other. The two companies are illustrated by two colors.

From my experience, the model, where we have two (or more) companies involved in the study in this way, helps to lower the effort for the companies over time. The first company is active in the first cycle, and the second company observes the project. For example, representatives of the second company are part of the reference team for the project. In the second cycle, the roles are reversed—the first company observes, and the second company is active.

Figure 12.1 shows the link between the two companies on a conceptual level. In practice, this link is established by the knowledge, results, and research tools developed in the project. Figure 12.2 presents how output from one company is carried over to the next company.

It is, naturally, more demanding to work with several companies in one action research project than it is to work with one organization. At the same time, it is also much more rewarding.

---

[1]Essentially, we called it phases, but this term is already used in this book to denote phases of action research.

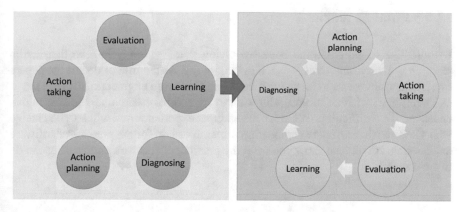

Fig. 12.1 Action research cycles involving multiple companies

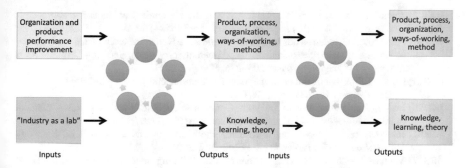

Fig. 12.2 Carryover of results and knowledge from one organization to another

First of all, working with more companies means that we can develop results that are more generic and more applicable in practice.

Second of all, each company has a different focus, which means that the research problem evolves as it is carried over. This leads to the ability to understand how different research problems are linked and how solving one problem opens up new possibility.

Thirds of all, and the most important in my opinion, is the ability to learn company to company. The researchers are only conduits in that knowledge transfer and at the same time being able to study this knowledge transfer. No models, techniques, and translations are needed when practitioners can meet and discuss a common problem. When that happens, we have achieved a self-sustained research environment where research in technology development is a natural part of software engineering industry.

12.5   Final Remarks

I would like to conclude the book by saying that I strongly believe that action research is a very important research methodology. As the title of one of the papers says, the action research can swing a balance in software engineering [dST11].

Therefore, I wish all of you, who want to try action research, all the best in this endeavor. It's a difficult task, but it's also a great experience and will let you change your view on what software engineering research can do for the practice of software engineering. It will also show you what the practice of software engineering can do to the research.

References

[DG02] Anna Dubois and Lars-Erik Gadde. Systematic combining: an abductive approach to case research. *Journal of business research*, 55(7):553–560, 2002.

[dST11] Paulo Sergio Medeiros dos Santos and Guilherme Horta Travassos. Chapter 5 - action research can swing the balance in experimental software engineering. volume 83 of *Advances in Computers*, pages 205–276. Elsevier, 2011.

[FJ19] Martin J Finkelstein and Glen A Jones. *Professorial Pathways: Academic Careers in a Global Perspective*. JHU Press, 2019.

[KD88] Bonnie Kaplan and Dennis Duchon. Combining qualitative and quantitative methods in information systems research: a case study. *MIS quarterly*, pages 571–586, 1988.

[Min01] John Mingers. Combining is research methods: towards a pluralist methodology. *Information systems research*, 12(3):240–259, 2001.

[RS17] Michael Roach and Henry Sauermann. The declining interest in an academic career. *PLoS One*, 12(9):e0184130, 2017.

[SHF+13] Miroslaw Staron, Jörgen Hansson, Robert Feldt, Anders Henriksson, Wilhelm Meding, Sven Nilsson, and Christoffer Höglund. Measuring and visualizing code stability–a case study at three companies. In *2013 Joint Conference of the 23rd International Workshop on Software Measurement and the 8th International Conference on Software Process and Product Measurement*, pages 191–200. IEEE, 2013.

Printed in the United States
By Bookmasters